The Organ
Thieves

The Organ Thieves

The Shocking Story of the First Heart Transplant in the Segregated South

CHIP JONES

GALLERY BOOKS
JETER PUBLISHING

New York   London   Toronto   Sydney   New Delhi

Gallery Books / Jeter Publishing
An Imprint of Simon & Schuster, Inc.
1230 Avenue of the Americas
New York, NY 10020

First Gallery Books hardcover edition August 2020

GALLERY BOOKS and colophon are registered trademarks of Simon & Schuster, Inc.

For information about special discounts for bulk purchases, please contact Simon & Schuster Special Sales at 1-866-506-1949 or business@simonandschuster.com.

The Simon & Schuster Speakers Bureau can bring authors to your live event. For more information or to book an event, contact the Simon & Schuster Speakers Bureau at 1-866-248-3049 or visit our website at www.simonspeakers.com.

Interior design by Davina Mock-Maniscalco
Maps illustrated by Christopher Hibben

Manufactured in the United States of America

10 9 8 7 6 5 4 3 2 1

Library of Congress Control Number: 2020935252

ISBN 978-1-9821-0752-9
ISBN 978-1-9821-0754-3 (ebook)

For Deborah

CONTENTS

The Organ
Thieves

PART ONE

Roots

CHAPTER ONE

Case of the Missing Heart

IN LATE MAY 1968, Doug Wilder was in his law office on a tree-lined street in Richmond, Virginia. He was winding down from a long day of work when the phone rang.

"They took my brother's heart!" the man on the other end of the line exclaimed in horror.[1]

As one of the best-known African American trial lawyers practicing in the state capital, Wilder was accustomed to taking random phone calls day or night. Accusations of rape, robbery, and murder were not uncommon, nor were other desperate pleas from mothers and fathers seeking help for loved ones who'd run afoul of the legal system. Even as halting steps toward progress had begun to bring incremental improvements in schools, housing, and jobs, his home state of Virginia was still moving at a snail's pace from under the heavy burden of centuries of discrimination.

But taking a man's heart from his own body? Wilder had never heard of such a thing. "I don't understand what you're talking about, not having a heart," he told the caller, William Tucker. "What do you mean? What happened to it?"

He started taking notes as Tucker described a deeply disturbing series of events that had just unfolded over the weekend. It all started when his brother Bruce went missing after work on Friday. It took a series of frantic phone calls—prompted by an insider's tip—to finally locate him at the Medical College of Virginia (MCV) on Saturday night. Then some bureaucrats hemmed and hawed before finally delivering the shocking bad news: his brother—who'd been rushed to the hospital with a head injury less than a day before—had died only a few hours earlier on an operating table.[2]

Bruce's body had been claimed and taken to a funeral home near the family farm. William was given Bruce's final possessions—among them his driver's license and a business card. *His* business card, William realized. It was for his shoe repair shop only a few blocks from the hospital. Why hadn't anyone called him sooner?

A day later, still numb from the news of his brother's death, William began the hour-long drive to the farm. He wanted to personally break the news to his eighty-year-old mother, Emma, and to Bruce's teenage son, Abraham, who lived with her. First, though, he would check with the local undertaker about the upcoming funeral. William's best-laid plans were shattered, though, when he learned more shocking details of his brother's treatment in an operating room at the Medical College of Virginia.

★   ★   ★

William Tucker's ordeal started with a hushed call from a friend inside the hospital. "Something's going on with Bruce," the friend whispered.

William put down a pair of shoes he was working on. It was early Saturday afternoon. He asked his friend to speak up and explain himself. His friend whispered something about a heart operation involving Bruce. Then the line went dead.

William stared at the phone and laid it back on its cradle. What was *that* about?

He tried calling the hospital a couple of times but couldn't get a straight answer. It took him a few hours to close up shop and drive over to MCV. By then it was after 7:00 p.m. When the hospital finally sent out some men to talk to him, he asked them a simple question: "Where is my brother?" William, a polio victim who used crutches, braced himself for the reply.

Bruce was dead, he was told, and "you'll need to make funeral arrangements." Nothing was said about an operation or anything about Bruce's heart.

★   ★   ★

On Monday morning, William Tucker swung by Jones Funeral Home in Stony Creek, Virginia. Mack Jones, the owner and mortician, apologetically informed William that while preparing the body for burial he noticed something bizarre: Bruce was missing his heart—and his kidneys.[3]

As William related his tale, Wilder put down his pen. This was too much to write down. After a silence, William asked Wilder if he'd represent him and the family and try to get to the bottom of what happened.

"Yes, I will," Wilder agreed. Though he tried to sound confident, he also knew there was something about the sound of this case he couldn't quite put his finger on. It was something that went to the dark heart of the city and state of his birth.

It had been almost ten years since Wilder graduated from Howard University School of Law in Washington, DC, but he still practiced law in the long, lingering shadow of the Jim Crow South. The courtrooms, jailhouses, and white-controlled bar association were all woefully behind the times and observed strict segregation. A black Virginian had no chance of having his or her trial being adjudicated by an African American judge for the simple reason that there *weren't* any black judges. Black jurors were also a rarity, since any defense attorney worth his salt would use the law to strike anyone of color from a jury panel.[4]

★   ★   ★

William Tucker went on to describe more of the peculiar circumstances surrounding his brother's demise. Bruce had been working at an egg-processing
plant not far from Wilder's law office. After work that past Friday, he was
relaxing with friends and passing a bottle of wine in the shade behind an
Esso station. He was sitting on a wall but lost his balance and hit his head,
rendering him unconscious. An ambulance was called. Bruce was quickly
transported to the nearby MCV, the state's largest teaching hospital.

That's how it started. But what happened *after* Bruce was treated in
the emergency room and later by the hospital's brain-injury specialists?
And why would he attract the notice of its heart surgeons? Wasn't it his
head—not his heart—that was injured?

From what Wilder could piece together from William's first account,
something simply didn't add up. It reminded Wilder of some kind of science fiction movie where doctors experiment on humans in the dead of
night. As William's friend had whispered from inside the hospital,
"They're doing some kind of experimental heart operation."

But *who*? Wilder wondered. And *why*? What happened behind the
walls of the big hospital on the hill?

★   ★   ★

William Tucker sounded distraught, and his first account took some
twists and turns that could be hard to follow at times: The frantic phone
calls to MCV . . . How nobody seemed to know even where Bruce had
been taken, much less anything about his condition—until someone
said he'd been transferred from the main hospital to nearby St. Philip
Hospital, a place Wilder knew well. Until recently it had been a segregated hospital solely for African American patients. The Civil Rights Act
of 1964 had forced all hospitals to end the separation of races in their
wards. So why had they sent such a severely injured black patient like
Bruce Tucker over to the still-second-rate facility?

The more Wilder heard from William, the more questions he had. Why hadn't the hospital given William time to get over to see Bruce when he was in such dire shape? Like the cobbler, Wilder ran a one-man shop, where he answered his own phone and even cleaned up the office. He couldn't just run out whenever an emergency arose. But why wouldn't William think he could wait a few hours if his brother was in such good hands at MCV, with some of the finest physicians in Virginia?

William finally managed to close his shop and get over to St. Philip sometime between 7:00 p.m. and 7:30 p.m. That's when he learned his brother had died more than three hours earlier—at 3:35 p.m. But *why*? From *what*? And if Bruce had been so near death, why hadn't anyone informed him so he could rush over to be by his bedside?

It didn't add up. One thing was clear to Wilder, though: questions needed to be asked on the family's behalf—and the sooner the better. Sure, Bruce Tucker was in bad shape when he'd been rushed to MCV. But the injured factory worker had another liability that had nothing to do with his job status or his medical condition: he was a black man with liquor on his breath. Because of that, Wilder knew that Bruce's odds for fair treatment were about as good as his own chances of ever getting elected governor.

How could a man go into the hospital with a head injury and come out not only dead but also with his vital organs missing? Something about the taking of Bruce's heart was particularly shocking. Wilder—a chemistry major in college who went on to work in the state medical examiner's office[5]—considered himself a rational, progressive-thinking man. But the *heart*? This still held a sacred place as the symbol of all human emotions. Who had taken it? he wondered. Who had received it—and why?

Wilder was the grandson of slaves. Early in life, he developed a thick skin to deal with the segregated world of the South that still plagued his hometown in 1968. As a result of his hard work, advocacy skills, and refusal to play by the old rules, the thirty-seven-year-old's legal practice was thriving.

But the call from the distraught brother had stirred up some bad childhood memories. Growing up in the 1930s and 1940s in the former capital of the Confederacy, Wilder heard rumors about what went on behind the fortresslike walls of the teaching hospital. There were whispered warnings from older boys: "You best stay away from MCV, or you might get snatched up by the night doctors!" It was like something from the pen of Edgar Allan Poe, who himself had once carried his own dark thoughts along the cobblestone streets of Richmond.

Between his law practice and earlier work in the Virginia medical examiner's office, Wilder knew doctors weren't perfect. Things happened in the course of medical treatments that were kept from prying eyes. But even in his worst nightmares, he never imagined a hospital would condone stealing a man's heart.[6]

It was an unseasonably warm day for spring in Richmond, so he switched on a fan by the open window. Kids were happily playing hopscotch on the sidewalk while young couples held hands as they took a stroll to enjoy this otherwise bright, sunny afternoon. Most of his neighbors were African American these days.

Not that long ago, Church Hill had been a mixed neighborhood where whites and blacks lived and worked together. It was named for St. John's Church, where Patrick Henry had famously declared in the run-up to the Revolutionary War, "Give me liberty, or give me death!" As Virginia was forced to open its public schools to black children in the early 1960s, many white families fled to avoid integration. Wilder always thought the white flight was a sad commentary on his community.

Something about William Tucker's story tugged at Wilder. He didn't entirely know what he was getting into, but he knew full well that he was in for one hell of a fight. MCV was not only a large medical school, but it also was a powerful one backed by big business and big government alike. As an aspiring politician, Wilder was keenly aware of how things worked around town. He had no doubt that with so much money, power, and influence at stake, MCV—which was funded by the state and was a major source of civic pride—was not a place to trifle with. It simply had too many friends in high places.

But, as he later observed, "I recognized that making a living was one thing, but I also had a role to play in representing those who were in danger of being left outside the system unless I helped them."[7]

Wilder hadn't paid that much attention to the recent news of the heart transplant on the front of the *Richmond Times-Dispatch*: "Heart Transplant Operation Performed Here at MCV." He recalled only that it was about helping a white businessman and it was a first for Virginia.[8]

The article had not said anything about the donor's identity. Now, he quickly surmised, William Tucker was filling in the major gap in the story: his brother Bruce was the unnamed "donor"—the guinea pig the MCV doctors used to jump into the heart transplant race. Doug Wilder was determined to find out why.

CHAPTER TWO

The Resurrectionists

For magic and applied science alike the problem is how to subdue reality to the wishes of men . . . both . . . are ready to do things hitherto regarded as disgusting and impious—such as digging up and mutilating the dead.

—C. S. Lewis[1]

THE STRANGE, SHADOWY MOVEMENTS around the medical college in Virginia's capital city may have struck some white residents as mere superstitions or folk legends. But in the century before young Doug Wilder heard such cautionary tales, they were heard not only in Richmond but also in other cities with medical schools—including New York, Boston, and Philadelphia.

By the 1830s and the start of its second century, Richmond was entering a kind of adolescence. It grew taller with factories and warehouses and—though whites tried to ignore them—slave-trading markets on the banks of the James River. The capital of Virginia was becoming a major industrial and business crossroads of the antebellum South. Its cobblestone streets were filled with Northern merchants, Southern farm boys, and recently arrived enslaved Africans laboring in the city's grain mills, tobacco warehouses, and ironworks. In hindsight, it seems only natural that old Richmond would help plant the seeds for some of the spine-tingling tales of early American fear and loathing as told by a moody itinerant writer named Edgar Allan Poe. At the apex of Poe's fears: being buried alive. It was a fear he shared with his readers: "To be buried alive is, beyond question, the most terrific of these extremes which has ever fallen to the lot of mere mortality," Poe wrote in "The Premature Burial." "The boundaries which divide Life from Death are at best shadowy and vague. Who shall say where the one ends, and where the other begins?"[2]

Poe's paranoia about the final closing of a coffin couldn't have been helped by an analogous fear—that of "night doctors" and grave robbers stalking local cemeteries. They typically plundered the final resting places of black slaves and white paupers. When it came to these hallowed grounds, there's proof, in Poe's words, "that truth is, indeed, stranger than fiction."[3] Ample evidence of this strange truth can be found not only in the archives of Virginia's flagship medical school but also in the history of the American way of practicing—and teaching—medicine.

★   ★   ★

Like many intercollegiate stories, the people and alliances that helped spark the founding of the first medical school in Virginia's capital city were driven by competition. Only instead of trying to win a sporting contest, this story begins with a young doctor who wanted to show his old classmates a thing or two.

Augustus L. Warner was a Baltimore native who'd attended Princeton University and completed his medical studies at the University of Maryland in 1829. Like other aspiring young doctors of his day, Warner believed in the value of hands-on medical education. Known as "anatomical instruction," it made dissection and study of the human body a vital part of medical school. This was considered a relatively new and progressive trend. It started in England and France, home of a number of celebrated physicians who voyaged across the Atlantic in the early 1800s to help the Americans catch up with their European medical brethren. Until that happened, American medical school tended to consist of about two years (sometimes only five months of class each year) of listening to long-winded lectures about what was known at the time about the human body, surgery, disease, birth, and death.[4]

Warner was eager to train doctors in his native Maryland on the subjects of anatomy, physiology, and surgery. Before long, his reputation spread south to the medical faculty at the University of Virginia, which was founded in 1819 by Thomas Jefferson in Charlottesville. Warner was offered the chair of anatomy, physiology, and surgery.[5]

He gladly accepted. But Warner's walks on the Lawn at Mr. Jefferson's Academical Village proved short-lived. He found that, unlike the more prestigious Northern medical schools that the Virginians aspired to match, such as Columbia and Penn, the medical faculty in Charlottesville was still following Jefferson's core curriculum of teaching by lectures alone—or "didactic teaching."[6] While UVA's doctors were well-grounded in natural science, they weren't benefiting from the hands-on clinical training—especially in anatomy—used by their Northern counterparts.

Warner was especially frustrated by the dearth of subjects for dissection and clinical cases for "demonstration"—that is, human remains for medical school professors to use in their hands-on demonstrations (or dissections) of human anatomy.[7] Warner saw a brighter future about seventy miles to the east in Virginia's burgeoning state capital city of Richmond.

★   ★   ★

By the 1830s, Richmonders knew their river city had come a long way. It had been more than two hundred years since the first British explorers sailed up from Jamestown to establish a new trading post for Virginia's original cash crop—tobacco. They initially made at least token efforts to form alliances with the indigenous people of the Powhatan tribe (who called their homeland Tsenacomoco). However, it didn't take long for the sword- and musket-bearing intruders led by Captain

Christopher Newport to run afoul of the people they called "savages."

Newport and his troops found what they saw as defensible positions on some hills where the Powhatan people were hunting, fishing, and raising their own tobacco and other crops.[8] The Native Americans would pay a terrible price in flesh and blood for the free farming tips they gave the English, who eventually founded a town on the hillsides. They named it Richmond because it reminded them of the view of the River Thames back home near London at Richmond Hill.

It took more than a century before Richmond formally became a town. By the time it was founded by William Byrd II, the Powhatan and other tribes had been wiped out by warfare, disease, and the encroachments of more invaders from across the ocean.

While some Americans may still embrace the romantic tale of Chief Powhatan's daughter, Pocahontas, the truth of Richmond's roots is much darker than any Disney narrative. Local historian Benjamin Campbell calls this "a piece of propaganda told to justify the effort and assuage the guilt of an unacknowledged war of conquest." Some 90 percent of Pocahontas's people, "those united under the paramount chief Powhatan, had been pushed out of Tidewater Virginia or killed in the first half-century of English conquest." Today, he notes, such policies would be considered genocide under international law.[9]

Some British-trained doctors joined in the genocidal killing spree, including "one particularly onerous case, [where] a Dr. John Pott, who was both a distiller and a doctor, prepared a cask of poisoned sherry for a celebration with the Patawomeck tribe." After a number of toasts to enjoying peace with the English, an estimated two hundred members of the tribe were poisoned and died on the spot—with many more slaughtered after the party was over.[10]

After losing their free agricultural advisers, the English colonists were left with the problem of how to tend their newfound top export back to England—tobacco. "Demand for tobacco expanded so rapidly that settlers who had not yet learned to plant enough food to feed themselves planted tobacco in every available corner," Campbell writes.[11]

It was an excruciating, labor-intensive enterprise. Tragically, Virginia's settlers—and eventually its plantation owners—filled their labor void with Africans forced into slavery. And Richmond soon became slave trading's heart of darkness.

By 1835, Richmond had established "the largest slave market in the New World except for New Orleans, the destination of many of the persons who were sold from Richmond," according to Campbell. In that year alone, forty thousand slaves were exported from Virginia to the Deep South, making the domestic slave trade "the largest single piece . . . of Richmond's economy" until the Civil War.[12]

★   ★   ★

By the time Augustus Warner moved to Richmond in the summer of 1837, the city had a thriving economy—one that mixed tobacco factories with ironworks, flour mills, and railroads.[13] It was a heady time for a young doctor ready to make his mark by starting another medical school—one he knew would give the facility over in Charlottesville a run for its money. Richmond physicians and leaders had been talking about having their teaching hospital for some time, so they were ready to embrace Warner when he announced the opening of "an office for the reception of private pupils" where he planned to "devote a large portion of his time."[14]

Warner promised to deliver fascinating lectures that would provide "minute examinations upon the several branches of medicine, dissection, anatomical demonstration and surgical operations during the winter."[15] (He was referring to the fact that in those days before air-conditioning and refrigeration, any human dissections needed to take place in cold or, at most, mild weather.)

Warner also promised to provide students with "the use of an extensive and carefully selected medical library and a cabinet of the therapeutic preparations in general use."[16]

His enthusiasm was infectious, and within a few months a small group of other doctors jumped on his educational bandwagon. The law required a state charter, and they would need as much public funding as possible. Therefore, Warner's planning group decided to seek a sponsor by petitioning Hampden-Sydney College to establish under its state charter a new medical school.[17] Hampden-Sydney was a small liberal arts college some sixty miles southwest of Richmond. It was more than a day's ride on horseback, so they proposed locating the school in Richmond. That way, "the student may obtain every advantage which he could possibly possess in the Northern cities."[18]

Using the coded language of a city and state founded on buying and selling Africans to work in fields and factories, Warner blithely bragged, "From the peculiarity of our institutions, materials for dissection can be obtained in abundance, and we believe are not surpassed if equaled by any city in our country. The number of negroes employed in our factories will furnish materials for the support of an extensive hospital, and afford to the student that great desideratum—clinical instruction."[19]

Translated: the "peculiar institution" of slavery not only gave plantation owners a steady supply of new labor, it also could be part of a morbid marketing scheme to gain a competitive edge for medical schools. What he didn't publicize, however, was the manner by which his plan would obtain a steady supply of fresh corpses. It hinged on stealing the bodies of slaves and free blacks, along with some impoverished whites. These groups often worked themselves to death on nearby plantations or were killed in the city's factories where safety was as foreign a concept as health benefits or a minimum wage.

Given the lack of legal or social restrictions, "The South did indeed have a unique advantage in its ability to provide adequate bodies for dissection," medical archivist Jodi Koste observes of MCV's roots. Quoting historian Todd Savitt, she added, "Blacks were considered more available and more accessible in this white-dominated society; they were rendered physically visible by their skin color but were legally invisible because of their slave status."[20]

Dr. Warner and friends began converting the old Union Hotel in downtown Richmond into a medical school with an infirmary, lecture halls, and dissecting rooms. Simultaneously, only a few blocks away they passed a living hell for new arrivals to their outwardly thriving city. By the time the medical department of Hampden-Sydney College opened its doors, the nearby slave market had become one of the city's fastest-growing enterprises.

The market was located at the base of Shockoe Hill—also the site of the governor's mansion and the stately capitol designed by Thomas Jefferson. The complex of buildings and slave jails formed the northern terminus of the American South's downriver slave trade.[21] Driven by the demands of the Southern cotton trade, "Virginia was shipping its surplus labor at great profit to the new cotton and sugar plantations opening in Louisiana, Mississippi and Alabama, and after 1845, in Texas," according to Campbell. As a result, "the population in Virginia of enslaved Africans remained essentially constant from 1830 through 1860."[22]

Richmond became a popular place for aspiring white physicians to live, but it was a terrible place for their potential dissection subjects to die. Grueling, physically demanding jobs often led to early death through exhaustion or accidents. Because of this, the seventy-five hundred slaves and eighteen hundred free blacks who made up about one-third of Richmond's population of twenty thousand easily satisfied the steady demands of the medical school.[23]

In his travelogue *American Notes*, English novelist Charles Dickens captured the pall that slavery cast over the city during his 1842 visit to Virginia. Riding on a train approaching Richmond from the north, he felt the oppressive sensation that "in this district as in all others where slavery sits brooding... there is an air of ruin and decay abroad which is inseparable from the system."[24]

Dickens—who'd make his mark decrying the poverty and injustice in England in bestselling novels such as *Oliver Twist* and *David Copperfield*—was sickened by what he saw during a brief stay in Richmond. Its "log-cabins... squalid in the last degree," "miserable stations by the railway side," and "negro children rolling on the ground before the cabin doors" contributed to a spirit of "gloom and dejection... upon them all."[25]

On a visit to a tobacco-processing plant, he saw an all-slave work-force running "the whole process of picking, rolling, drying, packing in casks, and branding" chewing tobacco. Dickens drolly commented that there was so much of the oily chewing tobacco that "one would have supposed that one storehouse to have filled even the comprehensive jaws of America."

Adding to the "gloom and dejection" for slaves working in the dank tobacco warehouses beside the James River was the deep void of legal rights and protections, even in death.[26] As Dr. Warner and his small medical school faculty set up shop nearby, they had no doubt they'd have an "abundant" supply of fresh cadavers to offer up to the first medical school classes. While the practice of grave robbing was technically illegal in Virginia, "Public officials generally ignored those engaged in grave robbing activities particularly when slaves or free blacks were the target," according to Koste. "They did, however, recognize the common practice and, in 1848, the Virginia General Assembly strengthened the law for 'violation of the sepulcher' by adding a jail sentence of one year and a fine of more than $500."[27] At that amount, the fine was only a third of the top dollar paid for slaves at the time.

Even though the law was on the books, it was rarely enforced. The medical school began to grow and build just a few blocks from where the Virginia General Assembly had passed the law.

★   ★   ★

Richmond professors were expected to increase the class sizes, which began at first as fifty-five to sixty-five students who attended two sessions that ran from October to March. Warner, who served as dean, joined other surgeons in conducting operations on living and dead subjects alike. Among the procedures listed in an annual catalog were tumor- and polyp-removal, amputations, and hernia repair.[28]

The 1844 catalog touted their underground supply of cadavers for the system: "While the student will have the opportunity of witnessing surgical operations" performed by their professors . . . "he can, from the cheapness of the *material*, practice them upon the dead body, and acquire the manipulation which is necessary for an operator, and a knowledge of the use of instruments."[29]

Promotional materials also extolled Richmond's mild climate in the mid-Atlantic compared to those competitors down in the Carolinas and Georgia. "There is certainly no city south of Virginia where the study of Practical Anatomy can be so advantageously prosecuted—the warmth of the climate in the more southern cities interfering with the duties of the dissecting room," boasted a faculty pamphlet of the day. "While at Richmond, not only is the supply of subjects ample, but the temperature is such as to allow dissection to be continued without interruption from October until March."[30]

The mild weather wasn't just travel-brochure material: without preservatives to maintain the corpses over any length of time, the more southern medical schools often found it difficult to teach anatomy except in the coldest months. Richmond's moderate climate in the upper South made it possible to hold longer sessions that could be touted for marketing purposes.

★　★　★

The medical school professors in Richmond spoke in a secret jargon similar to their peers at Harvard, Columbia, and elsewhere. The gauzy, semi-mystical lingo seems to have been adopted to provide a sort of verbal cushion. It softened the hard reality of an illegal activity that could not be easily explained or justified outside the confines of the dissecting room. So, for example, the grave robber was called a resurrectionist—a strange, religiously fraught term that would have been comical if the work had not been so despicable.

"Resurrection is a colorful description of a cemetery raid to raise a body from the dead to be used for the study of anatomy," historian Suzanne M. Shultz explains.[31] The term "resurrectionists" was coined "because it was commonly believed that the burial ground was sacred and that the removal of a body from 'God's Acre' was interference with the plan of Providence and the great Resurrection." Thus "resurrectionists" and "body snatchers" became synonymous.

Inside American medical schools of the early 1800s, the junior professor of anatomy assigned to solicit stolen bodies was called a demonstrator. The post often was coveted by young doctors trying to make their way up the medical school ladder. This was especially true of those aspiring surgeons who hoped to hone their skills on the contraband corpses.[32]

Still, it put young men who thought of themselves as respectable members of society among some disreputable characters as they did the dirty deeds of buying and delivering cadavers to impatient faculty members ready to teach anatomy and surgery. This clandestine medical hierarchy wasn't confined to Richmond, either. It was also commonplace in more northern climes, including Harvard University in Cambridge, Massachusetts. One well-known doctor, John Collins Warren, later reflected that "no occurrences in the course of my life gave me more trouble and anxiety than the procuring of subjects for medical lectures."[33]

The subterranean marketplace was teeming with guys who knew it was a seller's market. It was all the more difficult for the young demonstrators (equivalent to modern-day surgical residents) who feared they could lose their honor and reputations if their resurrectionist cronies called the police or tipped off the press. Faced with pressures of time, money, and reputation, some doctors in Richmond reached out to their rivals in Charlottesville. It didn't hurt that two of the demonstrators had been classmates at the University of Virginia: Dr. Carter Page Johnson in Richmond contacted Dr. John Staige Davis, a hardworking demonstrator at the UVA medical school. "Davis, in the relatively small city of Charlottesville, had to rely on bodies being shipped from more populous areas such as Norfolk and Richmond." Each had to deal with criminal elements, and they realized they were being played off each other. This was despite the grave robbers' repeated promises to be exclusive cadaver providers to each medical school.[34]

The Virginians were determined to fight back against suspected price gouging by the colluding resurrectionists. "Johnson, disturbed by the rivalry over bodies, proposed a plan where the two schools would divide subjects so that each would have the requisite number to support the instructional program," Jodi Koste writes.[35] Two-thirds of the stolen cadavers went to Richmond and MCV. The other third was hauled to Charlottesville and UVA. Details of this underground deal appears in the 1856 job description at MCV: "It should be the duty of the Demonstrator to make all arrangements necessary to secure subjects for the Professor of Anatomy and Surgery and for the students of this College and the University of Virginia and he will be expected to use the utmost diligence in guarding against all accidents which may serve to diminish the supply of material."[36]

In 1854 there was a dustup with the board of trustees of its parent college. As a result, the medical school severed ties with Hampden-Sydney and secured a new charter from the state legislature. The Medical College of Virginia was born.

Dr. Johnson, who'd worked himself to the bone to climb the faculty ladder, didn't live to enjoy the strange fruits of his labor. In the summer of 1855, the thirty-two-year-old surgeon sailed for England for some study and rest.[37] On his return trip from Liverpool in late

September, his paddle steamship, the *Arctic*, struck a smaller ship off the coast of Newfoundland. Several hundred passengers—including all the women and children on board—perished in the maritime disaster. It became a national scandal after it was reported that much of the crew and some male passengers took up space in the ship's limited number of lifeboats and survived.[38]

Johnson likely made the more honorable choice, though. The demonstrator was lost at sea.

CHAPTER THREE

The Anatomy Men

There are moments when, even to the sober eye of Reason, the world of our sad Humanity may assume the semblance of a Hell . . .

—Edgar Allan Poe[1]

Grave, n. A place in which the dead are laid to await the coming of the medical students.

—Ambrose Bierce[2]

CONTROVERSIES AND CONFLICTS OVER stealing human remains under the cover of night and in the name of scientific progress have a long, violent history. Well before antebellum physicians in Richmond started hatching schemes with their local resurrectionists, the usually sedate streets of Cambridge, England, were torn by violence in 1828 as the "Resurrection Riots" left an indelible impression on a medical school dropout who was studying religion at the university—Charles Darwin.

At the tender age of nineteen, the future father of evolutionary theory witnessed the raw, decidedly primitive side of humankind. He described a Cambridge street brawl as "almost as horrid a scene as could have been witnessed during the French Revolution. Two body-snatchers had been arrested, and whilst being taken to prison had been torn from the constable by a crowd of the roughest men who dragged them by their legs along the muddy and stony road. They were covered from head to foot with mud, and their faces were bleeding . . . they looked like corpses but the crowd was so dense that I got only a few momentary glimpses of the wretched creatures." Darwin wasn't sure, but he hoped the pair of grave robbers survived by being dragged into prison just ahead of their attackers.[3]

Charles Dickens also chronicled the grim business of grave robbing in *A Tale of Two Cities.* In the bestselling 1859 historical novel about the French Revolution, the character Jerry Cruncher, who works as a bank porter by day, tells his wife that he intends to go "fishing" during the night and do the work of an "honest tradesman." He sets out about 1:00 a.m. with a sack, crowbar, rope, chain, and other "fishing tackle of that nature."

His son, Young Jerry, witnesses the true purpose of the trip as his father meets two other "fishermen" who promptly raise a coffin from the ground and pry it open—all at the request of a surgeon seeking dissection matériel. Horrified, the boy runs home. But he soon summons up the courage to ask, "Father, what's a Resurrection-Man?"

The elder Cruncher—a scoundrel and wife abuser—tells him that a resurrection-man was a tradesman.

"What's his goods, father?" Young Jerry asks.

When Cruncher makes an evasive answer, the boy presses him. "Person's bodies, ain't it, father?"

When Cruncher confirms this, Jerry gushes, "Oh father, I should so like to be a Resurrection-Man when I'm quite growed up."[4]

The boy's macabre choice of a career path was well trod. Both in England and the United States, the plundering of graveyards regularly outraged the citizenry. Shortly before the Constitutional Convention was called to order in Philadelphia in the spring of 1787, the volatile issue of supplying medical schools with anatomy subjects stoked a full-scale riot in New York City. Underlying the mayhem were the nation's earliest protests about why black lives matter.

★　★　★

New York City in the earliest days of the republic was relatively small—with a population of about twenty-five thousand. Even with the high mortality rate of the day, it still left the medical professors at Columbia College desperately searching for cadavers.⁵ A class-based system for burials didn't help the doctors' public advocacy of their need for obtaining bodies for anatomy classes. Rather, the corrupt system reinforced popular notions that rich or otherwise well-connected whites would never see their loves ones' corpses whisked away in the dead of night. Working-class New Yorkers were painfully aware that the odds were high that one day they might visit a new grave only to find a dark hole where they'd last prayed over a loved one's shrouded body.

"There was a hierarchy for the eighteenth-century dead as surely as there was one for the living," notes historian Steven Wilf, with the ranking tied to the manner of burial.⁶

As another historian, Michael Sappol, writes in his sweeping study of anatomy and social identity in nineteenth-century America, *A Traffic of Dead Bodies*: "A gravesite's proximity to the church was linked to the social standing of the deceased: the higher the standing, the closer to the church."⁷ Given this wealth-based threshold to the underworld, he writes, the bodies of the upper classes "constituted a funerary community," one that was "symbolically protected by their enclosure and physically protected by wardens and hired watchmen."

The Gospel's teaching that "the first shall be last, and the last shall be first" seems to have been slighted by early New Yorkers, who, according to Sappol, believed that one's wealth, status, and family ties were the determining factors for burial on church grounds.

And, inevitably, it depended on one's racial identity. About 15 percent of the city's population was black, and whatever their societal status—free, enslaved, or indigent—they were laid to rest in what was called the Negros Burial Ground, "a segregated section of the potter's field, which was adjacent to the almshouse," according to Sappol. And that's where the trouble began.⁸

A respected surgeon, Dr. Richard Bayley, arrived to teach anatomy in New York. Bayley was well-known in American medical circles because he'd studied under one of the great British surgeons of the day—John Hunter. So between the anatomical plans of the popular Bayley and the growth at Columbia College, some keen-eyed African Americans began to notice an awful lot of nocturnal activity at the Negros Burial Ground.

Which was why a group of free blacks in 1787 petitioned for protections against medical students "making a merchandize of human bones." Their complaint read like a Gothic novel, filled with phantom medical students and their hired hands arriving "under cover of night . . . [to] dig up the bodies of the deceased, friends and relatives of the petitioners," who then "carry them away without respect to age or sex, mangle their flesh out of wanton curiosity and then expose it to beasts and birds." The petitioners asked the city's common council to stop the desecration of the African Americans' sacred space. One solution, they suggested, was restricting the use of dead bodies to only those convicted of capital crimes, which was another typical way of obtaining corpses.

Their plea was rejected because their community lacked the political clout to stop the carnage and the cover-ups. A year later, the black citizenry penned another outraged letter to the *New-York Daily Advertiser* complaining that "few blacks are buried whose bodies are permitted to remain in the grave," leading to gruesome sightings of swine devouring flesh and human flesh left out on New York's docks, "sewed up in bags."[9]

While New York's leaders kept their heads stuck in the Manhattan soil, the grave robbers managed to blow their cover when they raided the graveyard at the white-majority Trinity Church at the corner of Wall Street and Broadway. On February 21, 1788, after a report of the theft of a body of a white woman from Trinity's graveyard, the rector of the Episcopal church offered a large reward for information leading to the arrest of the grave robbers. "The city was in an uproar," Sappol writes. "The *Daily Advertiser* printed a stream of correspondence on the subject of grave robbery, including a defiant and inflammatory letter by 'A Student of Physic.'"[10]

While the debate raged at the intersection of religion and science, it took a group of boys peering in the windows at City Hospital to drive New Yorkers into the street in what was called the Doctors' Mob of April 13, 1788.[11]

After the boys were caught peeking inside the window of a dissecting room at City Hospital, "In some tellings, a medical student responded by waving a severed arm at the children to scare them away," Sappol writes. In other accounts the bloody arm was said to be hung out the window to dry. "What is certain is that a group of workmen assembled in front of the hospital, entered forcibly, and found some half-dissected bodies that they removed and publicly displayed. As the crowd grew larger and angrier, the hospital was sacked; some medical students were seized and roughed up."

As the violence and mayhem spread, it drew in a coterie of city and state leaders—including New York governor George Clinton, mayor James Duane, statesman and diplomat John Jay, and General Baron von Steuben. Meanwhile, Sappol writes, the crowd swelled to around five thousand, "carrying wooden staves, rocks, and clubs." The angry New Yorkers besieged a jail where medical students had been sequestered for their own protection. This siege prompted Governor Clinton to call up a militia force of about 150 armed men.

Undeterred, the crowd launched a volley of bricks and stones, with many striking prominent people trying to calm the rioters. This included Baron von Steuben—the Prussian-born American major general who'd fought with George Washington at Valley Forge—who suffered a facial wound, and John Jay, a founding father of the United States who would become the first chief justice of the Supreme Court, who "got his skull almost crackd," according to accounts cited by Sappol.[12]

Fearing a rout, "the militiamen opened fire and charged with bayonets," killing three rioters and wounding six more, Sappol writes. In the wake of the riot and the deaths, "sympathies for the protesters ran high," to the point where the local militia couldn't muster enough men to stand guard in the streets. This forced Governor Clinton to call up militiamen from outside the city to finally march through New York's streets and re-store order.

But in the wake of the rioting and deaths, "the old status quo was no longer tenable," Sappol writes.[13] "The Federalist establishment of the city was shaken," forcing grave robbers "to become more discreet and to forgo indiscriminate plunder of the graves."

Over time, New York's lawmakers led the way in trying to address this volatile issue. They adopted the 1789 "Act to Prevent the Odious Practice of Digging Up and Removing for the Purpose of Dissection, Dead Bodies Interred in Cemeteries or Burial Places."[14]

Still, the matter was far from settled—either in the Empire State or elsewhere in the young nation. No matter how much medical educators tried to sugarcoat it—avoiding even such hot-button words as "anat-omy," "dissection" and "cadaver"[15]—there was something contemptible about any system that inspired doctors to brag, as they did in Virginia's capital, about having an "abundant supply" of bodies. Well before the Virginians' braggadocio, America's medical schools had sparked a series of riots and protests. These actually predated the New York riots with what was called the Philadelphia Sailors' Mob of 1765. They also struck Baltimore in 1788 when a crowd sacked a local anatomy school "seeking to retrieve the body of an executed murderer."[16] Far from the Eastern academies, the public revulsion spread to Zanesville, Ohio, when a crowd rioted in 1811. Public unrest was also reported in New Haven, Connecticut ("riot against the medical department of Yale"); and in Woodstock, Vermont ("riot against the Vermont Medical College"). In-deed, Sappol's list of Crowd Actions Against American Colleges from 1765 to 1884 reads like a strange sort of travelogue of early America. Swedish immigrants invading a medical school in Des Moines, Iowa, to reclaim a body. Citizens taking to the streets in Saint Louis, Missouri, and across the Mississippi River in Illinois. Likewise in the Massachusetts cities of Worcester and Pittsfield. Across young America citizens were raising shouts and fists against the despoiling of their sacred grounds. Sometimes first responders led the charge. Such was the case in Rome, New York, where in 1854 volunteer firemen putting out a fire at the Eclectic Medical College were shocked to find dissected bodies. The discovery drove the firemen into such a frenzy that they threw the human remains out the window and trashed the rest of the school.[17]

★   ★   ★

Down in Virginia, anatomy riots had yet to break out. A young doctor named Arthur Peticolas was called on to step in as MCV's resident demonstrator after Carter Johnson was lost at sea. This was a difficult assignment for the aspiring surgeon who was also known as an artist and writer. "Peticolas suffered from asthma, which was exacerbated by his duties in the dissecting room."[18]

But neither his asthma nor his artistic temperament stopped him from doing whatever it took to illegally raise the dead for MCV—even when a key partner in crime quit in the winter of 1856. "To continue my lectures," Peticolas wrote a friend, "I was forced to play resurrectionist myself—by no means a pleasant profession when the snow is 8 inches deep and the thermometer near zero."[19]

Neither frostbite nor riots nor even the threat of arrest and jail could keep ambitious medical students from plundering the most vulnerable graveyards. Even as doctors acquired new cachet in the upper strata of society, the education of the American MD became inextricably bound to a system that would one day be seen as inhumane, unjust, immoral, and—more often than not—driven by deep-seated racial prejudice. So why *did* men who took the ancient Greek Hippocratic oath "to abstain from whatever is deleterious and mischievous" persist in inflicting such pain and emotional suffering upon vast swaths of the population?[20]

To find the answer, it helps to travel back in time to the Italian

Renaissance. Painters from Leonardo da Vinci to Michelangelo made human dissection part of pursuing their artistic callings. These masters, who were known as "art anatomists," were following in the footsteps of Antonio del Pollaiuolo (ca. 1431–1498). He was a sculptor, silversmith, tapestry designer, and teacher best known for his sculpture *Hercules and Antaeus.* Pollaiuolo's attention to physical detail was "dynamic," according to Shultz. But it's his sole engraving—*Battle of the Nudes*—that "clearly gives insight into his dissecting activities," she writes. "The figures almost appear to have been skinned; the underlying musculature is an excellent representation of true anatomic configuration."[21]

Michelangelo was introduced to dissection by a grave-robbing protégé of Pollaiuolo's and went on to study anatomy in Florence and Rome. "His paintings in the Sistine Chapel are the perfected works of a lifetime study of the human form assisted by anatomical dissections," Shultz observes. Similarly, Leonardo's richly detailed physiological observations would become bestsellers several centuries after his death with the nineteenth-century publication of his extensive notebooks.[22]

Thus, Shultz comments, "an alliance between art and medicine was forged early and the tradition has continued to the present day."

★ ★ ★

In nineteenth-century America, physicians and their protégés used anatomical studies—with dissection at its core—to distance themselves from other self-proclaimed practitioners of the healing arts. These included midwives still delivering babies on farms and in small towns, to big-city barbers who doubled as surgeons. This latter tradition was popularized in *Sweeney Todd*, a musical based on an 1847 story from London.[23]

Many American doctors had traveled abroad as young men to study under master surgeons in Paris, Edinburgh, and London. When they came home, they made anatomy fashionable. "In Philadelphia, New York, Boston, and Baltimore—even the rural South—a craze for anatomy flourished among medical students," Sappol notes. "Medicine now entered a new age of anatomical enthusiasm."[24]

A new wave of medical school graduates from Boston, Massachusetts, to Richmond, Virginia, to Columbia, South Carolina, could now shed outdated notions of medicine as a mere trade or craft. Doctors started acquiring more prestige as a profession informed by the latest scientific knowledge imported from Europe.

Gradually, applying to the top medical schools acquired the same sort of status for aspiring young men as law school. Women were mostly prohibited from obtaining medical degrees, an obstacle that would last well into the twentieth century. The men, though, were able to form a kind of professional "cult," in Sappol's words, eager to put as much distance as possible between themselves and less-educated healers.

Their challenge, writes Sappol, was to ensure that anyone who practiced as a medical doctor (MD) continued to "distinguish their cult from other healing sects, traditions and practice." This was accomplished by forming new professional networks such as the American Medical Association (AMA). When it was formed in 1847, the AMA pointedly excluded herbalists and "homeopathic physicians" (advocates of such "natural" cures as healing baths and other treatments that later would be called "alternative medicine"). In another early move with long-lasting consequences, the AMA erected a system of referring patients to consulting physicians, as well as a system of setting and collecting fees.[25]

The mid-century doctors also set higher standards for training and certification at medical schools. They published professional journals and took other measures to strengthen their scientific knowledge—including setting aside spaces for experimentation on animals and humans at colleges and universities.[26] They hoped to discover new cures for diseases, improve surgical instruments, and find novel techniques for treating diseases from cancer to tuberculosis. Such dreams of medical progress were consistent with other American aspirations—from the transcontinental railroad system linking the coasts to the telegraph lines that provided same-day communication. The possibilities for improving America's health seemed infinite and inspired audacious dreams of curing deadly maladies. The day might come, they hoped, when doctors would dare to operate on what was considered the symbol of human feeling: the heart.

Map of Richmond, Virginia, ca. 1850

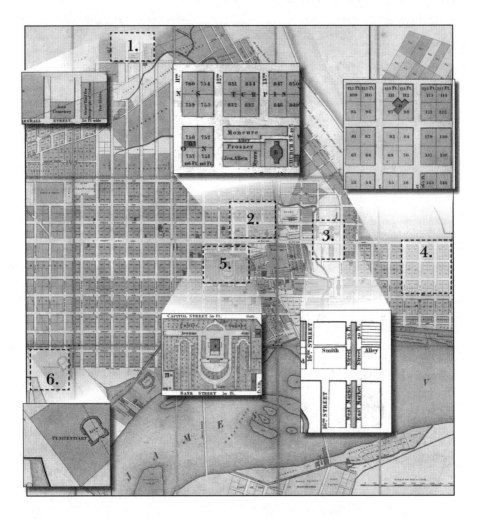

Legend of Key Sites

1. Graveyards
2. Medical College
3. Slave Markets
4. Church Hill
5. State Capitol
6. Penitentiary

CHAPTER FOUR

"The Limbo of the Unclaimed"

THE NEW MEDICAL SCHOOL building in downtown Richmond had a strange, brooding quality. It stuck out among the more conventional brick and wooden homes along Marshall Street and nearby Monumental Church. When it was first used in October 1844, this architectural anomaly was simply called College Building. It would take another half century before it was given a title worthy of its exotic grandeur:

The Egyptian Building.

From a distance, the sandy-hued structure looks like a cross between a small art museum and an enormous tomb. The medical school's lecture and dissection hall was the product of a mid-nineteenth-century architectural craze that evoked the grandeur of the Great Pyramids of ancient Egypt while taking up only a fraction of the real estate. Designed by one of America's leading architects—Thomas Somerville Stewart of Philadelphia—such Egyptian Revival structures were all the rage.[1]

When Richmond's medical school outgrew its first home in the Union Hotel, the faculty was ready to make a splash by hiring Stewart. His design of a nearby church, St. Paul's Episcopal, had wowed worshippers and tourists alike. For the church—located across the street from the capitol—Stewart chose another classical style, Greek Revival. But for the medical school's main lecture and laboratory building, he borrowed from rich imagery from the land of the pharaohs.

It was no wonder, then, that Richmond's pedestrians on nearby Broad Street tried to catch a glimpse of the grand project. Its tapered "battered walls" were thinner at the top than at the bottom.[2] This created a strange visual effect that made the four-story building seem higher than it really was. Its columns with squiggly decorations at the top and bottom evoked papyrus plants sprouting alongside the Nile, from which ancients scrolls were produced. There were many other touches that livened up Richmond's dowdy downtown with a taste of the Nile—from palm fronds to sun disks to twin snakes that seemed to have slithered right off Cleopatra's crown.

Yet for all the College Building's flourishes, two features in particular were tied more to function than to form: the flat, apparently windowless surfaces and the obelisks on the front and back flanks of the building. The windows were placed well above the line of sight, leaving it to the public's imagination to picture whatever the medical school doctors were doing inside. As for the obelisks—they were connected to a cast-iron fence that added to the look of a "sarcophagi," or—as the more learned passersby would understand—Herm figures.[3] The funereal visual effects were meant to serve as a sort of "No Trespassing" sign to curiosity seekers.

Yet for doctors then, and for many decades to come, MCV's central building came to embody the school's ambitions, which were rising as fast as a flooding Nile. The building was a local marvel to show off to applicants and prospective faculty alike. It gave MCV a bit of cachet and furthered the hope that one day it might be mentioned in the same breath as the great American medical schools of the day. These included Johns Hopkins in Baltimore, the University of Pennsylvania and Jefferson Medical College in Philadelphia, the Columbia College of Physicians and Surgeons in New York City, and Harvard College in Cambridge, Massachusetts. Like these esteemed institutions up north, Virginia's capital medical school now had a place for prospective physicians to study anatomy and dig deep into the inner workings and mysteries of the human body.

It was a symbol of pride that would connect the school's graduates for decades to come. Nearly a century later in 1940, MCV historian Dr. Wyndham Blanton captured this sentiment when he declared: "What old Nassau Hall is to Princeton, what the Wren Building is to William and Mary, what the Rotunda is to the University of Virginia, the Egyptian Building is to the Medical College of Virginia.[4]

"It is a shrine," he continued, "a sanctuary of tradition, the physical embodiment of our genius. It is a spiritual heritage. In a world often accused of cold materialism, with an ideology of human self-sufficiency, and an adoration of objects that can be handled and seen, there is a need for things of the spirit, if science is to do more than make life safer, longer, and more comfortable."

Yet, even in its earliest days, the activities behind the sweeping stucco walls with minimal windows also managed to make many people deeply uncomfortable. This was especially true for Richmonders who were hearing rumors about strange occurrences in nearby graveyards.

Given the building's glossy exterior, the medical school faculty quickly surmised that something had to be done to clean up the mess inside. This led to new job requirements for MCV's hardworking demonstrator, whose official duties were amended to make sure that the "Anatomical room, Dissecting room be kept as neat and free from offensive matter as possible, and in the removal of the refuse matter to provide that it be so done as never to give offense to the citizens."[5]

This directive must have given pause to young Carter Johnson before he was lost at sea. Neighbors were already complaining about the stench from the College Building that assaulted them when they stepped outside their homes in the morning.

As Johnson searched for a solution, he challenged the faculty to find an "appropriate place to deposit the refuse matter from the dissecting rooms" and the "dead room" where corpses were kept.[6]

An unnamed faculty member hit upon what must have seemed like an elegant solution at the time: the College Building used several wells to draw water to clean its dissection tables and some smaller laboratories. These water sources also helped with cleaning and quenching the thirsts of patients being treated in the infirmary in the Egyptian Building. One well also provided water to the horses kept at the hospital's stable. So when some of the first wells began to dry up, it was suggested they could be used as ad hoc trash dumps, or as they were later known, "limb pits."

At first, the demonstrator was given the task of making such "deposits in the sink" to keep the dissecting room clear of "offal." Soon the faculty hired a custodian to do the dirty work.

★   ★   ★

As the doctors tried tidying up, the city around them continued to grow—albeit in equally messy ways. Its most lucrative enterprise, slavery, was now threatening to tear the nation apart. By 1859–60, slave trading in Richmond generated more than $4 million in sales, second only to New Orleans. "Slave pens, public whipping posts and auction houses crowded several blocks in the center of the city," writes historian Lois Leveen. "Whites called this neighborhood Lumpkin's Alley, after one of the larger slave-trading establishments. Blacks called it Devil's Half-Acre."[7]

Despite this stain at the heart of the city, Richmond could otherwise be an alluring place. Young men and women could take in the sights, sounds, and smells of the city center near Capitol Square and the city's First Market. "Slave traders, country and town merchants, entertainment seekers, and those simply passing through filled the lobbies and parlors of the larger establishments," historian Gregg D. Kimball writes. "Listings of visitors to the major hotels ran in the local newspapers, providing information for those seeking family, business associates, and old friends."[8]

As they browsed through the paper, career-oriented young men with an interest in the healing arts would have noticed print ads in the *Daily Dispatch* late in the summer of 1859. They promoted the upcoming session at the medical school. "Every Facility will be enjoyed for obtaining a complete medical education, the advantages of Richmond in this respect having been fully tested by an experience of twenty years. The supply of material for Practical Anatomy is ample and at a very trifling cost."[9]

On the eve of the Civil War, the prospective medical student would have tallied up the semester's fees—those paid to each professor ($15), the demonstrator of anatomy ($10), matriculation ($5), and a $25 fee to be paid upon graduation to the college. And he would have been heartened by this reassurance from Levin S. Joynes, MD, dean of faculty: "Good room and board may be obtained in Richmond at prices ranging from $3 to $5 per week."[10]

As it promoted the session that would continue into 1860, behind the scenes MCV was starting to face more public scrutiny. Exactly how was it actually obtaining its "ample" supply of practical anatomy "material," all "at a very trifling cost" to the medical students?[11] Deep-seated suspicions in the black community had been acknowledged on the editorial pages of the *Richmond Dispatch*. It read, "Many of the negroes in Richmond are, for want of room and nurses, sent to the infirmary of the Medical College, when they are taken sick. Among them prevails a superstition that when they enter the infirmary, they never come out alive."[12] Adding to the suspicious circumstances, no doubt, was the infirmary's location inside the mysterious Egyptian Building.

MCV could endure such rumors from the black community, which had few legal rights and less political clout. But when the doubts arose from the white community as well, the college's leadership was forced to take action. As early as 1854, the faculty tried to address this touchy public relations issue by promoting new guidelines for handling deceased patients. Those earlier rules specified that "no body must be removed or interred until 24 hours have lapsed after death except at the express request of the friends or by direction of the attending Physician or Surgeon."[13]

Those cautionary rules seemed to address Poe's haunting fear of a premature burial by giving families the assurance they had at least one day to claim deceased loved ones. In 1860, war clouds started gathering over the South. In what may have been one of Virginia's last acts of cooperation with Washington, MCV said it was working with the federal government to build "a neat and substantial building near the accommodation of marines and other white patients who may need strict and careful nursing," according to a public notice in the *Richmond Dispatch*.[14]

Dean Levin S. Joynes laid out a cooperative arrangement "with the General Government by which sailors are received into their institution and properly cared for, and where . . . they receive the very best attention. In the new edifice the rooms are to be made light and airy," and to be furnished with warm and cold baths.[15]

But after issuing such bright promises of care for visiting US Marines and sailors, Dean Joynes made a startling assertion in an apparent effort to nip some rumors in the bud: "We are also authorized to say that no white person is ever dissected in the college; and that all patients who died there, are decently interred in the public burying ground."[16]

With publicity like this, was it any wonder that such dire rumors kept circulating around the College Building?

★   ★   ★

The public face of the college's chronic public relations problems was not the dean or the faculty. Neither was it the legion of white medical students who matriculated after the Civil War and through the rest of the nineteenth century and into the 1900s.

This dubious distinction would be held by a black man who spent his entire life living, working, and even raising a family in the bowels of the College Building. His name was Chris Baker. Between the Civil War and World War I, the man—who became known as "Old Chris"—would be reviled, romanticized, and also fondly remembered. It all depended on how one viewed the system that had hired him to steal, prepare, and help dissect bodies. Baker developed these skills despite never being taught how to read or write.

"Though he was technically a janitor, Chris Baker was actually a quasi-instructor" for the medical school, observes Dr. Shawn Utsey, a psychology professor who now chairs the Department of African American Studies at Virginia Commonwealth University (VCU). When Utsey first arrived in Richmond to teach at VCU, he noticed an image of Baker still used on a promotional brochure and thought, "This black man has some stories to tell."[17]

Baker appears to have inherited his position from his stepfather, Edward. He made Chris an apprentice in the care, cleaning, and acquisition of corpses. The younger Baker worked for more than forty years, from the 1870s until his death in 1919, with a series of MCV demonstrators and their hired grave robbers.[18]

Such clandestine duties became increasingly fraught with public exposure and danger in the days of Reconstruction. Even as the former capital of the Confederacy began rebuilding itself after being torched by its own fleeing troops, it didn't take long for Richmond's newly freed black citizens to taste the fruits of emancipation. By mid-1865, "secret political Radical associations" were taking shape in Virginia's major cities, including Richmond.[19] With that came something that would have been unthinkable only a few years earlier: black power.

"Richmond blacks first organized politically to protest the army's rounding up of 'vagrants' for plantation labor," writes historian Eric Foner, "but soon expanded their demands to include the right to vote and the removal of the 'Rebel-controlled' local government."

Other exciting changes followed, including an intense interest among African Americans to flex their newfound political clout. On August 1, 1867, for example, "Richmond's tobacco factories were forced to close because so many black laborers attended the Republican state convention," Foner writes. They were eager to embrace the party of Abraham Lincoln, who'd walked the streets of Richmond with his son Tad. Over time, the newly energized African American leadership would elect one hundred black men to the general assembly between 1869 and 1890.[20]

Other possibilities seemed within reach for the same people who had once been bought and sold at the base of their capitol's hill. In 1865, public schools were opened to serve more than one thousand black children. New stores and banks were built in the Jackson Ward neighborhood near MCV, which would become known as the "Black Wall Street of America."

With political and business clout came a new generation of black journalists and writers who dared to question the white-majority political establishment. No one landed more solid punches than John Mitchell Jr., the crusading editor of the *Richmond Planet*. Mitchell, who also became a city alderman, banker, and civic leader, was born into slavery. He soon learned to read from his mother and became known as a gifted student and orator. During Reconstruction, he worked for the government printing office in Washington, DC. The aspiring writer was encouraged by leading black intellectuals such as Frederick Douglass.

As Reconstruction gave way to the Jim Crow era in the early twentieth century, Mitchell was primed to speak out on a variety of issues, including the clandestine custodian living in the basement of the College Building. Even with the protections afforded by the medical school's all-white faculty, VCU's Utsey explained: "Chris Baker was living in a time where—for black people—it was very difficult to navigate day-to-day life, in terms of your economic safety and your physical safety."

Like other blacks hired by Southern medical schools of the day, Baker "was very prominent because of his association with the medical college," Utsey said. "He was being used by them, but he probably enjoyed that because it allowed him to provide, especially for his family, including his wife, Martha, and son, John." He was paid $360 a year, a livable wage considering his free housing in the basement of the Egyptian Building. "Old Chris," as he was known to each new generation of medical students, also made money on the side, serving as lookout for them while they gambled.[21]

In December 1882, "Old Chris" Baker had his cover blown. He was arrested, along with several white medical students, for attempted grave robbery at two African American cemeteries—Oakwood and Sycamore. The arrests were cheered by the *Virginia Star*, a black-owned publication with Republican ties. The news account focused more on the role of Baker as a traitor to his people than to the mendacity of the white MCV students.

"The notorious 'Chris' Baker, whom we published last winter as a grave robber . . . has at last been bagged by local police authorities together with three others of his adjutors. The names of three others are Caesar Roane, W.B. Meredith, and Wm A. Wyndham."[22]

"The last two are white medical students," the *Star* continued. "The other two are colored." After praising the "zeal and skill" of the arresting officers, the article took issue with a white Richmond newspaper—the *State*—over its support for MCV's pillage of the graveyards for educational purposes.

The *Star's* editors also presented an interesting dichotomy about the nighttime raids of black cemeteries and the official protection afforded the local elite white resting place: Hollywood Cemetery. The scenic riverfront cemetery offers sanctuary to two US presidents—James Monroe and John Tyler—along with Jefferson Davis, the former top Confederate.

Taking issue with the white-run *State's* position that "forays upon the sacred precincts of the dead are a necessary evil," the *Star* continued, "Besides, if they be, why not divide the honors between Oakwood and Hollywood alike, and between the two races? It has been claimed by many white men that Negroes are physically dissimilar to Caucasians. If that be true, then it is not fair to the white people that only colored ones should be dissected, and should be the only ones of whose physical structures the doctors have any knowledge."

They then offered this tongue-in-cheek suggestion for balancing things out: "We trust, therefore, that the carcass of the philanthropic writer of the *State*, after his demise, may be duly hauled up out of his silent grave by 'Chris' Baker, dragged, amid the irreverent jeers and curses of the unholy crowd, to the wagon, and finally hauled up on the dissecting table and carved in the most approved style, while many a vulgar joke will be cracked by the students at this excessive generosity to the profession."[23]

Though Baker, a black assistant, and the two medical students were convicted in Richmond court on December 20, 1882, they needn't have worried. The next day, Governor William Cameron issued a full pardon and everyone was sent home for Christmas.

It's instructive to contrast the sense of physical violation and moral outrage expressed in the black press to the paternalistic tone of MCV's later official account written by its historian, Dr. Blanton, some fifty years later. "The principal figure in the oft-repeated spectacle of grave-robbing was the college diener—in the South the negro janitor—whose exploits, real and imagined, made of him a character no longer existent in medical institutions. Armed with pick, spade, and lantern, the grave-digger fared forth alone or accompanied by a few adventurous medical students. A dark night, a sack, a cart and a shallow grave were all he needed to 'resurrect' the recently interred body."[24]

Blanton ignored the cries of injustice by Mitchell and other black journalists from the days of Jim Crow. Rather, he lifted up Baker and other "servitors of the Medical College" who "were viewed with wholesome respect in the college and particularly in the colored community."

This authorized history of MCV provides, in its own a way, a useful account of the blindness about the system that frightened generations of black children in Richmond—including its future governor L. Douglas Wilder.

"It was whispered among the negroes living in the vicinity that it was unsafe to traverse the nearby streets after dark," Blanton wrote. "Stories of the janitors stealthily creeping up behind stragglers on the street and throwing bags over their heads to smother their outcries as they were dragged away were common in the neighborhood. The unusual aspect of the Egyptian Building and the knowledge that here dead bodies were kept heightened the feeling of dread."

In his telling of the arrest of Chris Baker and his body-snatching posse, Blanton noted how easy the police and court system were on them. "In police court the next morning the culprits were fined and sentenced to imprisonment in the city jail. Here the two students, the two janitors, fed and provided for by sympathizers, made the best of their hard luck until Governor Cameron pardoned them."[25]

★   ★   ★

Still, in the years to come, gunshots would sometimes ring out near the Egyptian Building as unnamed assailants would try to pick off "Old Chris." For years, he and his kin stayed inside and rarely ventured out— at least in the daytime. Considering the ongoing resentment and occasional flare-ups over body snatching, Virginia's legislature passed a law to try to bring some order to the chaos. The 1884 "Act to Promote Medical Science, and to Protect Graves and Cemeteries from Desecration within the Commonwealth of Virginia" approved the creation of an anatomy board "for the distribution and delivery of dead human bodies." It gave MCV a privotal role, assigning to its professor of anatomy the task of chairing a committee to establish rules and regulations, appoint officers, and to keep official records "of all bodies received and distributed." One provision of the law ordered anyone working at an "almshouse, prison, morgue, other municipalities having charge of control over dead human bodies" to work with "the physicians and surgeons, from time to time . . . to take and remove all such bodies to be used within this state, for the advancement of medical science"—that is, dissection classes.

The measure also mandated that once a body was used for approved research, then "if any person claiming to be . . . kindred, or is related by marriage to the deceased, shall claim the said body for burial."

And in what appears to have been an effort to dilute the old system of resurrectionists and demonstrators, it included new standards for the care and transport of corpses. These ensured that the dead "shall be well enclosed in a desirable encasement, and carefully deposited, free from public observation."[26]

Anatomy programs were required to post a bond of $1,000, and body snatching was made a felony punishable by five to ten years in the penitentiary. Initially, the law seems to have curbed some of the illicit trafficking of corpses, since bodies now could be legally donated to medical schools.

And yet the crusading editor Mitchell knew from his sources that "Old Chris" was still being sent out on some late-night cemetery raids. Others occurred in broad daylight. In the summer of 1896, Mitchell learned that Baker had been sent to the nearby Virginia State Penitentiary to take possession of a newly executed prisoner named Solomon Marable. The fearless Mitchell promptly organized a group of angry citizens who rushed to the College Building "to reclaim the body of the convicted murderer after it was transported to the college and packed in a barrel of salt for preservation."[27]

To enhance Mitchell's story, the *Planet* included sketches of the scenes of the raucous intervention and protest. Their outrage was understandable considering the continuing desecration and plundering of African American burial grounds at a time when lynchings—meant to enforce white supremacy and intimidate blacks through terrorism—often went unpunished throughout the South.

As it was with anti-lynching provisions, the anatomy laws had mixed success—especially when it came to notifying families before a dissection was performed. "Waiting periods were sometimes ignored, and next of kin haphazardly notified," observes historian Michael Sappol. "The covert taking of bodies by professional and student body snatchers diminished markedly. However, as long as other states lacked similar legislation, commerce in bodies continued, albeit at a lower level."[28]

★   ★   ★

Grave robbing had other ripple effects through the US economy. One was driving the sale of affordable "penny death insurance" policies by Prudential and Metropolitan insurance companies. They found a fertile market by tapping into "the primary fear" of burial in a potter's field and the possibility of having a loved one's body wind up in a dissection room.

For American churchgoers, the possibility of protecting against these sacrilegious outcomes made such policies attractive. "The good burial was a reward and the bad burial (or no burial at all) a punishment," Sappol observes. "Anatomy laws drew a moral boundary between the respectable working poor and those below; a depth into which the working classes lived in a perennial terror of falling: the limbo of the unclaimed."[29]

It was a terror that would follow "Old Chris" Baker to his grave when he died at age sixty-four of cardiovascular disease on June 8, 1919. After living and working and getting shot at in graveyards for much of his life, his death certificate described his strange occupation: "Anatomical Man."[30]

PART TWO

The Race

CHAPTER FIVE

Breaking the Heart Barrier

OVER MUCH OF RECORDED history, dreams of replacing damaged limbs or diseased hearts have captured the imaginations of doctors, philosophers, and artists alike. One of the best-known healing visions concerned the "successful" transplantation of an entire leg of a Syrian man by the third-century physicians Cosmas and Damian. This legendary operation is depicted as a miracle of faith in several well-known paintings of the lives of these twin early Christian saints.[1]

Similar notions of healing through transplantation can be seen throughout history. In 600 BC, for example, the use of one's own skin to replace a missing nose was attempted. Some two millennia later, the Italian Renaissance surgeon Gaspare Tagliacozzi built on such ancient research and pursued his own pioneering work in facial reconstruction.[2] According to Clyde F. Barker and James F. Markmann, "the obvious extension of these methods was to use detached or 'free' grafts of the patient's own tissue or that of other donors."

It would take centuries—well into the twentieth—to understand why such attempts to graft skin or other organs onto the human body failed for various reasons, including problems with blood supply and the thickness of the tissue.[3] Like many medical breakthroughs—the use of anesthesia, the proper treatment of gunshot wounds—the discoveries that finally launched organ transplantation into the era of modern science came as a result of war and "began by chance."[4]

During World War II, Peter Medawar, a young Oxford zoologist with little previous interest in transplantation, was assigned to work with plastic surgeon Thomas Gibson to explore skin homografts for treatment of burned aviators at the burn unit at Glasgow's Royal Infirmary. They confirmed what some earlier researchers had noticed—using one's own skin to try to repair damaged skin or other defects usually failed. It took more scientific research on animals to put modern medicine on the right path to understanding the ins and outs of organ transplants. This was especially true of the role tissue rejection played in the process.

These wartime researchers revived earlier animal research as they peeled back some of the secrets of organ transplantation. One especially significant finding was that shared organs often worked best among twins—whether they were animals or humans.

Similar challenges were overcome by French medical researchers who paved the way for the first successful kidney transplants in animals. As early as 1912, the French surgeon Alexis Carrel won the Nobel Prize for his pioneering work in blood vessel suturing and organ transplantation.[5] In the years before World War II, Carrel remained a leading researcher in the field and even teamed up with the famous aviator Charles Lindbergh, "who approached him to discuss the possibility of a heart operation on a relative," Barker and Markmann write. The Carrel-Lindbergh collaboration led to the creation of a "pump oxygenator," which proved useful in the key operating room function known as perfusion (the passage of fluid through the circulatory system) to other organs and tissues.[6] Like many other medical innovators of their time, both men supported eugenics. Carrel would be accused of being a Nazi collaborator in Vichy France (he died before facing trial).[7] Lindbergh's early fame as an aviator was diminished by his support of Nazi Germany and his espousal of racial supremacy.

Despite the historical baggage of these transplantation pioneers, their work continued after the war. "In the 1940s and early 1950s, experimental dog kidney transplantation was actively conducted by surgeons in Paris and Boston," along with other, less-known figures from Denmark to London and even St. Louis, Missouri. In that river city, "Leo Loeb, an émigré from Nazi Germany working at Washington University . . . was one of only a few transplantation researchers."[8] Loeb made early breakthroughs in the genetics underlying organ rejection.

A pair of ambitious academic surgeons in San Francisco would soon harbor their own dreams of the potential of sharing organs—particularly the heart. But before they teamed up in the late 1950s, another seismic shift in the world of medicine and public health took place. This one was prompted by the chest pains of the best-known world leader of the day, the American president, Dwight D. Eisenhower.

It was April 23, 1955, and Ike, as he was known, was on the eighth hole of the Cherry Hills Country Club near Denver when he doubled over in pain. Not to worry, the president reassured his aides, it's probably just the hamburger with Bermuda onions he wolfed down between morning and afternoon rounds. The president had been on an extended vacation for more than a month in the Rockies—mostly fishing and golfing. But his pains were making his driver feel as heavy as an M1 rifle.

The sixty-four-year-old leader of the free world tried his best to maintain his broad smile and sunny persona. After all, bounding across the putting greens of America was one way the spry soldier-turned-president could maintain his facade of good health and humor. It also was a way to avoid giving any ideas about American weakness to the nation's adversaries. The Soviet Union had recently exploded its own thermonuclear bomb.

Between his heartburn and apocalyptic nightmares, it was little wonder that the former five-star army general might find it hard to keep up his cheerful facade. Finally, he couldn't take it any longer. He woke up in agony beside his wife, Mamie, at 2:00 a.m. She promptly called Ike's personal physician, Dr. Howard M. Snyder.[9]

Snyder had spent the past decade attending to the famously bull-headed Ike—first as an army doctor. In the parlance of the day, Snyder was a general practitioner—the sort of kindhearted, advice-giving, cocktail-sharing kindred spirit who made house calls and would later be immortalized by Robert Young in TV's *Marcus Welby, M.D.*

Dr. Snyder was used to guiding Ike through the panoply of health issues, large and small, common to any man in his sixties—particularly those involving food and digestion. No matter how much he tried to get Ike to cut back on greasy foods, Snyder knew his boss would probably consume what he wanted. Worse yet, Ike also didn't heed Dr. Snyder's repeated warnings about the dangers of smoking. Like so many men and women of the 1940s and 1950s, Ike had developed a nasty four-pack-a-day habit. He'd started smoking decades before as a young cadet at West Point, so Snyder knew the general's constant smoking had done its damage to his heart and lungs.[10]

As headstrong as Ike could be, the president also prided himself on having a soldier's capacity for self-control. At age fifty-nine he accepted his doctor's advice and managed to quit smoking on the spot—cold turkey. The old soldier had a funny way of doing it, though. He stuffed his pockets full of cigarettes to share with others. "He would pass them out to other smokers but not touch them himself, because this gave him a feeling of accomplishment and superiority," recalled former Detroit mayor Jerome P. Cavanagh.[11]

Now Dr. Snyder was trying to get a grip on a potentially lethal health crisis facing the most powerful, and perhaps irascible, patient on the planet. Had President Eisenhower finally suffered a heart attack or was this another case of heartburn?

Sensing the fallout if he made the more dire diagnosis, Snyder chose the easier path. He administered a shot of morphine to ease Ike's pain and remained by his bedside, hoping relief would come by morning.

It didn't. So when the president's chest pain returned, Dr. Snyder called for an ambulance to rush him to nearby Fitzsimons Army Hospital. An electrocardiogram (EKG) revealed that Ike had experienced the blockage in his left coronary artery, causing an "acute anterolateral myocardial infarction," also known as coronary thrombosis.[12]

After initial White House announcements that Eisenhower had merely suffered "digestive upset," the next day Americans awakened to alarming news. The president was fighting for his life in a hospital oxygen tent. They read about ischemia—the lack of oxygenated blood to a tissue. In the case of Ike's cardiac ischemia, the lack of oxygen-rich blood to his heart was probably due to coronary artery disease from the years of smoking. His bad diet didn't help things.

Americans heard another new medical term—angina pectoris, often shortened to angina. As they absorbed more details about the president's near-death experience, Americans were getting a crash course on the heart. It couldn't have come too soon. Most Americans were unaware of their own risk factors. Diet was one place to start. Smoking was another. A sedentary lifestyle was another contributor to heart disease. Was it any wonder that Americans' coronary arteries were as clogged as old kitchen sinks?[13]

For the next two months, coronary heart disease was the news of the day. It was on every front page, movie newsreel, and TV broadcast. Reporters and readers alike scrutinized the detailed press releases that Ike drew up from his hospital bed. The thirty-fourth president knew he could have followed the tradition of denying and covering up presidential illness and physical incapacities. As one example, Woodrow Wilson was incapacitated by a stroke in 1919, leaving the public in the dark for many months as his wife, Edith, served as the "secret president," screening all visitors and making major decisions as Wilson struggled to complete his second term in office.[14]

Before Wilson was Grover Cleveland. When he needed surgery in 1893 to remove a cancerous tumor in his mouth, he had it done in secret while sailing on a friend's yacht off the coast of Long Island.[15]

FDR was a polio victim who managed to turn his recovery into an inspiring story during the decade of the Depression.[16] But when he started to decline precipitously before the 1944 election, Roosevelt chose to hide it. He was abetted by the media, which was willing to cover up the news while the nation was at war.

Ike was different. He understood the importance of transparency and honesty for a democracy to flourish. Even as Dr. Snyder and other specialists urged him to minimize his condition, Eisenhower firmly instructed his press secretary, James C. Hagerty, to "tell them everything."

The stock market already had plunged. It lost $14 billion—or 6 percent of its value—in the two days after the heart attack was reported. This was the worst single day for investors since the start of World War II.[17] Ike wasn't about to risk any speculation about his condition.

Hagerty took his instructions literally, perhaps to a fault. "Eisenhower's case, in contrast to the illnesses of Presidents Woodrow Wilson and Franklin D. Roosevelt, set a new standard for disclosure," Barron H. Lerner observed in the *New York Times*. "Indeed, discussion of intimate details, like the president's bowel movements, made some people squeamish."[18]

The daily dispatches had an unintended consequence, helping to raise his countrymen's awareness of heart disease, diet, and exercise.

As he stepped off the plane in Washington with Mamie at his side, Ike flashed his famous smile and quipped, "I am happy the doctors have given me at least a parole, if not a pardon, and I expect to be back at my accustomed duties, although they say I must ease my way into them and not bulldoze my way into them."[19]

President Eisenhower would later have a small stroke during a White House meeting in 1957. He also would undergo surgery to remove an obstruction caused by Crohn's disease, an inflammation of the intestines.[20]

Ike's health dramas led many Americans to examine their own health habits. "Long before it was fashionable to do so, [Ike] became obsessed with maintaining a lower blood cholesterol level through strict dietary and weight control," writes Dr. Nicholas J. Fortuin.

The war hero's most formidable foe, it turned out, was himself. He continued to make some very ill-advised choices of food—refusing, for example, to give up pig knuckles. The president was also "prone to sudden, ferocious, purple-veined eruptions of anger, often over minor matters," Fortuin writes, citing the historical work of Clarence G. Lasby. "It is clear that after his heart attack he worked to control the frequency of these spells."

★ ★ ★

As the heart became a continuing topic of national interest, a young couple from New York City was having their own talks about the best path to follow in medicine. Like most doctors of the day, Dick Lower started out as a generalist—or what was called a general practitioner. In this capacity, he would deliver babies and treat children and adults alike. He would make house calls. Yet after flirting with the idea of moving to Maine and becoming the town doctor, Dick Lower had a change of heart.

One day, seemingly out of the blue, he asked his wife, Anne, "What would you think if I went into surgery?"

"Go for it," Anne encouraged him.

Dick was soon accepted into the surgical residency program at Stanford Medical School, which at the time was in downtown San Francisco. "So we went to San Francisco, bought a house, and thought we'd live there the rest of our life," she recalled.[21]

The elite medical school had other ideas, though, moving south of the city to its main campus in Palo Alto. This forced the Lowers to move again to avoid a long daily commute. But before leaving town, Dick ran into someone who not only changed the course of his life but, arguably, would also alter the course of medical history: Dr. Norman Shumway.

As a first-year resident on the general surgery service, young Dr. Lower was expected to work on "stuff that came up in the middle of the night," he explained later. "I got a call one night they needed some-one to help Dr. Shumway. I'd never heard of him."[22]

Dick had to look hard to find the guy conducting research in relative obscurity in the bowels of Stanford's aging facility. At the time, Shumway was something of a loner. His clinical duties involved kidney patients, but his passion was probing the inner workings of the heart.

Shumway had arrived from the University of Minnesota, hoping to work his way onto the A-team of Stanford's surgical residents. But his outspoken personality had rubbed some of the cliquey surgeons the wrong way. He was banished to the basement to supervise patients hooked up to an early version of a kidney dialysis machine.

Undaunted, Shumway was determined to find a way to test some of the advanced techniques he'd learned from surgeons in Minnesota who used extreme cold to treat damaged organs—including the heart.

By the time Lower found Shumway, he was impressed by how far he'd gotten in his animal research with minimal support from the sur-gery staff. All the while, Shumway had taken good care of his kidney patients.

Shumway gave him a tour of his basement empire. He was especially proud of some promising experiments using extreme cold to keep his dogs' hearts viable during operations.

"You better come work with me in the lab," he said with a sly smile. "You'll really learn to operate."

As Lower pondered the offer, he sensed this solitary surgeon was onto something.

Before he knew it—and before running it by Anne—Dick Lower agreed to join him.

CHAPTER SIX

Heart on Ice

THE PRECARIOUS STATE OF President Eisenhower's heart remained in the news throughout the 1950s. Yet the kind of innovative heart research that Dick Lower and Norm Shumway were perfecting usually stayed on the periphery of public consciousness. The nation seemed to have bigger problems to solve—from the impact of the 1954 Supreme Court decision ordering the desegregation of the nation's public schools to rising fears of a nuclear holocaust.

On October 4, 1957, Americans awoke to another shocking headline every bit as worrisome as Ike's heart attack. The Soviet Union had successfully launched an orbital carrier rocket (derived from an intercontinental ballistic missile), sending the world's first satellite into Earth's orbit. Overnight, it seemed, the United States faced a threat from above.

They called it *Sputnik*, or "fellow traveler." It had two radio transmitters emitting a continuous beep as it circled Earth. From London to Cairo, Tokyo to Washington, people went outside searching for signs of the satellite. It was a tiny aluminum alloy sphere—measuring 22.8 inches in diameter and weighing 184 pounds. Yet *Sputnik* had an outsize propaganda value. In Moscow, the Communist regime said the successful launch marked "a victory over American materialism." Soviet premier Nikita Khrushchev threatened to launch more rockets by the dozen—"like sausages."[1]

In Washington, a presidential adviser scoffed at *Sputnik's* importance, calling it "a silly bauble in the sky." This was an especially bad time for Ike. He was still suffering from the aftereffects of his heart attack as well as from lingering intestinal pain. Eisenhower was hardly at his best facing reporters eager to know how America's military was caught off guard by the Soviets' space program. What if they replace the harmlessly beeping "fellow traveler" with something less benign—like a nuclear bomb?

It was hard for the ailing president to honestly answer such questions. He couldn't reveal the recent innovations in America's high-altitude photography. "The Air Force had the capacity to take a picture from 55,000 feet of Ike's golf ball on a putting green," writes David Halberstam in *The Fifties*.[2] The crystal-clear, high-altitude reconnaissance photos soon would be taken by a top secret US spy plane. The U-2 was capable of soaring through the upper reaches of Earth's atmosphere at seventy thousand to eighty thousand feet. Ike's generals thought their spy planes were flying too high ever to be hit by Soviet air defenses—a bit of hubris that would soon fall to earth.

★ ★ ★

"The success of *Sputnik* seemed to herald a kind of technological Pearl Harbor," Halberstam writes. "Some saw it as a rebuke to America's self-indulgence. . . . Suddenly it seemed as if America were undergoing a national crisis of confidence."[3]

As the Cold War chilled Washington, another kind of science-based drama was unfolding in San Francisco. A cadre of CIA agents launched a series of secret experiments to explore the deepest recesses of the human brain. Their cloak-and-dagger operation was conducted near Stanford Lane Hospital in San Francisco, where Norm Shumway and Dick Lower were busy with their heart research.

In a covert operation called MK-ULTRA, the CIA from 1953 to 1964 conducted a series of ethically outrageous drug tests in San Francisco and nearby Stanford University in Palo Alto. They employed psychologists, psychiatrists, nurses, and other health practitioners to conduct clinical studies of a mind-altering substance that had been discovered in a Swiss lab: LSD.

Time health writer Maia Szalavitz described the CIA's clandestine effort as an "utterly-unbelievable-but-true story" that "involved using hookers to lure in unsuspecting johns for undisclosed testing, narcotics agents who slipped drugs into drinks, and a U.S. marshal who held up a San Francisco bar not knowing he was high on acid."[4]

It took years before journalists exposed these government-backed operations. The psychedelic spy craft would join other instances in American medicine where human rights were trampled in the name of progress. In the 1950s and 1960s, doctors and academic medical centers enjoyed so much prestige and authority that they often operated virtually unchecked from outside supervision. The notion of "informed consent" was nonexistent.

One example is the Tuskegee syphilis study, in which the US Public Health Service recruited hundreds of African American men and gave them the painful, fatal disease. Another is when Johns Hopkins Hospital researchers removed and exploited the cervical cancer cells of an unsuspecting Baltimore woman named Henrietta Lacks. In other cases, various drugs for a variety of diseases were tested on unwitting subjects, including those deemed "mentally defective."[5]

★ ★ ★

While the CIA was rewiring the brains of human guinea pigs around San Francisco, Anne and Dick Lower were living there in a much more conventional fashion. Anne had her hands full raising their young sons as Dick worked long hours with his enthusiastic colleague in the Stanford animal lab.

"Norm used to say, 'Beguile the tedium,'" Dick Lower said.[6]

If anyone could find research beguiling, it was this "tall, lanky country boy from Michigan."[7] When Shumway arrived at Stanford in the mid-1950s, he already had performed two tours as an army combat surgeon. This seemed to equip him with the emotional armor to shrug off any slights he may have felt early on at the prestigious medical school. Plus, he had a surgical weapon in his operating arsenal that most of his elders had never heard of: "total-body hypothermia." That is, the use of extreme cold to protect the heart during surgery.

Shumway had acquired this training while completing his postgraduate medical education at the University of Minnesota, known for its open-heart surgery program. He studied under two influential surgeons, C. Walton Lillehei and F. John Lewis. By the early 1950s, they were using extreme cold to operate on a patient's heart while blood circulation and breathing were handled by a heart-lung machine.[8]

Shumway's doctoral thesis on "the effects of hypothermia on the heart" argued that when used properly, extreme cold could lower the heart's temperature. In a later journal article from 1959, Shumway, Lower, and veterinarian Raymond Stofer detailed its beneficial effects. Hypothermia provided a safer alternative to what was then the most widely used method for heart stoppage during surgery—that is, the injection of potassium. The chemical's aftereffects often made it hard to restart the heart after a period of oxygen deprivation—anoxic arrest.

They continued, "Selective cooling of the heart is an attractive adjunct for anoxic arrest because of the need for abolishing coronary flow for a considerable interval of time in the surgical correction of cardiac lesions." By irrigating the pericardial sac "with cold saline" or similar solutions, the Stanford team reported they could avoid the "disadvantages of potassium arrest or coronary infusion with cold blood, yet it provides a dry, quiet heart for prolonged periods."

Using a heart-lung machine to handle breathing and blood circulation, they discovered they could take a full hour to operate "during cardiopulmonary bypass with blood at normal body temperature." That was three times longer than earlier operations that had about a twenty-minute limit, they wrote.[9]

The cooling technique also helped lower the level of electricity needed to shock the heart back to its normal rhythm when the operation was over.[10]

The innovations Shumway carried with him from Minnesota to California came at a time when heart surgery remained "pretty crude," as Lower later put it.[11] Working together, the Stanford duo was determined to take heart surgery to another level. They tested their theories on stray dogs plucked from the alleys of downtown San Francisco.

"The dogs became my project in the lab," Lower recalled.[12] The working conditions were less than ideal, or what one colleague called "relics of the past, even for the 1950s." They shared a single large laboratory with fourth-year medical students who were taking a mandatory course in dog surgery. The old washbasins were made of cement. The plumbing was exposed. "On rainy days, the silence of the dark and gloomy interior was interrupted by the sound of leaking rainwater being caught in buckets."[13]

Adding to the subpar conditions was the steady drip of negative comments they heard from peers and outsiders alike. "Some people thought they were crazy," Anne Lower later recalled. Some fellow physicians even objected to the very idea of operating on the heart. "They'd say, 'God didn't intend for you to do this—you're interrupting the blood supply.' "[14]

The local SPCA also criticized them for conducting animal research. As a result, the medical school was cautious about releasing any news of their research success.

Dick was undeterred, though. "It takes a certain kind of person who has the gall to cut into a person's chest," Anne explained. "That kind of person takes a risk to prove things that they know are viable."

One of the couple's early conversations reflects this sense of purpose. While they were moving their young family to San Francisco, Anne asked Dick about his underlying motive for becoming a surgeon.

"What's your goal?"

Thinking it over, he replied, "I want the respect of my peers. Those are the people who value me and know what I'm doing."

This never changed in the years to come. "All that mattered," said Anne, "was the respect of doctors who encouraged him to go on."

★　★　★

One early encourager was Dr. Roy Cohn, who, as acting chairman of Stanford's Department of Surgery, oversaw their work. Getting them out of their leaky lab, Cohn invited Shumway and Lower to join a team of pediatric surgeons who were leaving Stanford to work at the nearby Children's Hospital of San Francisco. Among them was Dr. Ann Purdy who—like Shumway—expressed disdain for some of Stanford's more established surgeons.

Dr. Cohn's liberating offer included funds for Norm to purchase a state-of-the-art heart-lung machine. In addition, when Cohn's caseload became too heavy, he shifted the work to Shumway. This gave Norm's career a boost and opened new research horizons. He also profited from the assistance provided by Raymond Stofer, who'd been recruited to run the research lab. The accomplished animal doctor helped Shumway create a custom-built perfusion system to keep the blood and oxygen flowing through dogs' veins during surgery. It also could be adapted for human use.

Shumway and Lower became a dynamic duo, aided by the resourceful Dr. Stofer. They shuttled from working with the dogs at Stanford Lane to operating on children at Children's Hospital, which required transporting their mobile system on the steep and challenging streets of San Francisco. Their first case involved the repair of a heart defect in a young woman by using Shumway's total-body hypothermia.

Biographer Donald McRae captures their comradery in *Every Second*

Counts: The Race to Transplant the First Human Heart: "They had solved the initial problem of transporting their heart-lung machine across town by hiring a van from Sparky's Delivery Service. They got a real charge when they roared up in a Sparky van. It was the kind of stunt you would expect from two guys called Dick and Norm."[15]

It wasn't all fun and games, though, and sometimes events left them shaken. One such early operation was on a boy "where a tiny piece of heart muscle was sucked back into the machine," entering the patient's brain and killing him. "Lower and Shumway were devastated."[16]

★ ★ ★

Sometimes Anne dropped by their lab. She loved listening to them debate the nature of their groundbreaking research. It was so new they struggled for the right words to describe it.

"What are we going to call what we're doing, Lower?" Norm asked.

Was it "autotransplantation"? The first part of the term—"auto"— referred to the self, and the second part to transplanting another's heart to help a patient live. Or perhaps a better term was "autoimmune transplant?" The prefixes were as endless as the possibilities they were pondering.

As they developed their own lexicon, they also grappled with a deeper, more philosophical question, Anne recalled. "When the heart is changed, is the person changed?" It would take nearly a decade to know for sure.

★ ★ ★

Success bred success. Dogs with transplanted hearts started living for more than a few hours to several days at a time. A week seemed within reach.

Their operations began by opening the dog's pericardium—the double-walled sac containing the heart and the roots of large blood vessels. Then the doctors used sutures to form what was called a pericardial cradle. After clamping the blood flow of its largest artery (the aorta), they immersed the heart in a cold saline solution that slowed its metabolism. The heart was in a state of suspended animation.

Now they could start repairing its defects. When they were finished, they released the clamp to the aorta. This restored the normal blood flow, warming the heart. A mild shock and—presto!—it started beating normally.

"Shumway had a great idea," Dick Lower reflected later, "which was if you cool the heart down, you can do just about anything with it." By cutting off the circulation of the heart, you can spend an hour repairing it. Then "the heart would start up beautifully."[17]

As they perfected their surgical techniques, Dick and Norm knew many obstacles had to be overcome before attempting to transplant a human heart. The most vexing one was tissue rejection—the same problem that had confounded medical researchers for centuries.

Animals and humans alike have immune systems to protect them from a legion of outside invaders, from germs to cancer cells to poisons. Every organic invader has proteins (called antigens) that coat their surface. Like an early-warning system, whenever the immune system senses these foreign bodies, it launches an attack of antibodies.

The same principle applies to transplanted organs. At first, the body's defenses (the immune system) detect the differences of the antigens on the cells of the transplanted organ. This can trigger a potentially damaging or deadly rejection.[18] This helps explain why some of the earliest success stories in transplantation occurred with identical twins, since they possess identical tissue antigens.[19] Such was the case in 1954, when Joseph E. Murray and a surgical team at Peter Bent Brigham Hospital in Boston performed the first truly successful kidney transplant from one twin to another.[20]

Otherwise, transplant surgeons had to use imperfect cortisone-like medications to try to trick the body's natural self-defenses from kicking in. These were called immunosuppressants.[21]

Yet they persisted, dreaming of the day they could replace "a dying heart with the still healthy organ transplanted from a human donor who had just been killed by an accidental head injury," McRae writes. "While it was still too early to tell, it seemed likely that, using their cold saline solution, they would be able to safely store a heart cut from a fresh corpse for at least an hour."[22]

That's when the clock would start ticking.

★   ★   ★

Notwithstanding their big dreams, they kept a low profile, content to be left alone to do their work. This changed overnight in late 1959 when Dr. Cohn was so "exhilarated by the success of Lower and Shumway's transplant experiment" that he bragged about it on local TV. The news quickly spread.[23]

One local reporter sensed the broader implications of the recent breakthrough. "The dog is still alive one week later," reported George Dusheck in the San Francisco *News-Call Bulletin*. "The daring experiment was carried out by Dr. Richard Lower, working with Dr. Norman Shumway at Stanford's new Palo Alto medical center." Then the reporter made a prediction that would capture the imaginations of newspaper editors around the United States: "Dr. Lower's feat, therefore, is a demonstration that when the problem of host immunity reaction is solved, the surgeons will be ready to install healthy hearts (presumably from victims of other diseases) in place of diseased hearts."[24]

It became a national story. On the last day of the decade—December 31, 1959—the *New York Times* ran an Associated Press account with a dramatic headline: "Dog Stays Alive with a New Heart."

> Two young Stanford surgeons have successfully transplanted a living heart from one dog to another. The mongrel male dog was alive today, a week after the operation.
>
> The experiment was carried out at Stanford University's new

medical center by Dr. Norman Shumway, 36 years old, and Dr. Richard Lower, 30. A medical school spokesman said he recalled a case in which another dog had undergone a heart transplant but lived only 7 ½ hours.

The operation by the Stanford doctors differed in one respect from previous attempts. They left in the host dog a portion of the wall of the auricles, the upper chambers of the heart, including the area where the entering veins carry blood back into the heart.

They explained that venous blood flows somewhat more slowly than arterial blood and was more likely to clot. Animals previously subjected to heart transplant operations died of clots.

The spokesman said the apparent significance of the operation was in getting the transplanted heart into the dog's body.

Many years later, Lower ruefully recalled this first brush with fame. "You would have thought the atomic bomb went off."[25]

It wouldn't be the last time.

CHAPTER SEVEN

Restless Genius

ACROSS THE COUNTRY FROM San Francisco, in a southern city not known for its willingness to embrace newcomers or new ideas, another academic surgeon was testing the limits of transplantation. His work took many forms and followed many hunches—from inserting monkey kidneys into humans to testing organ sharing between humans, chimpanzees, and, in one instance, a pig.

When it came to challenging medical conventions, few researchers could match the nerve and intensity of Dr. David Milford Hume. He was not yet forty years old when word of his pending arrival at the Medical College of Virginia made front-page news in the *Richmond News Leader*: "New Chairman of Surgery Arrives for Duty at MCV."

The headline reflected the high regard the public held for doctors in the 1950s and expressed a sense of hometown pride. "The Medical College of Virginia's new long-awaited professor and chairman of surgery has arrived to take over his joint responsibilities at the college and hospital. Dr. Hume, 38, comes from the Harvard Medical School, where he was assistant professor of surgery and director of the surgical research laboratory."[1]

Hume would be paid $15,000 a year in 1956, "in recognition of the importance of the professor of surgery," Dean John B. Truslow told the paper. The generous salary (equivalent to about $140,000 in 2020) was intended to allow the surgical chief to "devote more of his time to academic duties and research."

A black-and-white photo shows a serious, pensive-looking figure in a coat and tie—a true Harvard man who reportedly had a "warm personality." In this introduction to a reading audience across Virginia, David Hume seemed to step out of an episode of *Father Knows Best* or other squeaky-clean TV shows of the day.

He came across as a regular guy, starting by acknowledging the "tremendous opportunity" of his appointment. Hume also described his family's "rough trip" driving down south in a blue station wagon. "In addition to Mrs. Hume and him, the car contained their four children, a dog, a cat and parakeet," the paper said. The dog was a six-week-old puppy recently "born in Dr. Hume's research laboratory in Boston" and given to his oldest daughter for Christmas.

After this early, warmhearted introduction, though, it soon became apparent to his new colleagues at MCV that Hume had other sides to his personality. These hidden traits seemed to be more of a resemblance to the more conflicted actors of the day (James Dean, Marlon Brando) than to the wise and gentle fathers (Robert Young, Ozzie Nelson) out in TV land.

Yet, there was little doubt that the intense scholar-surgeon was held in high esteem by many leading academic medical researchers of the day. These included supervisors and colleagues at Harvard and its teaching hospital, Peter Bent Brigham Hospital.[2] The Boston hospital had achieved medical celebrity status in 1954 by conducting the first truly successful kidney transplant from one twin to another.[3] Hume was part of the transplant team that later was recognized by a Nobel Prize in Medicine.

"I have known Dr. Hume for the past 10 years and have consistently regarded him as the most outstanding of the young men here in surgery,"

J. Hartwell Harrison, MD, another noted surgeon at the hospital, wrote in a recommendation letter. He praised Hume's surgical skills and his "outstanding investigative work" and his laboratory skills. "Dave has a tremendous capacity for work," Harrison wrote, "and he is able to fulfill this because of his intense curiosity and desire to progress" in medicine.[4]

Perhaps the most influential plaudits that helped Hume land the job came from Dr. Francis "Frannie" D. Moore, the hospital's surgeon in chief and a nationally known expert on kidney transplantation. After lauding Hume's surgical skills, Moore cited his "active investigative program which he is conducting on his own right. His extensive work on renal transplantation is excellent evidence of his ingenuity and ability of his operative work." [5]

Hiring Hume had proven to be a balancing act for MCV's leadership. They wanted to snag a surgeon from a top-flight school with a strong research reputation. But they were somewhat limited by their own modest budget and wanted to find someone "young enough so that MCV could afford him."[6]

The medical school's dean, Dr. John Truslow, was a Harvard grad himself. So he sent an emissary to Dr. Moore asking for his advice, which was simple: Hire Hume, he said.[7] It was all Truslow needed to hear to offer him the job.

What Moore *didn't* tell MCV's emissary might have helped everyone in Richmond better understand the restless mind and domineering personality of their new hire. One story serves to illustrate the unique blend of brilliance and bossiness that would form the basis of what became the legend of David Hume. Some eight years earlier—in 1947—a young woman had arrived at Peter Bent Brigham Hospital clinging to life. She'd gone into septic shock from an abortion gone wrong and was suffering acute kidney failure. Finally, she slipped into a coma.

"Accordingly, we solicited the help of Doctor David Hume who went hunting for a prospective donor," Moore recalled. "We were fortunate to obtain a cadaver kidney later that day."[8]

The ensuing nocturnal operation had some of the elements of the nineteenth-century anatomy classes at America's growing medical schools—including Harvard and MCV. Moore, Hume, and others hurriedly worked to excise a kidney from the cadaver and attach it to the woman's thigh. This temporary measure allowed them to avoid renal failure—the complete shutdown of kidney functions. First, though, they had to overcome the objections of the hospital's administration about bringing such an "extremely critical" patient into the operating room.

These were the days before federal privacy regulations (HIPAA) and strict rules for obtaining a patient's prior consent to participate in a medical experiment. Across America, rule-bending surgeons usually encountered little interference. Sometimes a hospital administrator might complain about a breach in rules or operating protocols. Occasionally, transplant surgeons were dismissed as "mavericks" by colleagues who "widely criticized" their work."[9] Yet Hume seemed to relish his outsider role and was undeterred by any professional jealousy. Between 1951 and 1953, he performed nine kidney transplants at the Boston hospital. This included one transplant that functioned for more than five months before it was rejected.[10]

To early mentors such as Moore, Hume's zeal was born of an intense interest in science and saving lives. Later, Hume's critics would ask whether he sometimes went too far.

"In the dark of night," Moore later described the case of the young dying woman, "about midnight, when the kidney had been obtained immediately after the death of the donor, our little group, the urologist on the case, Hume and myself, proceeded to one of the end rooms on the second floor, and by the light of the two small gooseneck student lamps, prepared to do the transplant."

The Boston woman survived because of the experimental procedure. Though the transplanted kidney started to have problems, Lower would later note, "Fortunately by that time her own kidney had opened up, and she actually survived and left the hospital." In Lower's view, "That is really the first kidney transplant."[11]

It would not be recognized as such, however. That would come seven years later when Hume was on the surgical team of Dr. Joseph E. Murray, in Boston. This operation was recognized as the first successful transplant of the kidneys of identical twins and later would be cited when Murray shared a Nobel Prize.[12]

To Lower, the 1947 effort to help the victim of a botched abortion was quintessential Dave Hume: act first, seek permission later. In this case, the dimly lit, clandestine operation succeeded, with no one the wiser. No newspaper headlines, no hospital investigations, and—in those days before "malpractice" was every doctor's worst nightmare—no litigation.

Other parts of Hume's early body of work did receive ample publicity, helping build the reputation that led him to the Medical College of Virginia. In 1949, when he was in his early thirties, the *New York Times* ran a provocative headline, "Hormone Is Indicated in 'Seat of Emotion,'" about his presentation at a medical conference in Chicago.

"Experimental evidence was presented here today that the hypothalamus, a part of the forebrain designated as the 'seat of emotions,' secretes a vital hormone necessary for the activation of the all-important pituitary and the adrenal glands in response to stress," reported science writer William L. Laurence. "The evidence was offered at the annual clinical congress of the American College of Surgeons by Dr. David M. Hume of the surgical laboratories of the Peter Bent Brigham Hospital, Harvard Medical School."[13]

Noting the "great significance" of Hume's findings, Laurence added, "It not only promises to shed light on the mechanism involved in the body's response to stress under the influence of the pituitary-adrenal system, but also to provide a powerful agent for stimulating those two vital glands into activity, now known to be essential for the maintenance of health and for the prevention of a host of baffling ills, including arthritis, rheumatic fever and gout."

Laurence cited the brilliance of the Harvard doctor's "studies on animals" and how they reacted to stress when their hypothalamus glands were injured.

In an ironic twist, a later account of David Hume's MCV saga noted how often he induced higher levels of stress among fellow faculty members. "When the search committee from the Medical College visited the Harvard medical school to look into young Dr. Hume's record and interview him, they were told, in effect, that Hume would either give MCV the best surgical department it ever had or he would wreck it," historian Virginius Dabney wrote. It was a close call, Dabney added. "He succeeded in the former objective [raising the status of MCV's surgery department] and almost in the latter [wrecking it]."[14]

Hume was the son of a wholesale grocer and homemaker in Muskegon, Michigan. It was a village on the eastern shore of Lake Michigan with a rich history as a lumber town and, before that, a French-fur trading post and village of the Ottawa tribe.[15] Young Dave Hume dreamed of following his father into business, perhaps getting into real estate. A new dream emerged, though, after his brother-in-law, a doctor, convinced him to pursue a career in medicine.[16]

After transferring from a Michigan junior college, Dave Hume headed east to Harvard. He played football there on the brink of World War II. From there he went to medical school at the University of Chicago, gaining a colorful reputation as a student who studied, played, and partied hard.

"I met him when he was a medical student and I was an undergraduate," recalled Dr. Walter Lawrence, who became a noted cancer surgeon at MCV. "I played intramural football [against Hume] and I thought he was an obnoxious, loud-talking guy." Nonetheless, Lawrence said he developed a grudging respect for Hume's intellect, drive, and daring.

"I think everyone, including Lower, considered Hume in charge of everything," Lawrence said of Hume's control of MCV's surgical department. "Dr. Hume dominated the scene, without question."[17]

His work ethic stood out—even in a profession with more than its share of workaholics. His wife, Martha, recalled him saying, "I will be home for supper—and he wasn't home for three days. . . . That's the way he was. . . . He would get in the hospital and he would forget everything."[18] It was left to her to get their three daughters to dance classes, as well as providing for her husband's care, feeding, dressing, and other needs.

Though dinner was on the table by 6:00 p.m., he often didn't make it home to eat with his family or for their bedtimes. "I would make a plate for him and cover it with Reynolds Wrap and put it in the oven, and just let it sit there." By the time Hume ate the meal—often after 11:00 p.m.—it had congealed into a gray mass. "But he would eat it."

David Hume was driven by his outsize ambition but also by the expectation of MCV's leadership for him to help lift the college out of its decidedly second-class doldrums. "By the early 1950s, the nation boasted 80 medical schools of which 65 had full-time faculty," according to one account. "These schools were ready to take advantage of the huge appropriations from the National Institute of Health to support training programs in research. But MCV, like 14 other regional medical schools, held out, entrenched it seemed, in an older paradigm of part-time faculty and community private practice."[19]

When it came to national standings, Virginia's second "flagship" medical school (the University of Virginia also claimed that distinction) found itself stuck at half-mast. "If MCV was going to thrive, something had to change," said Dr. William Sanger, who led the medical school from 1925 to 1956. It didn't help faculty morale when the American Medical Association criticized MCV for its "lack of advanced research at the college" plus "the fact that so many of the faculty had been trained in Virginia," historian Dabney notes.[20]

After Sanger retired in 1956, his successor, Dr. Robert Blackwell Smith, continued the image upgrade. Hume was one among a number of promising young doctors who were hired to inject new life into a hidebound institution. By no means was this a charitable effort, since millions of dollars in new federal grants for health research were up for grabs.

The hard-nosed athlete and relentless researcher wasted no time in trying to move the ball down the field for his new medical team in Richmond. He was only too happy to tackle any obstacles that got in his way. He actually seemed to relish confrontation—a trait that was accepted at first as MCV tried to meet early demands for more personnel, equipment, and research space. His 1955 acceptance letter included a list of such requests, including "construction of a clinical research laboratory on the same floor with the ward surgical beds" and "enlargement of facilities for animal and laboratory space."[21] Putting the surgical ward near his research space would ensure he would keep potential human subjects in close proximity to his experimentation.

Hume made another demand that was key to seizing control of the surgery department: as chairman, he insisted that he preferred to deal "directly in matters involving his department, with the Dean of the Medical College and the Hospital Administrator, and that these dealings do not involve a committee."[22] Faculty appointments were the lone exception.

Hume soon became the talk of the hospital and—for better or worse—of the town. As a later account of his tenure put it: "He thrived on activity. He required little sleep, less food, and sustained himself with cigarettes and Coca-Colas."[23] As he worked to consolidate power in the surgery department, he began bringing in his own doctors, which often rubbed old-timers the wrong way.

"Hume could be brash, impetuous, and insensitive," Richmond physician B. Noland Carter II later observed. As Hume sought "to grab hold of the brass ring of new research dollars, he dismissed the enormous value that community physicians brought to MCV." Some doctors began resenting their alma mater, Carter said, because "when Hume came, he cleaned house."[24]

Martha Hume explained why. "He wanted to change the [way] medicine was [practiced] down here," she observed. "He thought a lot of the doctors were old southern types who were too conservative." He also didn't like the segregated hospital for black patients at MCV—St. Philip. Early on he turned down an invitation to join the elite, all-white Country Club of Virginia because of its policy against admitting people who were Jewish.[25]

★   ★   ★

When it came to changing the culture of his surgery department, David Hume wasn't subtle. His hard-charging personality left a trail of broken feelings and relationships. But he managed to win most internal battles by accomplishing his main directive from MCV's leadership—raising his department's national profile. He did so by doing what he loved best—operating on man and beast.

Like the Stanford surgeons, Shumway and Lower, he preferred to do his work without fanfare and in the privacy of his own operating room. The less people knew—including administrators and fellow doctors—the better. Once he had something to announce—a new development in kidney transplantation, for example—he would write a journal article or present it at a national conference. But until then, "Dr. Hume kept everything quiet," recalled his nurse, Kay Andrews Martine. "He didn't want a lot of publicity."[26]

He didn't always get his way, though. When the MCV hospital administrator learned he was operating on animals in the regular operating rooms for human patients, he was told to stop. He was also ordered not to operate on corpses, which he used to obtain kidneys for experiments.

Hume ignored the ban, though. When he sent some associates to retrieve yet another dead body from the morgue, an attendant tried to stop them. Hume, not one to listen to a lowly attendant, did as he pleased. When the administrator, Charles Cardwell, heard about it, he went ballistic.

A truce was called, though, and an agreement reached. Hume could use an abandoned labor and delivery room in St. Philip Hospital—the segregated hospital for black patients—to cut into corpses and operate on chimps, monkeys, and baboons.

This segregated system of medical experimentation took considerable creativity and logistics. It required moving patients, donated organs, animals, and sterilized equipment up and down elevators and through an underground tunnel linking the facilities. Somehow Hume and his close-knit team of surgical residents and nurses made it work.[27]

On one particularly busy night, Hume was operating on two sick patients at once: one receiving a cadaver kidney, while another was being prepared to receive a pair of kidneys from a monkey.

Nurse Andrews Martine vividly recalled the latter patient. "The [recipient of] the rhesus monkey was a used car salesman, and the reason I remember him pretty well is . . . in the city there were signs on the buses that said, 'Mad Man Dapper Dan' and the man worked . . . for Mad Man Dapper Dan."

Because the car salesman didn't have any family members whose kidneys might have proved to be a good match, "he was told there was no hope for him other than either a cadaver or the rhesus monkey. He knew it was experimental and he agreed to do this."

The dual transplant surgeries—one using a monkey's kidneys, the other taking the kidneys of a recently deceased accident victim—was one of the zaniest, yet most rewarding, nights of Andrews Martine's career. "I nursed both of them that night, and stayed twenty-four hours, to try to make sure they were taken care of."

The car salesman required the most attention during the postoperative period. Four intravenous lines stretched from arms and legs while he produced prodigious amounts of urine—so much that it began spreading across the floor. The nurse used Hume's empty Coke bottles to try to capture the overflow.

"I have never seen anybody put out that much urine," she recalled.

In the middle of the night the ailing salesman became agitated and started picking at his skin. The nurse dashed out into the hall to alert an on-call physician who was catching up on his sleep on a stretcher.

"It looks like he's going into the DTs [delirium tremens]!" she exclaimed. "He's picking at everything."

Yawning and rubbing his eyes, the doctor quipped, "Well, when he starts asking for bananas, call me."

It was no laughing matter for Dapper Dan's salesman who didn't survive the experimental operation that borrowed the monkey's organs. "The man literally peed himself to death," said Dr. Hume.[28] Presumably, the monkey also perished.

The legend of Hume's daring antics continued to grow around MCV. One case involved an attempted kidney transplant from a baboon to a human in which Dr. Hume purportedly was "running around the operating room" trying to keep the animal quiet, his nurse said.[29] Hume finally managed to sedate the primate and remove a kidney—which, his nurse recalled, then "was taken through the tunnel in a basin with a sterile cover over it." Word of the operation preceded it, though. The sight of a surgical resident carrying a baboon kidney didn't seem to faze the elevator operator.

"Is that the baboon kidney?" he asked.

★   ★   ★

Hume seemed happiest when he was working.

"He was very pleasant, very organized, very happy in the operating room," Andrews Martine recalled. "He would start his procedure. He would be ready. And there was always this communication back and forth" with the transplant team over at St. Philip.

One story serves to illustrate Hume's willingness to laugh at himself to lighten the mood in the OR. One day, Hume, who had bushy eyebrows, was gazing down at a patient's wound. Staring intently, he said, "What's that?"

"A hair," someone said. Then a resident or intern boldly suggested, "I think it's a Dave Hume bushy eyebrow."

Hume laughed at the joke, then took a hemostat and removed the offending hair. "He had a sense of humor on things like that," Andrews Martine said. "You would have thought he would have been very angry, but he wasn't."

He lived for the next challenge, no matter how far out it was. "His brain was constantly at work to try to create and come up with a new thing," Andrews Martine said. Hume had a natural charisma that attracted younger residents, fellow surgeons, and nurses alike. He encouraged innovation while giving everyone "enough rope to hang yourself," Andrews Martine said. Reflecting on Hume's nearly two-decade-long tenure at MCV, she said, "It was like a little family."

But it was a family that learned to keep secrets. One such case involved a young girl with cirrhosis of the liver.

Hume was keeping a small pig in his animal laboratory, so—in an effort to help the dying girl—he decided to remove the pig's liver and see if it could act as a surrogate organ. "You could see the steam [rising], to keep it warm and moist," Andrews Martine recalled of the animal's organ. Once Dr. Hume figured out a way to attach the girl's arteries to the donated organ, she said, "We ran her blood through the liver."

It was a form of human-animal liver dialysis. The idea was to keep the girl alive until Hume could find a proper human donor. "But the girl didn't make it."

Such setbacks aside, Hume never lost his enthusiasm for the next big thing. Whenever an accident victim with little hope of survival was brought into his operating room, Hume was careful to make sure "the heart was beating . . . and then they would take the kidney out." At that time in the early to mid-1960s, there was no reliable method available for transporting donated kidneys to recipients. So, his nurse explained, "We were so afraid that they would have kidney damage that, you know, they would keep the patient going."

Hume never seemed to lose his sense of boyish wonder when he saw a gray kidney taken out of a dead body. As the organ was revived with fresh blood, Hume exclaimed, "Oh it's getting pink!"

And once the kidney began to function normally, allowing the patient to produce and excrete urine, "he was beside himself with excitement—every time, I mean, it wasn't just one. It was every transplant he was excited about."

Not everyone shared his excitement, though. Nor was everyone a fan. One attending staff nephrologist—a kidney disease specialist—refused to provide dialysis treatments for Hume's patients to purify their blood when the kidney wasn't functioning normally. "They did not believe in transplantation," Andrews Martine explained. "They thought it was heresy; they thought it was awful."

Some pushback was inevitable, though. Sometimes nurses from other departments would still be grieving the loss of a patient. They were hardly in the mood to turn them over to Hume's residents seeking "cadaver donors" of kidneys. "They felt like they were sacrificing someone in order to transplant."

Still, as other patients survived and returned to normal life, word spread about the surgeon with the healing touch. Young residents began to talk like him and even walk like him. Dr. Hunter McGuire Jr., a surgical resident at the time, experienced both doubt and awe working with MCV's star surgeon. The surgery department "flourished because Hume tried techniques and grafts and stuff like that," including taking out skin cancers (melanoma).[30]

McGuire came from a long line of Virginia doctors who'd seen plenty of war, bloodshed, and upheaval. He was the great-great-grandson of Dr. Hunter Holmes McGuire, who served as Confederate general Thomas J. "Stonewall" Jackson's surgeon in the Civil War, amputating the rebel general's left arm in a failed effort to save him after he was wounded by friendly fire at the Battle of Chancellorsville in 1863.[31] A statue of Dr. McGuire—who went on to a distinguished career after the war and became president of the American Medical Association—is on the capitol grounds in Richmond. The Hunter Holmes McGuire VA Medical Center is named for him.

A century after his ancestor survived the carnage of Virginia's battlefields, young Dr. McGuire endured his own professional fields of fire. He was especially concerned by David Hume's failure to fully explain the risks of experimental procedures to unsuspecting patients. "People didn't know what he was doing."[32]

Even so, as he looked back at his ethically challenged mentor, McGuire conceded that "all these things made the residency very exciting. . . . Something new and fresh was happening all the time."[33]

With Hume's growing reputation came more fame and power— within the hospital and beyond. "The personality of Hume [and] his presence was so impressive and so charismatic" it was palpable, McGuire remembered. When the elevator door opened, "you could sense Hume's presence on the elevator without being able to see him." And if he wasn't on the elevator, McGuire added, "He was running up sixteen floors just to prove to people he could do it."[34]

His patients "loved him," nurse Andrews Martine said. "They looked on Dr. Hume like he was God, and when he came into the room, they all felt better." In an age when "bedside manner" was still part of the health-care lexicon, Hume "would sit on the side of the bed and talk to them very gently . . . he was very kind. And the families loved him, too." His daily rounds in the surgical wards became a kind of performance, with patients and families crowding the hallways to catch a glimpse of the famous Dr. Hume.

He even celebrated anniversaries of transplant patients at his farm west of Richmond. At one such soiree for a one-year transplant survivor, Hume's nurse drove up the driveway only to find people scrambling outside the farmhouse. In his zeal, Hume had managed to shatter a kitchen window with a champagne cork.

In another instance, Hume learned that one of his recent kidney-transplant patients was pregnant. She'd flown in from Chicago for a checkup and learned from an X-ray exam that she was five months along. At Hume's invitation, she stayed in the hospital on bed rest until she carried her baby to full term. When a healthy girl was delivered, "Dr. Hume was like the father of the baby, the way he was acting in the delivery room," Andrews Martine said. "He was so excited this baby girl was born normal."

His nurse provided rich details of one side of David Hume—the one his supporters would come to embrace. Loyalty to patients, shared excitement over research advances, one big happy family. Yet there were plenty of other people—from senior surgeons to residents to other nurses—who saw Hume as arrogant, pushy, and often unconcerned about breaking the rules and ethics of his profession. Well into the 1960s, there was little to no regulation over how most patients were treated in medical experiments at MCV and other large teaching hospitals. "I think Hume liked having a large public hospital populated by people who had no say in what happened to them," observed Hunter McGuire, who knew Hume both as a surgical resident and as a member of MCV's faculty.

Given the hospital's role in providing care to indigent patients—many of whom were African Americans—"They were great subjects for research," McGuire said. "And there was no problem getting informed consent because they wouldn't understand the information anyhow . . . [Hume] was not into that."[35]

Dr. I. N. Sporn recalled his own concerns while following Hume with other interns and residents in the late 1950s. "I remember his interviewing an African American man who was in kidney failure and saying to him, 'If we don't do something, you're going to die. But we can transplant a kidney into you and you'll get well.'"

Sporn was bothered by the incomplete information given to the patient. Outside his room, he asked Hume about the exchange. Wouldn't it have been better, he asked, to let the patient know his body might *reject* the transplanted kidney? And shouldn't the patient have been told he might die of complications during the operation? Shouldn't Dr. Hume have let him know that transplantation was in fact an *experimental* procedure?

Hume seemed unconcerned and brushed aside his questions.

"He was in control," observed Sporn, who went on to become a respected nephrologist (a specialist in kidney disease). "The patient just did what he said."[36]

A more ethical approach to conducting medical research, Sporn believed, was to adhere to the Nuremberg Code—the guidelines that grew out of the 1947 trial of the leaders of Nazi Germany for experimenting on humans in concentration camps. With this in mind, when speaking with potential test subjects, he always used the word "experimental" and provided other details of such unproven treatments.

Once he'd provided as much information as possible, "most patients—probably nine out of 10—decided not to participate as experimental subjects" for various reasons, Sporn said. "I thought that was about the right ratio."[37]

Though he had his share of doubters and critics, Hume also had a legion of defenders. This included some who said they witnessed Hume's high bar when it came to matters of life and death.

Dr. Ronald K. Davis, a surgical resident, observed Hume's adhering to the conventional definition of death in the early 1960s—that is, the cessation of a heartbeat, pulse, and breathing. "During this time of early transplantation," Davis said, "many of us remember bringing up patients from the emergency room who were dead, and how Dr. Hume insisted that the last breath be taken before the organs were removed to be transplanted elsewhere."[38]

He recalled the case of a fourteen-year-old boy repairing a truck when the engine's fan came loose—penetrating his skull and piercing the frontal cortex of his brain. "He was declared dead."

Hume waited, though, resisting any temptation to claim the patient's healthy kidneys for someone else. As he did so, the boy's eyes popped open, and he began to regain consciousness. He soon went back to school—never knowing how close he'd come to becoming an unwitting organ donor.[39]

In those days, the concept of brain death was foreign to most doctors and nurses, much less to the average American. So was the notion of requiring "informed consent" for organ donations, experimental surgery, or other clandestine activities commonplace at MCV and other medical schools.

In *The Immortal Life of Henrietta Lacks*, Rebecca Skloot reveals the accountability gap when it came to explaining medical procedures and tests to patients in the 1950s. She poignantly details how Henrietta Lacks, a busy homemaker and the mother of five children in Baltimore, died at age thirty-one of cervical cancer. Her gynecologist at Johns Hopkins Hospital had examined her cervix, and, following a biopsy of her cells, found some to be cancerous. He shared those cells with a colleague, Dr. George Gey, a prominent cancer and virus researcher, who in turn shared her cells with medical researchers across the nation. Lacks's husband, children, brothers, sisters, and other family members were kept in the dark for decades after her 1951 death and the involuntary donation of the "HeLa" cells named for Henrietta Lacks. Her fast-growing cancer cells were "bought, sold, packaged, and shipped by the trillions to laboratories around the world," Skloot writes, helping to fuel "some of the most important advances in medicine: the polio vaccine, chemotherapy, cloning, gene mapping, in vitro fertilization."[40] But not a penny was paid to them. It took Skloot's relentless research and book—along with the Lacks family's own efforts—to finally win recognition for Henrietta Lacks's contributions to science and medicine.

Even as a cancer researcher at Memorial Sloan Kettering Cancer Center began injecting HeLa cells into unsuspecting prisoners and other test subjects in New York, Skloot writes, "There was no formal research oversight in the United States." While some state and federal laws along those lines had been introduced early in the 1900s, they were quickly squelched by doctors or researchers "for fear of interfering with the progress of science."[41]

Such was the status quo at the Medical College of Virginia as David Hume followed his instincts. It was a kind of medical Wild West, with no sheriff in town to keep order.

"He didn't need to ask the patient's permission," Dr. McGuire explained. "He sort of just did it. And he continued doing that sort of thing here . . . to his advantage and to our advantage. He would have us as residents do experiments on patients without asking their consent, or patients not knowing it had been done."

McGuire added, "There was no institutional research committee that he had to deal with, so he just did anything he wanted." But despite many reservations about the surgical chief's sometimes Machiavellian methods, McGuire also could see that he saved many lives and helped advance medical knowledge, especially in kidney transplantation. "Transplant surgery and immunology marched ahead faster than it would have without him."[42]

Hume's sometimes heavy-handed management style eventually caught up with him. In June 1962, Dr. Lewis Bosher, the hospital's most senior heart surgeon—finally couldn't take him anymore. In a battle of big-time egos, it seems fitting that it began with a conflict over who would get to operate on a key part of the body: the thorax.

In a letter to Hume on June 11, 1962, Bosher criticized Hume's edict removing a number of his surgical duties. It particularly galled Bosher when Hume assumed responsibility for all surgeries involving "direct thoracic aneurisms." This would deprive him of the chance to operate on patients with a particularly life-threatening condition—acute dissecting aneurysms. This occurs when the layers of the artery weaken from a variety of causes and, as a result, allow blood to get between the inner and middle layers. This, in turn, is often associated with an arterial aneurysm, the ballooning or bulging of a weakened section of the vessel. The concern is that as blood continues to be pumped through the vessel, the pressure exerted on an aneurysm causes the layers of the vessel to split, thus creating a false path that could rupture the vessel entirely.

But it was the professional type of rupture that threatened to tear apart the surgery department. Hume was chipping away at Bosher's patient load—including pediatric heart cases, the veteran surgeon complained. "I have not the slightest inclination to believe that this or any part of it is in the best interest of teaching, patient care or even research."

Bosher, sounding a bit like a Virginia Cavalier ready to fight a duel, said he had no choice but to challenge Hume's decision. He would take his complaint directly to the president, dean, and board of visitors of MCV.[43]

Bosher also took his challenge public—starting with a letter to the editor of the morning and evening Richmond newspapers. As a respected surgeon, he already knew some of the editors well. These included James J. Kilpatrick, editor of the *Richmond News Leader*.

Hume wasted no time in counterpunching. In a lengthy letter dated a week later—June 16, 1962—he wrote medical school dean William F. Maloney, calling the "alteration of Dr. Bosher's duties . . . a purely administrative" matter.

He went on to cite an earlier letter from MCV president Smith that supported Hume's right to make his own administrative decisions— which, after all, had been part of his original contract when he was hired away from Harvard.

Furthermore, Hume noted that Dr. Smith had reassured him that he was "well within his limits of the administrative authority and responsibility he is expected to exercise as chairman of the department." In the earlier letter from January 29, 1962, Smith warned Bosher that any more resistance of the chairman's order would be "regarded as willful defiance of properly constituted authority."[44]

Hume proved to be a relentless, vengeful foe. Dr. Bosher soon found himself overmatched in such institutional combat. He was playing by the rules of old-fashioned collegiality that Hume had rejected from the start. McGuire, who knew both men, explained the culture clash: "Bosher was scrupulously honest, and because of his scrupulous honesty, he despised Hume. And Bosher was a threat to the charismatic chief of surgery" should he ever blow the whistle on his wide-ranging experiments and "things he did without proper consent." These could have been used "to do Hume in."[45]

After hints of a lawsuit by Bosher, eventually by midsummer of 1962, the executive committee of the MCV board of visitors took up the matter and finally issued an edict to clearly state the lines of authority within the surgery department. Hume had survived a serious and public challenge to his authority. Bosher's attempted coup was backed by many of the disgruntled physicians around town who'd lost practice privileges and prestige under Hume's regime.

Even so, Hume could console himself by basking in the admiration of the younger generation of residents and surgeons he'd brought onto his staff. He was the medical equivalent of General George Patton— revered by most of his men but scorned by many of his peers. Hunter McGuire Jr., who praised Hume's clinical skills, remarked on the dark side of his genius. "Hume was also a completely unconventional, un-disciplined brat, naughty bad boy, who loved bad boys and recruited them."[46]

The surgery chief's celebrations were legendary—including one at an annual Christmas event that led to the trashing of the nearby Valentine Museum, a treasured part of old Richmond. Its leader banned all future parties by anyone from the medical college.

He also threw parties inside the hospital, consuming a "fish house punch" that McGuire called "very powerful and very deceptive and made everybody very drunk." Hume and his all-male residents invited nurses to join them in the department library on the eighth floor of the main hospital, behind a bank of elevators. There they would share the heady brew and party through the night. This went on for years until a well-connected visitor to the hospital ran into a gaggle of Hume's residents stumbling out of the elevator. One threw up at the visitor's feet. This led to yet another ban—this one straight from the governor—who "issued orders for no more alcoholic parties on state property."

McGuire also described Hume's nocturnal habits during a professional conference at the Homestead, a resort in the mountains of western Virginia. As he was preparing to deliver a paper to the Southern Surgical Association, McGuire recalled, "I was very nervous . . . so I wanted a good night's sleep." He didn't get one, though. "Hume was drunk on the floor in my bedroom," he said, laughing. "So that was kinda life with Hume."

Another early member of Hume's surgical team, Dr. H. Myron Kauffman, recalled his mentor's three main characteristics: "One is when he focused on something, he was totally focused on it to the exclusion of everything else in the world. His second characteristic was kindness and loyalty to his troops. If you were one of Hume's men, he was behind you 100 percent and immensely thoughtful. He even volunteered to co-sign the mortgage on my first home. But if you were his enemy," Kauffman warned, "[Hume] was unrelenting for those who crossed his path."[47]

★ ★ ★

David Hume was a rising star at the Virginia medical college and in the eyes of his colleagues around the nation. But it wasn't enough. By the early 1960s, he had his eyes on the biggest medical prize of all—conducting the first human heart transplant. He knew he couldn't do it alone, though, and started scanning the professional landscape. At the top of his wish list: Shumway and Lower at Stanford. Hume had studied their papers and heard others in the transplant community sing their praises. They seemed the most likely doctors to win a race that would be as historic as putting the first man on the moon.

Out in Palo Alto, the surgeons and friends had forged ahead with their research and refinements of the removal and transplant of dog hearts. Furthermore, they were chipping away at the pesky problem of organ rejection—focusing on drugs to suppress the body's natural defenses.

For all their success, though, the pair seemed stuck on the periphery of the nation's top surgeons. Often they were more of an object of curiosity than universal acclaim. When they spoke at professional conferences, the auditorium was sometimes virtually empty. Ironically, considering their aversion to publicity, Shumway and Lower seemed to generate more interest in the media than from their peers. This was especially true of science and medical writers and editors who took the time to pore over the surgeons' journal articles. These journalists—including the San Francisco reporter who'd drawn attention to the weeklong survival of the dog at Stanford—were perceptive enough to follow the pair's steady progress.

On October 11, 1960, the *San Francisco Examiner* reported, "Six whole hearts have been transplanted from one dog to another by a group of Stanford surgeons. Drs. Lower and Shumway, having pretty well perfected the surgical technique involved, now are concerned with the problem of long-term storage of the hearts, looking toward the day when a young human heart from an accident victim can be kept long enough to be transplanted into a man whose own is worn and failing."[48]

Other academic surgeons around the United States and abroad were also in pursuit of this dream. Foremost among them was Dr. Adrian Kantrowitz at Maimonides Medical Center in Brooklyn, New York. Kantrowitz was described as a "force of nature" by biographer Donald McRae. Like Hume, Kantrowitz had to buck his hospital administrators to conduct his research and try to win the race.[49]

Shumway—the master of applying extreme cold to protect organ transplants—was Hume's first choice to try to lure to MCV to start his own program in Richmond. The feeling wasn't mutual, though. Shumway "could not, in the end, escape the central flaw in Hume's character,"

McRae wrote. "Hume was stubborn to the point of being, in Shumway's laconic phrase, 'sorta pig-headed.' "[50] The Stanford surgeon also suspected that Hume was "a compulsive meddler" who would be difficult to work with. It seems likely that Hume's well-publicized dispute with Dr. Bosher and others had reached Shumway through the professional grapevine.

Shumway rebuffed Hume's offer to come to Richmond. But he also urged him to make the same offer to Lower. In the spring of 1965, at a meeting of the American Thoracic Society in New Orleans, Hume approached him. *How'd you like to join me at MCV and head up your own transplant program?*

Lower hesitated. If he was going to ask Anne to move their growing family from sunny California, New York would be acceptable, or perhaps Boston. But *Richmond, Virginia?*

Neither he nor Anne was particularly fond of the South, especially in light of the continuing crackdowns on civil rights crusaders—from the brutal murders of freedom riders in Mississippi to little girls tragically perishing in a church bombing in Birmingham, Alabama. More recently, in 1965, they'd watched on TV the revolting scenes as Martin Luther King Jr. and his marchers were beaten and brutalized in Selma, Alabama. Would Richmond—the former capital of the Confederacy—be just as primitive and violent?

Yet, Lower also felt compelled to consider what became an alluring offer from Hume to head his own surgical transplant team. He agreed to pay a visit—knowing he'd come highly recommended.

"Lower's the guru," Shumway said.[51]

CHAPTER EIGHT

The Glass Jar

RICHMOND, VIRGINIA, WAS KNOWN for many things in the 1960s—from its country cooking to its Southern hospitality to its insatiable appetite for history (albeit still full of Jim Crow narratives). Then there was the pungent smell of tobacco that hung over its downtown. If you were a motorist in the north-south corridor of Interstate 95, you likely caught a whiff at the tollbooths that made you stop and support the local road system. As you searched for coins, you might get a free hit of nicotine.

Richmond was home to the world's cigarette behemoth—Philip Morris—creating thousands of high-paying blue-collar jobs for men and women alike. It also offered good-paying jobs to Richmond's sizable African American population. Together they ran the increasingly automated, high-volume cigarette-making machines that satisfied America's craving for Marlboros and other popular brands. The sales continued to spike despite the damning report by the US Surgeon General in 1964. That was the government's first official warning about what many doctors already had been cautioning patients: smoking will shorten your life.

Philip Morris had a research and development center that could be glimpsed off the interstate.[1] It would be a fleeting look, though, because the low-slung brick buildings—which resembled a college campus—had their windows painted black. Inside, highly paid chemists, engineers, and even a few behavioral psychologists were hard at work developing what the US Food and Drug Administration would later call a "nicotine delivery device." Yet for all the harm the tobacco company continued to wreak on the nation's health, Philip Morris always managed to make billions of dollars in profits. It did so by adapting to the changes in the political, legal, and cultural climate.

The same couldn't be said, however, of the nearby public hospital that treated thousands of Virginians each year for heart disease, lung cancer, and emphysema. This was especially true of MCV's years of hand-wringing about finally stamping out its racist practices.

Dr. Hunter M. McGuire was just a young resident in 1964 when he was asked to attend various administrative and board meetings that gave him a front-row seat on the hospital administration's sluggish response. He recalled visiting the medical school's president, Dr. Robert Blackwell Smith, and the awkward response of the change-averse president. "I . . . told him the fact that MCV hospitals were not integrated, were still socially segregated, racially segregated, was just something that we couldn't stand any longer. Whether you thought it was good or bad was not important; practically, it [integration] had to be done, and it had to be done quickly, voluntarily, before someone came and told us to."[2]

President Smith "just sat there with sweat pouring down his forehead and trembling. He just couldn't stand those sorts of things." His nervous reaction to the mere mention of allowing blacks into medical school and opening up hospital wards to people of all hues likely stemmed from a spate of recent bad publicity.

On May 28, 1962, the News Leader's front page ran an article with this headline: "Negro Student Barred from Social Affairs. Leads M.C.V. Class." The embarrassing article began, "A Negro student at the Medical College of Virginia's School of Medicine is to be graduated Sunday with the highest academic standing in the 88-member class, but has been excluded from some social functions attendant to the graduation."[3]

The invitation-only functions included a dance for graduates of the class of 1962, an alumni social hour, and a buffet luncheon. Medical students and their proud parents could mingle with the elite members of MCV's board of visitors and distinguished alumni. The social functions also allowed newly minted doctors to make critical career connections in Richmond and around Virginia.

But because of MCV's race-based restrictions, the top-ranked student from the class of 1962, Charles F. "Charlie" Christian, was kept out because he was black. Christian, a much-admired army captain and Korean War veteran, came from humble origins in rural Virginia. His rags-to-riches story should have provided public relations gold to the medical college. Instead, he was barred from a host of the graduation-week events, including a dance at the landmark John Marshall Hotel.

The *News Leader* reported that "his exclusion from the social functions" along with five other black students set to graduate from MCV "were the subject of sharp disagreement" at a recent faculty meeting. To their credit, the medical school professors voted by a seventy to fourteen margin to end the university's ban on black students at university-sponsored social events.

Perversely, MCV president Robert Blackwell Smith initially tried to defend the school's apartheid policy. He said it was meant to "conform to the social customs of the community." MCV was still blindly carrying out an exclusionary policy that its social functions were open only to students who had received official invitations. And, he said, under this Catch 22–like exclusionary rule, "Negroes are not issued invitations."[4]

Smith's attempt to defend something so indefensible sparked outrage off campus as well. The president of the Richmond NAACP, Dr. J. M. Tinsley, dismissed the MCV's president's explanation. "This type of decision by MCV makes headlines for the Communist papers. Dr. R.B. Smith says that this action is the 'policy which conforms to tradition.' He should have said it is the policy which conforms to prejudice."[5]

Faced with a chorus of condemnation on the eve of MCV's commencement ceremony, the board of visitors reversed the policy. "Any graduating Negro who shows up at any of the commencement weekend functions will not be denied." While hardly a warm welcome to Christian and his fellow black graduates, the college's governing board said it reached its decision "to the end that any possible embarrassment to anyone concerned might be avoided in the future." Christian, for his part, avoided the limelight and chose not to comment on the affair. So did the "five other negro students graduating this Sunday from MCV."[6]

★　★　★

Such institutional slights and injustices would take more years to address, leaving in their wake a troubled legacy and emotional scars for Dr. Christian and other black doctors of the 1960s and beyond. The earliest signs of change at MCV and other Southern medical schools could be traced back a decade or more before the problems in Richmond made headlines. In 1950, a Texas law school student—Heman M. Sweatt—was refused admission on the basis of his race to the School of Law at the University of Texas. The US Supreme Court ruled in his favor in *Sweatt v. Painter*. The case successfully challenged the "separate but equal" doctrine of racial segregation that had been the law of the land since the 1896 case of *Plessy v. Ferguson*. The 1950 case from Texas would set the stage for the landmark case four years later of *Brown v. Board of Education of Topeka*, which led to federal orders to open the nation's public schools to black children.

After the 1950 Supreme Court decision, MCV's board of visitors took up the sensitive issue of racial desegregation of the medical school and its related professional schools. Dr. William Sanger, who was then president of the college, informed his board that a black student had applied to the school of physical therapy, an event that in another time or place would be routine. But not at MCV and not in the Virginia capital of 1950.

Sanger immediately contacted the state attorney general's office for legal advice. He also asked the applicant to take a battery of tests "to determine whether he was eligible to be admitted, as it was difficult to deal with a case without knowing the qualifications of the applicant in detail." Then, predictably enough, Sanger reported that "the Negro candidate for admission to our school of physical therapy had apparently not met entrance requirements based upon both academic record and performance on the college record examination . . ."[7]

Sanger and his board of white businessmen and civic leaders tried to stick to slow-moving changes. The Supreme Court decision finally forced their hand, though, and the board chairman "was informed that it was the sense of the Executive Committee that race shall not be a consideration in the admission of students."[8]

Following that decision, "the president presented to the Board the application of Miss Jean L. Harris, a Negro, for admission to the 1951 class of the School of Medicine."[9] And by late 1951, the new classes at MCV included a small group of other African American students: two in the dietetics program; two in physical therapy; one in the School of Pharmacy.

All the while, though, MCV kept open its segregated St. Philip School of Nursing until it finally closed in 1962—the same year as the Dr. Charlie Christian debacle. Along the way, a small number of black women were quietly admitted to the MCV School of Nursing. The Richmond medical college may have been crawling at a snail's pace toward equality, but any social progress in Virginia's capital was bound to attract national attention—especially in magazines for and about African Americans. In 1955, *Ebony* ran a cover photo of a smiling Dr. Jean Harris, wearing a crisp white smock, with her glasses in one hand and a stethoscope in the other. "Virginia's First Negro Medical Grad" *Ebony's* cover announced.[10]

★ ★ ★

Tensions between the city's black leaders and hospital officials were like a virus lingering just below the surface. The distrust dated back to the 1880s, with John Mitchell's columns in the *Richmond Planet* to stop the plundering of local African American cemeteries to supply bodies to MCV. And while laws and customs finally put an end to grave robbing, Richmond's underground economy left behind deep reserves of enmity and distrust. In fact, many years before Richmond NAACP president J. M. Tinsley criticized the college for its insensitive treatment of Charlie Christian, he was busy calling out MCV over the sad state of the segregated wards of St. Philip Hospital.

In late 1943, he released a letter he wrote MCV as chairman of the "Committee to Investigate St. Philip Hospital" that exposed the unsanitary and unsafe conditions black patients faced in the segregated facility. The fact that Tinsley, a respected Richmond dentist, penned his letter in the thick of World War Two—while many black Virginians served in the military—added poignancy to his plea.

"Dear Sir," he wrote Dr. Lewis E. Jarrett. "The recent rat incident has set fire to rumors, smoldering for many years, of the existence of unwholesome conditions at St. Philip Hospital. These rumors relate not merely to the present incident, but also to conditions existent throughout the hospital, and this incident has served to excite and intensify further rumors which, whether true or not, nevertheless have a disastrous effect upon public morale and confidence in the administration of this public function."

Dr. Tinsley noted that he was writing on behalf of more than one hundred civic organizations. He noted earlier complaints, "all growing out of the rat incident." He also lamented the sense among "a large portion of the population, and the vast majority of that class of the people directly affected," that MCV had only tried to "whitewash" the situation in an effort "to soothe the resentment" roiling Richmond's black community.

Dr. Tinsley sought "a fair and objective investigation" by "a group whose only interest is to ascertain the truth." With that in mind, Tinsley asked for permission "to conduct an independent investigation of the hospital, without supervision and by methods of our own selection, with a view to possible alleviation of the unfortunate consequences above stated."[11] Faced with public humiliation, the hospital's administration finally agreed to a series of upgrades at St. Philip, including renovations and improvements that helped to mitigate the rat infestation, at least for a while.

In years to come, Dr. Tinsley and his wife, Ruth Nelson Tinsley, became active in the struggle for civil rights in Richmond, a city not normally equated with the sort of violence Americans witnessed on their TV screens from the Deep South of the 1950s and 1960s. But the image of Ruth Tinsley being manhandled by two white city policemen, one handling a German shepherd, ran in *Life* magazine on March 7, 1960. Mrs. Tinsley was arrested after a sit-in demonstration outside a downtown department store—Thalhimers—that refused to serve lunch to nonwhite customers. A *Life* caption described the pair of policemen "manfully hustling 58-year-old Mrs. Ruth Tinsley into custody."[12]

During this period of social unrest, the resident physicians of MCV had their own take on the deplorable conditions the Tinsleys had fought to eradicate. The young white doctors called St. Philip "the Black Hole of Calcutta." Despite its problems—or perhaps because of them—the segregated hospital was seen as a prime training ground for new white doctors. "If you wanted to train in medicine you wanted to work at St. Philip," explained one MCV alumnus. "That's where you saw every disease in the world."[13]

This was Richmond, Virginia, in the mid-1960s—a conflicted Southern city where old, racist habits died hard. Its reputation could

make it difficult to recruit new doctors to MCV and other local practices. But the historical baggage wasn't enough for Richard Lower to say
no to David Hume's recruitment offer in 1965. Anne Lower said she
never doubted Dick would seize a rare opportunity to run his own transplantation program.

"I knew Hume was an innovator who appealed to Dick's ego," she explained later. Yet when her husband first broached the subject, "I yelled,
'Never!' I couldn't imagine going to the South."

Ever the loyal companion, though, Anne gave up her initial resistance. Within a few weeks, the Lowers were landing at Byrd Field on the
outskirts of town. Upon first meeting Hume, she found him impulsive
and brash, "a diamond in the rough." After they loaded their suitcases in
his car, "David was driving like a crazy man. He was definitely a personality. . . . Life was going to be very interesting and Dick knew this."[14]

They were invited to stay at the Humes' suburban home. After
drinks and dinner, Anne got up and yawned. It had been a long day of
travel. Dick took her cue. "I think we'll slip up to bed," he said, aware of
something his hosts didn't know: Anne was pregnant again.[15]

Hume was disappointed. To him, the welcoming party was just getting started. He loved a stiff drink and late-night bull sessions. Why
didn't Lower let his wife go upstairs alone, leaving the men to talk?
There was so much to discuss if they were going to get off to a running
start in the heart transplant race.

The next morning, Hume called Shumway at his Stanford office to
see if he'd made a mistake. "What is it with this guy?" Hume asked. "Is
he all right? I mean . . . it's ten thirty and he goes to bed."

Shumway laughed it off. "Naw, he's all right, David. The problem is
that he's a little bit of a sex maniac, you know. You see all those children
he's got—just figure it out!"

After pulling the Virginian's leg, Shumway reassured him that Lower
was absolutely the right choice to start a heart transplant program.[16]

Lower didn't disappoint. He got right to work to achieve their shared vision of creating a center of research excellence. "The main reason I was so eager to come to MCV and join the faculty is that it was clear there was more expertise in managing organ transplant patients here than in any place in the world," he later explained. "Hume's team was on the cutting edge of ways of using newer immunosuppressant drugs" to treat the rejection of new organs. And "they were ready to embark on a major liver transplant program. They were already renowned as having the best kidney transplant program in the world, or at least one of the best. So it seemed the ideal place to launch a heart transplant program, and this was what Hume was determined to have happen here at MCV."[17]

It didn't take long for Hume to tell him just how determined he was that a history-making heart transplant would happen first in his surgery department. Lower had hardly unpacked before Hume posed a question that would become a kind of professional mantra. "Could you do one tomorrow?"[18]

There was still a steep learning curve and a host of problems to solve. For example, they discussed the possibility of using organs from the dead in different ways. Hume already had successfully transplanted kidneys from dead patients into living ones—typically with the approval of the donor or his family.

What would happen, Lower wondered, if they also received permission to remove a beating heart? That might be the clearest path to performing a human heart transplant. But would they be able to resuscitate the heart, he asked, and would it function normally?[19]

There were other issues as well, not only for the MCV surgeons but also for their peers across the United States. The main one: What constitutes life and death?

This central dilemma was exacerbated in 1953 with the invention of a machine that acted as a surrogate heart and lung for the body. The cardiopulmonary bypass machine (CPB)—also called simply the Pump—"pumps the blood, and, using an oxygenator, allows red blood cells to pick up oxygen, as well as allowing carbon dioxide levels to de-

crease. . . . This mimics the function of the heart and lungs, respec-
tively."[20]

It was a great leap forward in the operating room. Like many innovations, however, the Pump—along with its cousin, the ventilator, which
kept oxygen going through the lungs and to the brain—sometimes led
to "confusions and controversies about when death occurs in a critical
care setting."[21]

Doctors across the United States in the 1950s and 1960s began to
notice an unintended consequence: since various ailments could typically incapacitate a person's ability to breathe, the CPB and the ventilator allowed doctors to, in a sense, do an end run around the grim reaper.
"Although it does not treat the underlying disease," such machinery
"may stave off death, often for months or even years."[22]

The ventilator alone created "a set of ethical and philosophical
complexities," according to the Council on Bioethics. The first question
was whether keeping a patient on artificial life support was always "in
the best interest of the patient?" In many cases, the bioethicists noted, a
devastating injury—such as a car wreck or a gunshot wound—leaves a
patient unable to breathe spontaneously. This means "there is little
chance that use of a ventilator will lead to much improvement in the patient's condition. The reason for this is that an inability to breathe spontaneously is often the result of a very serious injury to the brain."

Furthermore, the council reported, "Saving a patient from death
after such an injury turns out, in many cases, to be an ambiguous sort of
success. This ambiguity often leads physicians and patients' loved ones
to decide that death should be allowed to come even when the ventilator
is capable of putting it off for a time."[23]

Lower was familiar with these vexing issues, since he'd started performing heart surgery right after the introduction of the Pump and the
ventilator. He could see he needed to reach some kind of gentleman's
agreement with Hume about what lines they would not be willing to
cross in this race to be first with a heart transplant.

"The concern was over, first of all, whether we could use a cadaver or whether we could use the concept of 'brain death,'" Lower explained. "There were no protections in the courts. It was not a generally accepted principle among physicians and laypeople alike. There were also concerns about whether it would be acceptable."[24]

If there was any consolation, it came from knowing that other transplant surgeons around the world were facing the same conundrums. The year before the Lowers landed in Richmond, a transplant experiment had gone awry at the University of Mississippi Medical Center. Dr. James Hardy, known for conducting the first open-heart surgery in the state, had been appalled by the surrounding segregationist practices as well as the violence of its White Citizens' Council that led to the abduction and murder of three civil rights workers in Mississippi in 1964.

Hardy decided to take a huge risk. Though he'd gained approval to remove the beating heart of a dying patient, the surgeon knew the chances of finding a healthy human heart and getting the family's permission—as his superiors required—were remote in a small town like Jackson, Mississippi.

"And so," writes Donald McRae in *Every Second Counts*, "determined to be first to the heart, Hardy ordered the purchase of four chimpanzees." Since chimpanzee kidneys had worked in humans, "Hardy saw no logical reason why a chimp heart should not be used in the same way."[25]

This led to one of the early debacles of the heart transplant era. Hardy decided to transplant what would become known as a "monkey heart" into the chest of a dying, sixty-eight-year-old white man, using what was known as "the Lower-Shumway" technique from Stanford. He hoped to excise most of the man's heart—leaving some of its upper cavities in place—then quickly replace it with the chimp's heart. (The chimp's lifeless body was whisked out of the operating room and dumped in the hospital incinerator.)[26]

After a brief period of beating normally, the chimp's heart, "which was far too small for the man it was supposed to support, simply stopped." Hardy tried to massage it back to life but to no avail. The patient was dead. But because of a deceptive press release from the medical college, the Associated Press mistakenly reported that the university transplant team had taken the heart from a dead man—not from a chimpanzee. Though the human recipient soon expired, the AP reported that this was "perhaps the first successful heart transplant in the world."[27]

After the *New York Times* printed a more accurate account—clarifying the use of the chimp's heart—Hardy's career was severely damaged. "Hardy had not won the race, as he had hoped," McRae wrote. "Rather he had become embroiled in a freak show that focused on the use of a chimp and the deceit of the hospital."[28]

With these and other controversies in the air, Lower chose to proceed with caution. His timidity was soon challenged by Hume, who managed to get the tacit approval of a key state official to use transplanted hearts in their research program. They were told this could pass muster as long as they took the heart from an accident victim considered brain dead. The donor's family also should provide prior consent, they learned.

As Lower later explained it, "[Hume] got [Geoffrey] Mann, who was the chief medical examiner for Richmond at that time, to say, 'I got no problem with this. You can have an accident victim and [neurologically] say he's brain dead.' "

Under such circumstances, Mann said, "Go ahead and use the organs." He said this was permitted under the Virginia statute that allowed corpses to be used for anatomical study.[29] Despite Mann's informal opinion, however, Virginia law in the mid-1960s did not recognize the concept of brain death. This was a matter, instead, for debate by medical ethicists at leading universities, including Harvard. At that point, however, "brain death" was not recognized in the Code of Virginia. State law cited a more traditional definition known as "biological death"—that is, the cessation of a patient's heartbeat, pulse, or breathing.

The law cited by Mann to Hume dated back to the nineteenth

century, when the 1884 general assembly passed its "Act to Promote Medical Sciences, and to Protect Graves and Cemeteries from Desecration within the Commonwealth of Virginia."

Lower later explained how he and Hume handled such hard, potentially controversial, issues. "In a few instances we got permission from the family of the donor of the kidneys" to agree to "also take out the heart."[30] In one such case, Lower said he "took a movie of that heart beating in a jar." It was kept alive by cooling it in a bucket of cold saline, then, working with his perfusionist, he pumped warm blood back into the heart before shocking it back to a normal beat.

"We actually got these hearts to resume beating in a little glass receptacle. Some of them would beat so hard you could hear the hearts out in the hall," Lower marveled. "We got pretty excited about this because like, in fact, without breaking any rules or anything, you could probably transplant one of these hearts and it could support life."[31]

Lower soon learned to keep a lid on his growing excitement. Not long after his beating-heart experiment, he was invited to speak to a professional group of doctors in Richmond. The group included some older doctors eager to hear the star surgeon from Stanford. Lower thought it might help to explain his work by showing a short film of the beating heart in the glass jar. Afterward, a couple of doctors approached him at the lectern.

"I want you to settle a bet," one said. "My friend thinks that's a human heart, but I say it came from a dog. Which is it?"

Lower nodded. "Sorry, your friend wins the bet. It was a human heart taken from a cadaver."

"God help us!" his inquisitor exclaimed as he turned and walked away.

Lower suddenly realized, *Maybe Virginia is too conservative for me.* His caution—and his resistance to Hume's eager entreaties—was clearly warranted. It wasn't just the general public that didn't understand heart transplants. Plenty of doctors didn't, either.[32]

CHAPTER NINE

Foreign Exchange

DAVID HUME WAS USED to hearing from medical professionals who wanted to observe his kidney transplant program. He saw such queries as validation of his own research and journal articles, as well as a sign that his surgery department's reputation was drawing notice since the arrival of Dick Lower. One spring morning in 1966, Hume received an urgent letter from another interested visitor, from the University of Cape Town, South Africa.

"Dear David," the letter began, "I am really sorry to be pestering you." As Hume read on, he quickly realized that he'd failed to get back to the correspondent, Dr. Christiaan Barnard.

The up-and-coming South African heart surgeon was trying to finalize his plans for a three-month study program at MCV in May 1966. But as the letter from March made painfully clear, he had not heard back from Hume in more than month. "I am a little anxious that I have not heard from you."

Barnard went on to politely query Hume about the status of his request to secure a "working post for me in your renal transplant unit." He underscored the importance of receiving an official invitation from Hume. "There isn't much time left," to gain the approval of his superiors in Cape Town, Barnard wrote.

"So I am only awaiting the final word from you."[1]

He listed a number of medical and academic degrees, including MD and PhD. Dr. Christiaan Barnard was also an associate professor at the South African university.

For Hume, it was another administrative task fallen through the cracks. It wasn't the first and it wouldn't be the last. Sometimes even the medical school dean couldn't get Hume to respond to queries—even when it involved funding issues. Paperwork just wasn't the busy surgeon's thing. His supporters saw this as a small price to pay for his genius. Finishing a Coke, Hume set to work to make things right, starting with inventing a post for the persistent surgeon from Cape Town. He would need to help him find accommodations—a task that could prove challenging considering his native land. South Africa's all-white government was known for its brutal system of racial segregation and discrimination—apartheid. What would Barnard think about where he lived? After all, it hadn't been long since Virginia's capital city had its own system of apartheid. Racial equality remained a distant dream. It had been only a year since black patients were allowed into the MCV hospital.

Hume dictated a reply to one of his secretaries, trying to allay Barnard's concerns.[2] By late June, the Afrikaner professor wrote back, thrilled to be firming up plans for a three-month sabbatical in Virginia. "Dear Dave," Barnard wrote, "Thank you very much for your letter of June 7 and for your kindness in making it possible for me to come and work with your unit and learn how you handle the renal transplant problems." He shared his travel plans, including his arrival in late July and plans to report in by August 1. "I shall be on my own, for the first few weeks at least, and would be glad if you could locate accommodations for me somewhere near the hospital."

Some form of compensation seemed to be on the table as the South African expressed his thanks "for the arrangements you are making to augment my limited finances while I am there, this is indeed very kind and greatly appreciated."

Still, Dr. Barnard's anxieties—no doubt fueled by Hume's earlier inattention to his pleas for a timely response—were still evident in the last letter he sent before leaving for the States.

"Please would you confirm the arrangements . . . and let me know when and where you have been able to arrange accommodation for me; I hope this will not be too much trouble, but it will really put my mind at rest to know that I will have somewhere to stay nearby."

The letters offer some of the details of Dr. Christiaan Barnard's 1966 journey to Richmond. Like their author, the communications were rich with ambiguity, nuance, and flattery. While he professed to be coming to observe Hume's vaunted kidney transplant program, Barnard had an ulterior motive. He wanted to learn from MCV's other star surgeon, Dick Lower, taking in all he could about transplanting animal hearts and battling tissue rejection.

"The big battle in a heart transplant was not going to be placing a new heart, but in getting it to stay there," Barnard wrote in his autobiography, *One Life*. "This was our problem. Unless we could control this immunological rejection, there was no basis for attempting a heart transplant."[3]

Though singing the praises of Hume's kidney research, Barnard knew there were bigger issues to address involving the body's immune system. By coming to MCV, he hoped to find some possible solutions. The Richmond teaching hospital offered a rare opportunity to learn from two masters in their respective fields. In Hume, he could absorb the latest advances in kidney transplants; in Lower, he hoped to get a front-row seat to a legendary figure who'd made a human heart transplant seem tantalizingly close.

Barnard wrote, "In kidney transplants, ways had been found to prevent, or at least delay, rejection—indicating we would soon be able to transplant a heart." If the human body "could be conditioned to accept a kidney, it could take other organs, especially something as basic as a pumping muscle . . . The kidney had become a stepping stone to the heart."[4]

There were other connections to be made during his three-month sabbatical at MCV. In the mid-1950s, Barnard had traveled to the University of Minnesota to study under Dr. Walt Lillehei, who explored the use of extreme cold. This was the same body of research Norm Shumway brought to Stanford and further developed with Dick Lower.

Barnard seemed to have harbored another reason for coming to Richmond. He wanted to reconnect with a former colleague, Carl Goosen, who had moved from South Africa to work at MCV. The fellow Afrikaner was trained as a perfusionist and had played a key role in many of Barnard's early heart surgeries by operating the heart-lung machine for him and his brother, Dr. Marius Barnard. Once he learned as much as he could from the MCV surgeons, Christiaan Barnard hoped to convince Goosen to return home to work with him at Groote Schuur Hospital in Cape Town.[5]

It would be a difficult pitch to make, though. Goosen "loathed his fellow Afrikaner," who had often "screamed at him" during the intricate heart surgeries. Barnard's anger seemed to stem from the frustrations of practicing in a pariah nation like South Africa, where he feared he might be destined to labor in obscurity. He felt a sense of professional jealousy as he saw other transplant surgeons—such as Hume's mentor in Boston, Dr. Francis "Frannie" Moore—receive national acclaim from the likes of *Time* magazine.[6] In one instance, *Time* used its cover—usually reserved for movie stars, politicians, or astronauts—to celebrate the work of innovators like Moore. The article gushed over how "under the bright lights that illuminate the surgical incision with brutal clarity, the achievement of the surgeon and his assistants becomes one of the greater glories of science. Man may strain ever further into space, ever deeper into the heart of the atom, but there in the operating room all the results of the most improbable reaches of research, all the immense accumulation of medical knowledge are drawn upon in a determined drive toward the most awesome goal of all: the preservation of human life."[7] Another surgeon who received star treatment was Barnard's former classmate in Minnesota, Norm Shumway.

Reading the magazine in distant Cape Town, Barnard "felt his throat constrict at the mention of so many surgeons with whom he was acquainted," according to McRae. He didn't mind the coverage of Dr. Moore or his former mentor at the University of Minnesota, Dr. Walt Lillehei, "but the appearance of Shumway into that exalted list ate into him."[8]

Barnard, a minister's son, rebelled against his strict upbringing and could be hard on his staff and colleagues, who sometimes tried to distance themselves from him. These included Goosen, who, "weary of Barnard's abuse" was "keen to start a new life in America," McRae wrote. In a strange twist of fate, the newly arrived perfusionist began working for Dr. Lewis Bosher, who had his own tussles with an ambitious, sometimes testy surgeon—David Hume. So it was that "Goosen discovered that life at MCV was only marginally smoother than at Groote Schuur. Bosher had fallen out with Hume and been demoted after the appointment of Lower, who now worked in an adjoining lab. For all of Lower's deft interpersonal skills, the atmosphere at MCV could be prickly. Yet Goosen enjoyed the comparative peace of life without the Barnard brothers."[9] His peace was soon to be shattered.

Compared to Richmond's usual dog days of summer, Christiaan Barnard's arrival that Monday morning could hardly have been timed better. Stopping by a newspaper box to scan the local weather prediction, he saw a sunny day ahead with a high in the eighties and possibly low nineties—hardly enough to make a native Afrikaner sweat. He wore a coat and tie to make a good first impression. Next to its weather prediction, the *Times-Dispatch* posted on its masthead the number of papers printed that day—151,435—backing up its claim to have the "largest morning circulation in Virginia." Barnard appreciated the fact that Americans didn't mind blowing their own horns. He wished his fellow South Africans could do more of that.

The paper was full of local, state, and national news. President Johnson had ordered a defiant machinists' union to get back to work and end a twenty-four-day-long strike that was crippling travelers on a host of airlines—Eastern, National, Northwest, Trans World, and United. South Vietnam's strongman leader—Premier Nguyen Cao Ky—was up to the same sort of power plays Barnard knew all too well back home. The Afrikaner leadership had recently sent a black freedom fighter and accused communist—Nelson Mandela—to serve a long, backbreaking sentence on Robben Island prison.

Barnard walked along Broad Street, which was filled with state government workers, doctors, and nurses entering the looming brick buildings of the medical college. He marveled at the easy way America's white and black workers seemed to intermingle without any sign of police making sure everyone stayed in their place. He hoped no one would ask him to explain his country's separation of the races. He knew from experience at medical conferences around the world—and from his time in Minnesota—that there was no easy way to present his life story.

As the son of a church pastor, Chris Barnard grew up in the Dutch Reformed Church side by side with "nonwhites." His fellow congregants "were a mixture of European, Malayan and Hottentot—an indigenous, pre-Negroid South African people, today almost extinct," he wrote.[10] They were labeled as non-European, or, more common, "coloreds." Barnard's father ministered to these people who were scorned by the white majority. For this he received a fraction of the salary paid those who took the pulpits at the more affluent churches of the descendants of Dutch traders, the Afrikaners.

Early on, Barnard—himself an Afrikaner—witnessed the injustices suffered by his neighbors "living in primitive conditions—suffering sickness, hunger, and all the inherited ills of social outcasts."[11]

He hadn't grown up in privilege, but most of his new acquaintances in America probably would not believe it—except, that is, for his former assistant, Goosen. When Barnard arrived at MCV that morning, he made it a point to drop by. He hoped his old colleague would be pleasantly surprised.

Goosen later recalled the otherwise routine start to his week in a laboratory when "he heard the loud braying that had haunted him for so many years." His first thought was that "he had gone suddenly insane. He had been in Richmond for a month, and it now sounded as if an especially convincing impressionist had come to town." His mind wasn't deceiving him, though. "The nightmare voice belonged to the real Chris Barnard."

Ignoring Goosen's obvious dismay, Barnard chirped, "I thought I'd find you here. Listen, man, when are you coming home?"[12]

Goosen was speechless.

The new arrival from Cape Town tried to blend in, following doctors on their rounds, inquiring about their cases of severe kidney or heart disease. Many of the patients had traveled long distances in the hope of finding relief from the talented physicians, particularly Hume and Lower. On this stage, they were the stars while Barnard was "just another visitor looking at kidney transplants."[13] The cochairman of the surgery department, cancer surgeon Dr. Walter Lawrence, described Barnard as "just a guy who seemed to be hanging around. He wasn't participating much in our meetings."[14]

It took a few weeks, but Christiaan Barnard finally made his presence felt in the MCV surgery department. It happened during an otherwise routine morning round when Hume and his coterie were discussing a particularly challenging case of a young man who'd fallen gravely ill because of a failing liver. As they examined the man, who was a shade of yellow, Hume explained his treatment plan. "He was being treated by an interesting technique, which consisted in giving fifteen pints of blood, one pint at a time, while withdrawing the same amount—an exchange transfusion," Barnard wrote later. This "diluted the poisons that had accumulated in the body as a result of liver failure." Hume hoped to give the liver time to recover by regenerating healthy tissue. "If given a rest," Barnard observed, "it can often repair itself."[15]

He knew Hume had plenty of experience employing sometimes exotic measures to treat kidney failure. Barnard, never a wallflower, seized the moment and spoke up. Why not try a liver cross-circulation with an animal, he asked, as you once did with a pig? This time around, he suggested, perhaps you could also employ extreme cold and use some heart-lung machines.

Hume, clearly fascinated by the bold proposal, asked, "Have you ever done it?"

"No," Barnard replied, "but I don't see why it can't be done—for example, with a baboon."

One of Hume's surgical residents objected. "The baboon has natural antibodies in his blood against a human being."

Barnard enjoyed the chance to debate the staff. "I'll get rid of them," he vowed.

"How?" Hume asked.

"I'll take a baboon and cool him down, wash out his blood with water, then fill him up with human blood of the same group as your patient. That will be your baboon with human blood."

Hume was fascinated. "You believe you can do that?"

"Yes, I can do it."[16]

Barnard had reason to be confident because he'd once treated a similar case of liver failure. In Cape Town, he'd drained the dying patient's blood and restored him with a fresh batch. But the treatment plan he was suggesting to Hume was one step beyond. *Hooking up a dying human with jaundice to a living baboon so his liver can clean the man's blood.*

Hume, a natural gambler, decided to roll the dice. His staff sprang into action on an experimental procedure that would take not one or two but *three* heart-lung machines. It was the only way to pull it off.

Before they could begin, they had to overcome a major hurdle that surprised the South African. "I discovered then that America has almost everything, but it is very low on baboons." Following a number of urgent phone calls to zoos, a baboon was found. It would arrive the next day by air freight.

The next morning, Barnard performed the risky procedure before "a small crowd of doctors and students with movie cameras." He was getting a bit of the star treatment he craved.[17]

Barnard worked fast with the heart-lung machines—hooking the baboon to the first one. This machine helped lower the animal's temperature to 5 degrees Celsius (41 degrees Fahrenheit), "a deep enough hypothermia to prevent brain damage during the period when the animal would be without blood circulation." Then he "cut the pump and quickly drained the baboon of all its blood."[18]

Using a second heart-lung machine, Hume and Barnard purified the baboon's blood with a multi-chemical brew called Ringer's lactate solution. By doing so, they replaced the baboon's electrolytes and fluids.

Then came the moment of truth. They connected the third heart-lung machine to run the patient's blood through the baboon's newly cleansed liver. It could now, in effect, act as a surrogate organ for the young man's own failing liver. At this critical moment, just as human blood flowed into the baboon, its heart began beating irregularly. It went into atrial fibrillation.

"I knew it," Hume said darkly, "that baboon's going to die."

"Just wait, Professor," Barnard reassured him. He warmed the human blood in the animal's body and applied an electric shock. Much to everyone's relief, the baboon's heart started beating normally. It survived the operation and so did the young man.

The next morning, Barnard visited the brown baboon, who was alert and sitting up in its cage, contentedly munching an orange. Now the primate was the star of the show, bathed in bright lights and curiously eyeing the doctors and students with their cameras "still recording his new existence—an animal form, living with human blood."

Barnard jokingly suggested that Hume might have to consider

another scenario if he tried this again. "Suppose the patient wakes up to find he's practically in bed with a baboon—what next?"[19]

Lower and Hume continued pushing the boundaries of transplantation, including a number that cost animals their lives. In those days before animal rights became mainstream, the surgeons occasionally ran afoul of the SPCA. Yet back home, each doctor was an animal lover. The Lowers had three dogs, while the Humes always kept pets on their farm. If anyone called or wrote to complain, Dick Lower's answer was polite but firm. "Do you want us to experiment on people? We need to experiment on dogs, pigs, and baboons first."[20]

While it was relatively easy for Lower to write off animal advocates as well-intentioned idealists, it wasn't so easy to ignore Hume's nagging to get the transplant done. "He was pushing Dick," Anne Lower said of Hume.[21]

There was more than professional pride at stake: millions of dollars in federal grant money likely would flow to the winner of the heart transplant race. The conundrum, as Dr. Lower put it later, was "where are you going to get a heart?"[22]

In the fall of 1966, soon after Christiaan Barnard returned to South Africa, Lower seemed to get an answer to his question. A car accident victim in Richmond suffered a brain injury and was being kept alive on a ventilator. A possible recipient for the donor heart was a man in his forties who'd suffered a heart attack that had caused severe damage to the organ. But he was young enough to be a candidate for a transplant that would save his life. "It looked like the perfect situation," Lower said later.

He ordered his transplant team to prepare a couple of operating rooms for the world's first human heart transplant. Just one more thing was needed: proof from the blood bank that both men—the donor and the recipient—had compatible blood types.[23] Without a match, the fortysomething man's body probably would reject the heart of the comatose accident victim. This would create a host of complications that could kill the recipient during the operation.

Hume seemed somewhat oblivious to the problem of the blood match and urged Lower on. "*C'mon*," Hume implored. *"Do it!"*[24]

Lower, cautious by nature, wouldn't be hurried. His concerns proved to be correct: the two men's blood types were incompatible.

MCV's moment in medical history was scrubbed. Years later, Lower explained why. "I knew if we were going to do it, particularly if it was going to be the first transplant, we should do everything right." They might "have learned some things . . . but it would have been a terrible blow psychologically" if the world's first heart transplant patient had died on the operating table.[25]

Lower couldn't have known it then, but his surgical skills and transplant technique had been closely observed and recorded by the curious visitor from Cape Town. He listened to former assistant—Carl Goosen—rave about Lower's delicate touch when operating on dog hearts. After that, Barnard began brushing up on journal articles by Lower and Shumway he'd previously ignored. He also began spending more time in Lower's dog lab.

Dr. Lower was only too happy to welcome the inquisitive visitor and explain his transplant methods. He reasoned that just as he'd been trained by some great surgeons, he should be equally generous with Barnard. Wasn't that how science and medicine made progress?

When Lower saw Barnard and Goosen outside his door, he "allowed the two South Africans into his lab with a cheery wave" and invited them to watch him work.[26] Barnard was entranced by the Richmonder's use of hypothermia to switch a heart "from one dog to the other with a minimum of fuss and drama."[27]

After one such operation, according to McRae's account, Barnard whispered to Goosen in their native tongue, "*My God, is dit al wat dit is?*" ("My God, is that all it is?")

Lower must have overheard them as he sutured shut the dog's chest. But he was too absorbed to give it much thought.

"Lower was an elegant surgeon" and "completely honest," observed his younger colleague, Dr. Hunter McGuire. "Lower was also a little bit of an adolescent, perpetually."[28] That may be as good an explanation as any about why Lower didn't worry about Barnard's long, close scrutiny.

Goosen, sensing his former boss's intentions, tried warning Lower through his perfusionist—Lanier Allen. But after the message was relayed to him, Lower seemed unconcerned. Barnard may have been a bit pompous, but that was hardly unique among surgeons. The South African was a relative novice and probably years away from ever attempting a human heart transplant.

Lower laughed and brushed off his assistant's concern, saying, "You guys have been drinking."[29]

CHAPTER TEN

Finish Line

IN EARLY 1967, THE race to put the first man on the moon blew up in America's face. As three astronauts huddled inside the first lunar command module, a series of tragic events would mark the end of innocence for the nation's space program. The accident served as a cautionary tale for others, including ambitious heart surgeons, about the price of victory. Sometimes taking a leap into the unknown could cost human lives.

Gus Grissom, America's second man in space, led the crew of Apollo 1. He was joined by Ed White, the first American to perform a spacewalk, and rookie astronaut Roger Chaffee, a navy pilot who cheerfully predicted, "I think it will be a lot of fun."[1]

The fun faded with the late-afternoon light of January 27, 1967, as the crew fidgeted inside a cramped capsule more than two hundred feet above the Kennedy Space Center. They were trying to solve some annoying problems such as the foul smell from the oxygen tank and crackling on the radio. While some of the issues were relatively trivial, they weren't happy to be working on them so near the launch date, only a month away. They were eager to continue the mission that began in 1961, with President Kennedy's challenge to Congress "to achieving the

goal, before the decade is out, of landing a man on the moon and returning him safely to Earth."

It was a lofty goal, to be sure, making it all the more bothersome for
the astronauts to be dealing with what seemed like sloppy work by their
engineers. This included the garbled radio transmissions while they
were still on the launchpad. Grissom, the ship's forty-year-old commander, gruffly joked about the poor communications, "How are we
going to get to the moon if we can't talk between two or three buildings?"[2]

Grissom knew from personal experience how NASA's squeaky-clean
image wasn't all it was cracked up to be. As the second American in
space, he'd suffered one of the few embarrassments in the early days of
the Mercury program when his capsule filled with water and sank. This
forced him to abandon the capsule and swim for dear life.

Sadly, on that winter day in early 1967, Grissom's luck ran out when
someone shouted inside the capsule, "Fire in the spacecraft!" Before
anyone could respond, its oxygen-filled interior "became engulfed in
flames," according to science writer Hanneke Weitering. "Heat caused
the air pressure inside the spacecraft to rise, making it impossible for the
astronauts to open the hatch, which was designed to open inward. After
about 30 seconds, the spacecraft ruptured."[3]

NASA's ground crew desperately tried to rescue the trapped space-
men, but it was too late. Grissom, White, and Chaffee quickly died of as-
phyxiation.[4] Their immolation led to an investigation that found a stray
spark in a bundle of wires. Grissom's last-minute doubts proved to be
prophetic. The tragedy led to a redesign of the capsule—one that reduced the high level of flammable materials and gave future astronauts
an escape hatch should another fire break out on the launchpad.

In Richmond, where MCV's transplant team was on a mission to
win the heart transplant race, another lesson could be drawn from the
tragedy of Apollo 1. "It seems as though political pressure to get to the
moon in the height of the space race might have led NASA officials to

overlook safety concerns in favor of beating Russia to the moon," Weit- ering wrote. One former astronaut's comment seemed to apply to the heart transplant race as well: "NASA was attempting to do something that had never been done before, and that comes with an inherent risk."[5]

On that day in early 1967, Dick Lower and Dave Hume had little time to process the sight of the smoldering carnage on the Florida coast. They were too consumed with their own kind of medical launchpads. Like the early space program—which launched dogs and chimps into orbit—they were busy using animals to test their theories and surgical techniques. This was often a grueling, all-consuming enterprise. Their wives were their copilots. Upon landing in Richmond two years earlier, Dick bluntly told Anne Lower what to expect. "You've got to talk with the children," he said, "and you've got to tell them I won't be here for two years."[6]

Anne and her kids managed to adjust to his long absences. "There was a lot of time," son Glenn recalled, "when we didn't see him. He'd leave in the morning and come back late night." Yet the surgeon's son came to understand why his father spent so much time at the office. "Nurses would tell me, 'Your dad is so amazing. He spends so much time with patients and families, and never delegates things to others.'"[7]

In those days, Glenn Lower recalled, he used to clip out newspaper articles for his social studies class to learn more about current events. On that fateful Saturday in early 1967, the *Times-Dispatch* included a wide world of headlines—from a mysterious Chinese army division which "Turns Against Mao" to an article on Egypt's President Nasser sending Russian-built bombers to attack Saudi-backed forces in Yemen.

But there was one more hopeful story that involved space explora- tion. Representatives of the United States, Great Britain, and the Soviet Union signed a "space treaty" at the White House seeking to outlaw the use of nuclear warheads or other weapons of mass destructions in space exploration. "Let us hope we will not wait long for solution of earthly problems," said Soviet Ambassador Anatoly Dobrynin.[8]

Despite the ambassador's best intentions, many Americans probably shared the darker view of Richmond-born novelist Tom Robbins about "the international situation—desperate as usual."[9] Still, in many ways it could be said that the *local* situation in Richmond was improving. After years of hard work and sacrifice by the black community, Virginia's capital was showing signs of advancement. Much of this was due to the courageous work of the Richmond Crusade for Voters—a coalition of black businesses, social clubs, professional groups, and churches. In the decade following David Hume's arrival at MCV in 1956 the voting power of African Americans had increased by a whopping 400 percent—to 32,500.[10]

These gains came as more African Americans moved to the state capital—a trend that mirrored much of the South's overall urban migration in the 1950s. This, in turn, helped increase the influence of civil rights organizers willing to put their bodies and lives on the line to desegregate schools, stores, and workplaces. "We were the original revolutionaries," said Dr. William Thornton, a podiatrist who was one of the Crusade's founding members.[11]

The voting power helped a new generation of black leaders take their seats in the monochromatic chambers of power. They included civil rights attorney Henry Marsh (later to become mayor) and another young attorney, L. Douglas Wilder. Reflecting on the early obstacles he encountered, Wilder said, "When I first started the practice of law, everything was segregated—the courtrooms, the jails, and the bar association. There was not a single African American judge sitting full-time in any court in Virginia."[12]

Though he didn't consider himself a civil rights activist, Wilder worked to change the system "by representing African American folks in the courts." It took hard work, including serving as his own office receptionist and custodian. "Before long, I had a thriving practice. My reputation was earned by being a damned good trial lawyer."[13]

Richmond's white establishment predictably tried to maintain the status quo and cling to power. Historians John V. Moeser and Rutledge M. Dennis describe the "white response" to the rising tide of black political power as "one of terror" not only in the city, but throughout the entire commonwealth. "Virginia's particular brand of oligarchy and paternalism was unlike the racial politics in the lower South where trenchant race-baiting was more prevalent, a feature most scholars attribute to the lower states' basically rural economies and high black population."

The entrenched white leadership in the general assembly and governor's mansion was occupied by alumni of such tradition-bound colleges as the University of Virginia, Virginia Polytechnic Institute (VPI), and Virginia Military Institute (VMI). These were men who felt completely at ease with "the oligarchy's 'velvet glove' approach to both the lower- and-middle-class white population and to the entire black population." And they were "shaped by a code of 'gentlemanly' behavior that was almost 'royalist' in tone and behavior."[14]

Their heritage led them to protect Richmond, the royal city of the Confederacy. Such defensive impulses were driven by the collective sense of lost honor and pride still venerated along Monument Avenue. The old wounds opened up after the passage of federal civil rights legislation in the mid-1960s. President Lyndon B. Johnson, overcoming his own segregationist past, had managed to get Congress to approve his sweeping legislative package to create his Great Society program. Predictably, giving more power and resources to black citizens didn't sit well in the South. The Virginia countryside was dotted with rebel flags waving defiantly toward LBJ and his congressional allies. In Richmond, such animosity usually was expressed in a more genteel fashion. It was best served with a polite smile, a touch of passive aggression, and the sweetness of a country club daiquiri.

"As Virginia's 'special place,' Richmond and its politics are inextricably entwined with the state," write Moeser and Dennis. "Consequently, a challenge to Richmond's political order constitutes, by definition, a challenge to the state's."[15]

Such challenges took on new meaning after passage of the Voting Rights Act of 1965. The historic law made it a federal crime to keep blacks away from the voting booth, thus violating rights guaranteed in the Fifteenth Amendment. In Richmond, the business elite responded by creating "Richmond First." Though it sounded like a chamber of commerce spinoff, the group's chief aim was to suppress black voting power. The business cabal held a series of secret meetings between white city council leaders and their suburban counterparts.

"Word began circulating in the legislative halls that if blacks were to acquire control of Richmond, they would proceed to destroy the monuments of Civil War heroes" on Monument Avenue. Such shocking predictions led the Virginia legislature to pass a law granting the right of eminent domain over the city's monuments to the state Attorney General.[16] The measure—which embodied the refusal of many white Virginians to honestly confront the past—would cast a long shadow over the state well into the twenty-first century.[17]

Meanwhile, over on the medical school campus, the Richmond transplantation doctors focused on their work. Hume kept prodding Lower, hinting that he was being too timid about the medical equivalent of shooting for the moon.

"Let's do this!" he urged. "Let's get going!"[18]

Lower *was* going—but at his own pace. Though he may have come across as being overly cautious with humans, when it came to animals, Dr. Lower didn't mind pushing the research envelope.

On a Sunday night in late May 1967, Lower called another heart surgeon into his basement operating room. "Lock the doors," he ordered.

On the operating table was a newly deceased man. His sides had fresh stitches left from a recent procedure when Hume had taken out his kidneys. Lower confided to his assisting physician, Dr. Richard Cleveland, that he'd rather Hume not hear about what he planned to do with the cadaver. It would only add to the incessant pressure to perform a human heart transplant. But, in fact, that's exactly what he had in mind. But it came with a twist: the heart of the man on the table would not go into another person. Instead, it would be transplanted into a living, breathing baboon. Lower wanted to see if a baboon could serve, in effect, as a host to keep a heart viable until a human recipient could be found.

Cleveland felt uneasy. It wasn't just the cloak-and-dagger aspect of their midnight operation. He was more concerned about the ethically fraught terrain they were entering—mixing the organs of people and primates. After what had happened to James Hardy in Mississippi, Cleveland "was paranoid that both their careers might be ruined by the attempt," according to McRae's biography. "Yet Lower had been researching cardiac transplantation for seven and a half years. He was ready to work with a human heart."[19]

Both doctors knew what could happen if word ever leaked about this experiment, with its science fiction optics. Despite his assistant's misgivings, Lower worked quickly to remove the corpse's heart and preserve it in an icy saline solution. Then Lower opened the baboon's chest and attached the still-viable human heart to its arteries and veins.

"It soon began to beat inside the baboon's chest," McRae wrote. "Lower had done it. He had transplanted a human heart." In mordant homage, he dubbed the clandestine procedure a "reverse Hardy."[20]

The operation ultimately ended strangely, though, as the man's heart was too big to allow them to sew up the animal's chest. When it was over—with the baboon joining the long line of animals who died for scientific progress—Cleveland "let slip a thankful sigh." He was glad to know that "only he and Lower had seen the surreal transplant. Their careers, at least for a little while longer, were safe from scandal."[21] Lower never published the results of his audacious experiment.

But while caution often held sway in Richmond, some of the techniques that Dr. Christiaan Barnard had brought back with him soon would be put to the test. Though he was far from solving the deadly riddles of organ rejection, Barnard was determined to transplant a heart from one human being to another "at the earliest opportunity."[22]

As a warm-up, he decided to attempt the first kidney transplant on the African continent. He chose the best available Afrikaner surgeons, including his brother, Marius, a cardiac surgeon who'd returned from America after laboring under the Texas-size egos of heart surgeons Michael DeBakey and Denton Cooley. Other nurses and specialists, including bacteriologists "trained to detect infection at the first onslaught," were added to Barnard's Cape Town transplant team.[23]

Normally, a surgeon only stayed in charge of a patient during the operation and the immediate postoperative recovery period. Transplants demanded a different kind of medical protocol because "the operation would be followed by a struggle to control rejection." Barnard said he decided to "personally direct the postoperative antirejection battle."[24]

By the fall of 1967, he had found his subject for his trial run on the kidney. Mrs. Edith Black was a middle-aged white woman with badly diseased kidneys. Barnard assured her he could help her. He would replace a single kidney that would serve to filter her blood, remove waste, and add water to create urine. In a reprise of his MCV procedure with Hume (but without the baboon), Barnard removed both of her diseased kidneys and hooked Mrs. Black to a dialysis machine. The wait for a proper donor began. This required a patient with a "normal and healthy" kidney, with a compatible blood type, and who was "free of infectious diseases."[25]

Unlike Lower, Barnard didn't lose any sleep pondering the difficult questions raised by the sharing of human organs. He knew he was protected by South Africa's loose legal requirements for organ removal. These required only "a postmortem of any person dying from unnatural causes—such as an auto accident or a death for non-certifiable reasons," Barnard wrote. "The body is opened up, its organs examined, and it is then closed up for burial. During the postmortem, one or another organ may legally be removed for purposes of teaching and study, provided the parents or relatives give consent."[26]

The door was wide open for him to win the heart transplant race. "We intended to operate within this law, putting the kidney or heart within a new body, rather than in a bottle on a shelf." Time was the main issue. Permission would have to be obtained quickly, "before the organ became unserviceable."

To avoid what he called "hasty decisions, or charges of pirating living bodies," Barnard kept an arm's-length distance on the process. "We decided that none of the doctors involved in the transplant would pronounce on the death of a potential donor." This would be handled by a separate neurological team.[27]

The emergency department at Groote Schuur Hospital, known as the "casualty department," was put on alert to find a kidney donor. As the days passed, six potential donors were considered, but each was rejected for one reason or another. Finally, Barnard learned of a seventh candidate, "a colored youth with severe brain injury from an auto accident." Once the young man was declared dead, Barnard said, he received the family's permission to take his kidneys.

"We moved him into the operating room, removed the left kidney, and proceeded to put it into Mrs. Black" with "surprising ease." This involved anastomosis—or connecting tubular structures. In this case, they connected the renal artery of the donated kidney to Mrs. Black's hypogastric artery (also known as the internal lilac artery). After a ureter was implanted into the bladder, she began to secrete urine. Soon she was sitting up in bed. A few weeks later, Edith Black was feeling good enough to return home and resume her normal life.[28]

South Africa's newspapers—eager to promote anything positive about their scorned nation—hailed Barnard's handiwork as a major breakthrough. But the foreign press couldn't resist having some fun with headlines like "Mrs. Black Gets Black Kidney."[29]

In his memoir, Barnard put his own spin on the story. "Mrs. Black—with a kidney whose potentials of rejection or tolerance did not depend on the color of skin—left the hospital to begin a normal life."[30]

★ ★ ★

If heart surgeons and other medical professionals had been gamblers, then the smart money would have been put on Stanford's Norm Shumway to win the heart transplant prize. Lower, on the other hand, didn't enjoy such front-runner status. This was evident in early October 1967 at a convention of the American College of Surgeons in Chicago. Lower spoke to the gathering of surgeons before his old colleague. He played a "short film featuring a large brown-and-white mongrel running around and wagging her tail," according to McRae. "She was one of the two dogs that had been alive for more than fifteen months since receiving new hearts in Virginia."

After eight years of laboratory experience, Lower humbly declared, "We are now quite convinced that cardiac transplantation is a perfectly feasible procedure from the technical as well as the physiological standpoint."[31]

When it was Shumway's turn to take the podium, he sounded far more confident than his old partner. "The time has come for clinical application," he declared.[32]

Brooklyn heart surgeon Adrian Kantrowitz, sitting in the audience, elbowed his assistant in the ribs. *"Did you hear him?* Shumway's gonna do it!"

About a month later—on November 20, 1967—Shumway announced that his Stanford team was prepared to conduct the first human heart transplant. The countdown began. All they needed was the right patient and a willing donor.[33]

Two weeks later, the front page of the *Richmond Times-Dispatch* was filled with a story and pictures about the death and destruction that had swept through Central Virginia during a windstorm. A retired bank president had been electrocuted to death as he tried to douse a fire caused by a downed power line, tripping on a wire as he did so. An army family at

Fort Lee was injured when its trailer overturned. A local high school gym was a mess of mangled steel.

But the news that dominated the front page on Monday, December 4, 1967, extended far beyond local weather. Beside the picture of the storm damage was a headline that seemed to blow away the hopes and dreams of Drs. Richard Lower and David Hume, along with their colleagues at MCV.

Human Heart Transplant Held Success
First Operation of Kind Performed in South Africa

"A South African hospital reported Sunday the world's first successful human heart transplant," the Associated Press reported from Cape Town. "Surgeons removed the heart of a young woman who died after an automobile crash and placed it in the chest of a 55-year-old man dying because his own heart was damaged.

"When the transplanted heart was in place, it was started beating by an electric shock. Dr. Jan H. Louw, the hospital's chief surgeon, said, 'It was like turning the ignition switch of a car.'

"Groote Schuur Hospital said the man was in satisfactory condition late Sunday but that the next few days would be a critical period."[34]

The organ donor was twenty-five-year-old Denise Ann Darvall, a bank employee who perished in the car crash along with her mother. Following Christiaan Barnard's instructions, neurosurgeons had used an electroencephalogram (EEG) to measure her brain activity. When none was found, they pronounced her dead. The young woman's father had quickly given his legal consent to take her heart, allowing Barnard to start operating a half hour after she was declared dead.

The wire service described how a team of five cardiac surgeons—supported by more than three times that many other doctors and nurses—had "transferred" the woman's heart to Louis Washkansky, a

Lithuanian-born businessman, in a five-hour-long operation. A picture of the oblong-faced recipient ran beside his well-dressed wife in a mink coat. "Louis Washkansky," the caption read, "Whose Health Was Failing, and Wife."

The story provided plenty of clinical details, including how doctors used heart-lung machines on the donor and the recipient to keep them alive or their organs viable. They learned that Washkansky, whose actual age was fifty-four, had diabetes and had been on the hospital's critical list after suffering two heart attacks in recent months. At the time of the transplant, his ailing organ had shrunk to only a third of its pumping capacity, leaving him weak and gasping for air.

"When the transplant was completed, electrodes were placed against the heart walls, and a high current was switched on for a fraction of a second." Then, Dr. Louw said, "The heart started beating immediately."

Miraculously, it seemed, a man on the brink of death—breathless and blue—quickly acquired a ruddy hue. More clinical details were supplied, including how doctors were treating Washkansky for possible rejection of the donated heart.

The article also took note of the fact that "surgeons at Stanford Medical Center have been reported by the *Journal of the American Medical Association* to be ready for a heart transplant, whenever the ideal donor and the ideal recipient appear there at the same time." Now this seemed irrelevant. South Africa had won the race. Everyone else—whether at Stanford, MCV, or other medical centers around the country—would be vying for second place.

The turn of events left a bitter aftertaste with the fraternity of American heart surgeons. The AP story took a while to name the leader of the transplant team in Cape Town, but Drs. Hume and Lower knew: "Heading the team of five cardiac surgeons was Prof. Chris Barnard." This initial report made Barnard sound like some sort of underling, "one of the professors in Louw's department."[35] Soon enough, though, Barnard would be made the leading man in this international medical drama.

The heartburn didn't stop there for the MCV doctors. Another article on the front page was headlined, "Surgery Team Chief Worked at MCV in '66."

"Dr. Chris Barnard, the leader of the surgical team that performed the first human-to-human heart transplanting . . . spent a few months last year at the Medical College of Virginia studying transplant procedures."[36]

Barnard's three-month fellowship in Richmond, where he was allowed to observe and even participate in some transplant experiments, was described. Lower was quoted as saying his own human heart transplant efforts were "still in the laboratory research phase," wrote *Times-Dispatch* science writer Beverly Orndorff.

Lower told the local reporter that he'd be following Barnard's breakthrough operation "with interest." The comment seemed to express a degree of polite skepticism about the Afrikaner's qualifications to join the ranks of great transplant surgeons.

A sense of failure crept into the newspaper's coverage. Orndorff knew enough about the recent history of transplantation to call Stanford "one of the main pioneering groups" in the "more than eight years of laboratory research in animals, particularly in dogs."

MCV, by contrast, came across as something of a laggard. Orndorff had interviewed Hume and Lower many times over the years about their transplant work. Now he cited Lower's efforts to determine "whether dead, non-functioning hearts could be successfully transplanted and resuscitated."

Notwithstanding such nods to the earlier work at MCV, the impression left by the morning paper was as inescapable as the damage from the previous day's windstorm. Dogs and corpses once had seemed fascinating; now they were yesterday's news.

Pouring more salt into their wounded pride, the heart surgeons at MCV and Stanford knew full well that Barnard had used the Shumway-Lower transplant technique and collectively felt he had recklessly used it before he was ready. If Barnard had been more careful and ethical about it, they felt, he would have waited until *his* work on dog hearts was more advanced. Lower's skepticism was captured when he later remarked of Barnard, "I don't think he gave a damn about ethics."[37]

He would stifle his criticism for many years, though. At the time neither he nor other American heart surgeons wanted to sound like sore losers. But a counter-narrative to Barnard's victory lap soon took hold among surgeons.

"His motive was his outsized ambition to make his mark and surpass his former colleagues at the University of Minnesota, among whom was Shumway," wrote Dr. Peter A. Alivizatos, a general surgeon in Dallas. "His excuse for doing an operation for which he was not prepared was the inability of his American colleagues to proceed because of the prohibitive legislation [laws about brain death of possible donors]."

Barnard fully "realized his advantage: in South Africa only the agreement of two doctors was required to declare death in a case of irreversible brain injury, even before the heart had stopped. It was the ace up his sleeve!"[38]

Christiaan Barnard, for all his well-documented flaws, would later agree with the Americans. "You have to recognize that in South Africa we didn't have the legal restraints of other countries," he confided to British medical writer John Illman. "I didn't even have to ask permission to do that first transplant. I just told the hospital authorities after I had done it. Can you imagine that happening anywhere else in the world?"[39]

However one judges the events leading up to the first human heart transplant, Lower's burden proved to be a heavy one. Dr. Alivizatos, who was a surgical resident with him at MCV, vividly recalled the pain in Lower's voice when he recounted the story during a lecture at the medical school.

"In 1966 I did not proceed with the heart transplant and God never forgave me for my hesitation. So glory and reputation went to Cape Town, South Africa, and not to Richmond, Virginia."[40]

Whatever regrets he felt seemed to be tempered by Lower's natural loathing of self-promotion. The avid fly fisherman and hunter always preferred a day out in nature rather than a conference under the bright lights. His son Glenn recalled weekends in rural North Carolina where fellow professionals came to hunt and get away from civilization.

"They all had nicknames for each other," Glenn Lower said. "His was 'Doctor Nice.' "[41]

While David Hume's response to the news from South Africa wasn't recorded, there's no doubt that "Barnard's scoop . . . rankled MCV's surgery department considerably," Orndorff recalled. As for the man known as "Doctor Nice," his response was much more muted—at least to the newspaper. "The low-key Dr. Lower said he was 'sort of relieved' when Barnard performed the first human heart transplant, because he got all the heat."[42]

The South African surgeon loved the camera and the camera loved him. This quickly became apparent in the hours after the operation when he allowed a CBS crew to film his patient, Louis Washkansky, from the doorway of his room. Barnard even helped by moving a microphone to his patient to capture the sound of "Washy's" newly beating heart. The reporters in the hallways were mesmerized.

From Cape Town to London, and Paris to New York, Christiaan Barnard began receiving the kind of accolades usually reserved for Hollywood stars. He was variously described as "handsome" and "boyish," "lean" and "tanned."[43] Despite the ongoing injustices and human rights abuses around him, Barnard proved to be a natural-born goodwill ambassador. "See, we South Africans aren't the bad eggs you overseas people so often describe," he proclaimed at a news conference. "Have a look around this hospital yourselves and see if you can notice any difference in the kind of treatment that we give to the European and Colored patients in our wards."[44]

Though Barnard's "ethnic references were shaped by the semantics of apartheid," McRae notes, "most of the foreign press in attendance were seduced by the intense Afrikaner. He looked as if he had been waiting for this moment his whole life." As a physician, Barnard should have been giving his fragile patient, Louis Washkansky, his full focus and time. Instead, he put postoperative considerations such as "arterial flutters" and urine output on the back burner. They couldn't compete with the siren song of fame and fortune.

Barnard's dreams were fully realized when he appeared on the covers of three major newsmagazines, a rare trifecta in those days: *Newsweek*, *Time*, and *Life*. For only 35 cents a copy, *Life*'s readers could revel in a story rich in medicine, love, marriage—and the story of the brave surgeon. The cover promised a story worthy of its own screenplay:

A dying man lives with a dead girl's heart

The color photograph shows Washkansky gamely smiling, with a sheet drawn up to his chin. His head rests on a pillow. On his left is an unnamed nurse in a mask. Her dark, twinkling eyes hint at a smile, along with the doctor beside her. The caption reads,

Louis Washkansky, recipient of the historic transplant, smiles after regaining consciousness

Inside, another headline explains: "Her Husband Got the Heart. . . . His Daughter Gave It."

In a two-page-wide photograph, a neatly coiffed woman wears a simple round-collared dress with a coat hanging over her shoulders. She appears to be trying to keep warm as she leans forward, clutching a large purse in her lap. With her head bowed slightly, she listens to a distinguished-looking man who—for reasons not explained—appears to be wearing a bathrobe.

"The lady at the left, Mrs. Anne Washkansky, is full of gratitude—

her husband has been saved from sure death by the gift of a new heart," it begins. "The man with her, Edward Darvall, is full of grief, for he has lost both his wife and daughter in an auto accident. But he draws some consolation from the fact that it is his daughter's heart now beating in another's chest."[45]

Life quickly summarized the details of the now-legendary story—the car accident that took Darvall's life . . . her father's consent . . . pulling Mrs. Washkansky's husband back from the brink of death.

The magazine also explored several other heart transplants that followed Barnard's.

"A few days later surgeons at Maimonides Hospital in Brooklyn, N.Y. transplanted a heart from a just-dead baby to a baby born with virtually no heart function. But the transplanted heart worked for only a matter of hours before it stopped."[46]

The magazine includes a hauntingly beautiful picture of the Cape Town donor—Denise Ann Darvall—with curly black hair, dark eyes, and a shy smile. Barnard—dapper as a film star—appears in a suit and tie instead of his white coat.

Life also provided a detailed account of how Barnard had removed Darvall's heart and transferred it to Washkansky. The lessons Barnard had learned back in Richmond were never mentioned.

"Carefully clamping the major arteries, the team began the painstaking extraction," the article explains. "When they had a nearly intact heart in their hands, except for a small portion of its back wall, which they had abandoned in the donor. The recipient's heart was cut away in a similar fashion, though a larger piece of its rear wall was left as a foundation for the new heart. All that was left to do was join the two—a job that was extremely difficult because of the difference in sizes between the two hearts."[47]

As it happened, it wasn't the difference in the sizes of the hearts that caused problems. "Though his new heart went on beating steadily, it was

his own body—and the possibility that his system would reject as foreign tissue the very heart that was keeping it alive—that was causing the
greatest worry for his doctors."

The worry was well founded. Even as the press speculated about a
possible Nobel Prize for Christiaan Barnard, Washkansky was starting to
slip away. This didn't stop his attending surgeon from maintaining a busy
interview schedule. "While Barnard had restricted local press access to
his patient, he could not resist any overture from a powerful international
media outlet," McRae notes. "These included intrusive moments from a
BBC reporter who asked [Washkansky] how it felt as the Lithuanian-born
Jew to have a Gentile's heart beating in his chest."

Washkansky struggled to answer the strange query. "Well, I never
thought of it that way. I don't know."[48] That interview was shut down,
but the patient's medical problems weren't so easily handled.
"Washy's" condition deteriorated and he developed pneumonia.
Phone calls were cut off. In a moment that captured the hyperbolic atmosphere, "Dr. Christiaan Barnard was giving an interview to NBC
television when he got word that Mr. Washkansky had pneumonia."[49]

Nearly three weeks after the historic operation, his patient's demise
was evident as Washkansky struggled to breathe and his "hands and feet
were as cold as a corpse's. Barnard knew that Washkansky was dying, but
he could not nail [down] the reason," writes McRae.

He tried treating him for bacterial pneumonia, but this failed. Thinking of his time in Richmond, he recalled David Hume mentioning a
seemingly mystifying condition "in which the lung seemingly attacked
itself" in a kidney transplant patient—what Hume called "transplant
lung." Barnard remembered how the MCV surgeon had prescribed "a
concentrated course of powerful" drugs to suppress the rejection.

"Barnard decided to follow the Hume method, even if it meant they
would be traveling even further down the tangled road of antirejection
treatment."[50] There was simply no map for this course of treatment; the
drugs could just as easily lower his patient's natural immunity.

The desperate measures backfired, and after a painful bout with double pneumonia and other infections, the undersize heart that had served Louis Washkansky for eighteen days stopped beating. In his haste and his distraction, Barnard had misdiagnosed the early signs of rejection.

"Pneumonia, not rejection, had killed Louis Washkansky," McRae writes. "If Barnard had attacked the infection immediately, as he would have done in a normal patient, it seemed likely Washkansky would still be alive. The surgeon, instead, had devastated a dangerously ill man's immune system in a misguided attempt to overcome a nonexistent pattern of rejection."[51]

Though Barnard was devastated, it failed to slake his thirst for fame. A second transplant candidate—one who seemed to have better prospects for survival than "Washy"—was identified. With that in mind, Barnard should have stayed in Cape Town for preoperative work. But he was blinded by the bright lights of fame. If he made any fatal errors in judgment, Barnard also seemed to have an uncanny knack for rationalizing them.[52]

Before long, he jetted off to Washington for a special appearance on CBS's *Face the Nation*, along with two other emerging stars of heart surgery: Adrian Kantrowitz, who had performed the second heart surgery in Brooklyn, and Texas heart surgeon Michael DeBakey. When he saw the guest list, Barnard was glad to see neither Shumway nor Lower had made the cut. Accompanied by his long-suffering wife, Louwtjie, Barnard also received an invitation to visit the president of the United States—Lyndon B. Johnson—at his ranch in the Texas Hill Country. (LBJ had suffered a heart attack himself more than a decade earlier and would ultimately succumb to heart disease.)

Barnard was a natural on TV. In his *Face the Nation* appearance hosted by veteran CBS correspondent Martin Agronsky, he managed to outshine his fellow surgeons by appearing to be both humbled by the hard lessons of Washkansky's death and to have learned from them.[53]

News accounts of the interview cast Barnard as a brilliant, handsome rising star. The *Washington Star* called him "South Africa's winning answer to Dr. Kildare," while New York's tabloids called him "Dr. Charisma" and "A Real Heart-Throb!"[54]

After he successfully transplanted a second heart in late January 1968, Barnard left Cape Town again to continue his victory tour.[55] He appeared on yet another major magazine cover—*Paris Match*—and entered a recording studio to make a novelty album. This "featured the beats and cadences of his Afrikaans accent as he talked, rather than sang, about the first human transplant."[56]

Landing in Rome, he was swarmed by screaming fans. Some rushed to touch him as though he possessed godlike healing powers. Barnard was more interested in getting in touch with two of Italy's most glamorous actresses, Gina Lollobrigida and Sophia Loren.

Ultimately, his time with the jet set would crash and burn. Years later, British writer John Illman, who coauthored a book with Barnard, called him "a bundle of moral contradictions. He was an outspoken opponent of South Africa's apartheid laws. He advocated for euthanasia as a humane and compassionate end to human suffering. But he was also known to those who worked with him closely as a loud-mouthed tyrant."

Further complicating matters, "Sex and women—especially young ones—were certainly important to him," Illman wrote. "His fame had placed intolerable strain on his first marriage of 21 years to [Louwtjie], a nurse who had helped to support him while he developed his surgical career and with whom he had two children."[57]

Not everyone was drawn to the South African surgeon. On a swing through London, he appeared on BBC's *Tomorrow's World* in a show titled "Dr. Barnard Faces His Critics." Among them was the conservative British columnist Malcolm Muggeridge, who joked that the TV program should have been dubbed "Dr. Barnard Faces His Adulators." Muggeridge surprised Barnard by comparing his heart transplant to the totalitarian eugenics predicted by Aldous Huxley in *Brave New World* and George Orwell in *1984*.

"Why was it," Muggeridge demanded to know, "that this operation was first performed in the Union of South Africa? Was it because in the Union of South Africa there were more brilliant or more audacious surgeons? Was it because in the Union of South Africa there was better equipment, finer facilities? Or was it, I suspect, that, because of the vile doctrine of apartheid, life is held cheaper?"

Barnard tried to defend himself. "I think we have fairly good surgeons in South Africa," he replied. He said he was simply trying to treat a sick man and relieve human suffering.[58]

Muggeridge may have used Barnard as a prop in his own morality play. But he made a valid point about the blurred lines of ethics and law that the heart surgeons were starting to cross. In most cases, the physicians were left to navigate by themselves, with no clear road map to help them find their way.

PART THREE

Reckoning

Map of Richmond, Virginia, ca. 1968

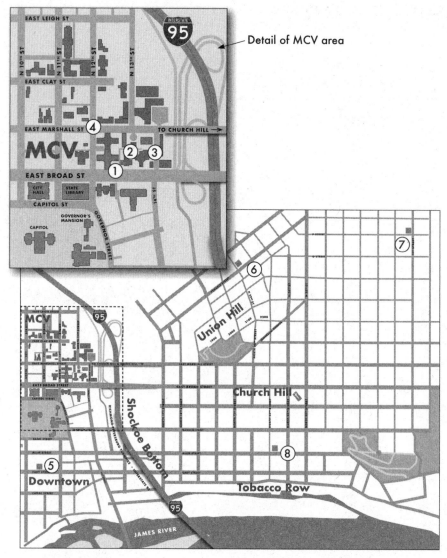

Detail of MCV area

Legend of Key Sites

1. MCV Hospital (West)
2. Saint Philip Hospital
3. Egyptian Building
4. State Medical Examiner's Offices
5. Esskay plant, 1114 E. Cary St.
6. Esso station, 2200 Venable St.
7. L. Douglas Wilder, Attorney-at-Law, 3026 P St.
8. Tucker's Shoe Repair, 2304 E. Main St.

CHAPTER ELEVEN

The Fall

3:00 p.m., Friday, May 24, 1968

BRUCE TUCKER'S FRIENDS LIKED to gather behind the Esso station on Church Hill, catching up on gossip, news, and sharing a joke or two. In the shade behind the gas station, the group passed around a bottle of wine to mark the end of another hard workweek.

Though drinking in public was against the law, they knew if they kept to themselves and didn't get too loud, nobody would notice. They could blend into the tree-lined neighborhood of comfortable homes, brick churches, and small businesses and offices. It was friendly territory for these working-class black men. As long as the sun was still up, they were reasonably certain they wouldn't be hassled by the police.

Bruce Tucker settled back on a brick wall. Lighting a cigarette, he took in some of the latest news. There was a story in the *Richmond Afro-American* about a preacher arrested in a civil rights protest after his son had been handcuffed.[1] The black-owned newspaper served its news straight up—on that everyone could agree. It was better than the morning *Times-Dispatch* or evening *News Leader,* which only gave the white point of view.

As everyone shared the wine, the talk turned to Dr. King's assassination in Memphis and the city's striking sanitation workers. If it could happen to Martin, couldn't it happen anywhere? The recent arrests of the Richmond pastors made them wonder.

Though Bruce Tucker and his friends were hardly acting like angels, if anyone needed help, they knew it was right around the corner at a large Baptist church—the Temple of Judah. The wine kept flowing along with the conversation about the news of the day. Another big story was the Poor People's March as some of the Washington-bound marchers planned to stay in Richmond that night on their way north.[2] Like the Memphis sanitation workers, these marchers were trying to improve the economic status of African Americans.

Bruce Tucker was never able to attend high school, but he always tried to support himself. He'd worked for years at a nearby food-packing plant, where he learned more about sorting eggs than a mother hen. At age fifty-four, he figured he might be packing eggs until he was eligible for his Social Security pension.

He'd left his family farm in 1954 in search of a better job in the city. During his boyhood and teen years in his native Dinwiddie County, he slept in a room crowded with his brothers and shared the limited space, food, and attention with several sisters, too. His parents, Spencer and Emma, had done the best they could, working odd jobs and raising crops on a small plot of land. As he got older, Bruce could see his career options didn't stretch beyond the rows of his family's soybeans. Virginia's capital, only an hour's drive to the north, beckoned.

He was following in the footsteps of his younger brother William. Even though he'd contracted polio in his youth, William was bright and had a strong work ethic. His crutches didn't deter him from learning the cobbler's craft. Eventually he earned enough money to open his own shop. Tucker's Shoe Repair was on East Main Street, not far from where Bruce found work at the egg-processing plant. The shoe business was as steady as delivering newspapers, eggs, or milk. Just as folks would always need something to eat and drink and read in the morning, they'd also needed to keep their shoes in good repair. By

1968, there were more than thirty shoe-related businesses around town.[3]

Bruce made more than $3,000 a year working at the plant—enough to pay the rent in a rooming house about a mile away from Church Hill.[4] He also sent $175 a month to his mother down in Dinwiddie. That helped support his only son, Abraham, who was a fourteen-year-old freshman at the county high school. Bruce's wife had left a few years before, so it made sense to leave Abraham down on the farm.[5]

A breeze picked up from the south. A storm was brewing. The after-work bunch passed the wine one last time. There was plenty more news to discuss—like how the Richmond Braves, a minor league baseball team for Atlanta—had won the night before over the Mets' minor league club at Parker Field . . . and how up in DC, Frank Howard of the Washington Senators was leading the American League in hitting with a .348 batting average and seventeen homers.

A thunderstorm rumbled. Storm clouds gathered. Then someone shouted behind the Esso station: *Bruce!* Like Humpty Dumpty, the egg man had fallen off the wall.

6:00 p.m.

The Allied ambulance blared through the tree-lined streets, its siren echoing off Church Hill's two-story homes with narrow porches and tidy yards framed by azaleas and peonies. Reaching Broad Street, the ambulance turned right and shot down the hill toward the medical college.

It only took a few minutes to reach the emergency entrance at the base of the tall brick MCV hospital. Opening the back of the ambulance, the attendant cautioned the hospital orderlies to go easy. The patient had been drinking, he said, and may have had a seizure. He had a nasty-looking contusion on the back of his head. It was already wrapped in bandages. The patient was lifted on a gurney and whisked inside.

An ER doctor, noticing the deep gash, ordered an X-ray. Afterward, a nurse began a chart for "Tucker, Bruce," and jotted down what little was known about him at that point. "The Allied ambulance driver stated he had a seizure 'earlier today' and refused to come to the emergency room . . . fell down and was brought to E.R. On admission he was disoriented, combative with flaccid right arm and leg." Tucker's blood pressure was high—216/100. The X-ray revealed a fracture at the base of his skull.

11:00 p.m.

The on-call neurologists determined that the blow to the back of Tucker's head had caused his brain to shift five millimeters (about two-tenths of an inch) to the right. He had suffered a "subdural hematoma"—a collection of blood between his cracked skull and the left side of his brain.[6] He also had a severe bruise—or contusion—at the base of his brain. The brainstem, as it's known, serves as the main neural pathway connecting the brain's vital functions to the spinal cord. This pathway controls breathing.

The neurologists ordered two emergency surgeries—a craniotomy, the drilling of a hole into his skull; and a tracheotomy, an opening into his windpipe to help him breathe.

Those procedures would take nearly three hours into the wee hours of the morning. If he made it.

Midnight, Saturday, May 25, 1968

While Tucker's skull was being drilled and his breathing passage opened, word of his dire condition reached the surgery department. The early conversations among the surgeons had little to do about his chances for survival but rather concerned using him for another purpose. No one was discussing whether he might recover and be rehabilitated. No one talked about him going home. Men like Tucker, arriving with alcohol on their breath and seemingly no one to claim them, were often written off as "charity patients." They weren't expected to pay their bills, with the hospital absorbing any expenses.

Considering Tucker's dire condition and poor prognosis, some of the on-call surgeons wondered whether he might be a good candidate to donate his heart for a transplant. That was the word passed along to Dr. Lower by his staff. Lower had been in close consultation with MCV's cardiologists about the possibility of a heart transplant in a last-ditch attempt to save the life of a patient suffering from severe heart disease. His name was Joseph G. Klett. He was a businessman from the town of Orange—about an hour's drive north in Virginia's horse country.

The ailing businessman had been repeatedly hospitalized—twice at the University of Virginia over in Charlottesville and, for the past three weeks, at MCV. Technically, Klett was still under the care of a cardiologist, Dr. V. Eric Kemp. But after much consultation, the surgeons had concluded that a transplant was probably Klett's only hope for survival. He was handed off to Lower as a potential transplant patient.

It soon became clear to Lower that time was running out on Klett, a former New Yorker who'd moved to Virginia to run a metal products company.[7] His coronary disease was so severe that it blocked the much-needed blood supply to nourish his heart and keep it pumping. His end was a matter of days, and maybe just hours, away. Indeed, Lower wondered whether someone so sick could even survive a heart transplant.

As fate would have it, Klett had reached the same age, fifty-four, as the brain-damaged man, Bruce Tucker, who also was hanging on for dear life, one floor below. It was late, so Lower hurried home to try to grab a few hours' sleep. He knew that once Dave Hume heard the news—which he surely would through his hospital network—he would be bouncing off the walls like one of his baboons. Lower was leery of hearing anything more from Hume about finally doing a heart transplant.

There was little traffic as he rumbled over the cobblestones of Monument Avenue, past the shadows of the statues of Stuart, Lee, Jackson, and Jefferson Davis. Passing the homages to dead generals, Lower thought of a living hero—Norm Shumway. Now there was a man he truly admired. Unlike Hume, Norm wouldn't allow himself to be swept up by the hype surrounding what should be a carefully calibrated and delicate operation. Everyone who mattered in surgical America's circles knew Norm could have won what the media called "the transplant race." But he'd refused to be rushed.

Now he thought of his own responsibilities. He pictured Mr. Klett, gasping for breath, counting on him to do something—*anything!*—to keep him alive.

Lower shuddered to think of the frenzy that had followed Shumway's first heart transplant—only the third in the world, and the first for an adult American. A near-riot had ensued outside his operating room at Stanford Hospital. He thought about Shumway's funny, firsthand account of the media circus, with fifty or more reporters clamoring for news. Some of them even scaled the walls and tried to climb through the windows. Anything for a scoop.

Since Norm's brush with history more than five months earlier, it seemed like everyone was jumping on the transplant bandwagon. This was happening despite the low odds of survival; most lived only for a few weeks or less with their borrowed hearts. Only Norm, with his droll sense of humor, could capture the misguided priorities.

"Suddenly," he wisecracked, "heart transplants were being done in places where one would hesitate to have his atrial septal defect closed!"[8]

Norm knew the highs of heart surgery, but he also knew the lows. This was experimental medicine, after all, particularly because of the unsolved problem of organ rejection. Shumway's first heart transplant recipient, a retired steel worker named Mike Kasperak, initially had done well with his new heart. But he succumbed after only a couple of weeks after his stomach started to bleed badly. This was tied to damage to his liver and kidneys from years of living with heart disease. Kasperak—like Joseph Klett and Bruce Tucker—had been fifty-four years old.

Lower got home and tried not to wake up Anne and the boys. He couldn't stop thinking about the risks of replacing the heart of someone like Joseph Klett whose body had suffered so much. There was simply no way of knowing if he would survive the procedure or its uncertain aftermath.

If only he could be as relaxed as Shumway was before his first heart transplant. As Norm prepared to remove the heart of a forty-three-year-old housewife whose brain hemorrhage left her in a coma, someone asked, "Do you think this is really legal?"

"I guess we'll see," Shumway replied.[9]

2:05 a.m.

After three hours of extensive treatment for his head injury, Bruce Tucker was rolled out of the operating room in slightly better condition than when he'd arrived at MCV some eight hours before. Some of the pressure on his brain had been relieved by the burr holes, and the tracheotomy was helping him breathe.

In the recovery room, nurses attached an IV line so he could be fed intravenously and receive medications each hour to relieve his pain and keep him hydrated and stabilized.[10]

3:00 a.m.

Following Lower's orders, his staff called Richmond police headquarters. The police were sorry, but they had no new information about Tucker: no missing-person report; no phone calls from his family; nothing. They could only confirm the address recorded by the ambulance crew: 109 E. Charity Street, on the city's north side. This was considered a rough neighborhood, only a short drive from MCV. The arrival of a police cruiser with white cops surely would not be welcome.

Nonetheless, the police agreed to drive over to Tucker's home address. A black-and-white cruiser was dispatched. Taking side streets from downtown, they soon passed the roar of traffic on Interstate 95.

The cops made a left on East Duvall, driving parallel to the interstate, then turned right on North First Street. Passing the Greater Mt. Moriah Baptist Church, they turned left and reached the address. One of the patrolmen knocked on the front door. After a while, someone finally appeared at a second-story window.

"We're looking for the family of Bruce Tucker," the cop said. "Can you help us out?"

The man in the window said he didn't know anyone of that name.

"Are you sure?"

"Yes," the man said, closing the window firmly.

The cops had little choice but to leave. There was no active investigation and no search warrant. As they pulled away from the darkened house, they knew they could let the MCV doctors know they'd done their best.[11]

CHAPTER TWELVE

His Brother's Heart

9:30 a.m., Saturday, May 25, 1968
MCV Hospital

DAVID HUME WAS JACKED up, and not only because he'd consumed his usual morning snack of doughnuts and Cokes. *This is it*, he thought, *we're finally going to do it!*

Dick Lower, by contrast, was trying to approach this Saturday in the surgery department like any other day. After getting a few hours' sleep, he'd driven back to the hospital for his morning rounds. The possibility of a heart transplant was looming in the back of his mind, but he didn't want to ignore his other patients. Despite his best intentions, any veneer of normalcy was shattered by Hume at a staff meeting he called with a special guest—Dr. Abdullah Fatteh. The young physician was on duty for the state office of the medical examiner a block away.

"It seemed so exciting that day," recalled Dr. Walter Lawrence, vice chairman of the surgery department. "Hume was so excited about the whole thing—much more than Lower—because it had finally come to happen at his place." A heart transplant was within their grasp.[1]

Pacing like a football coach before a big game, Hume developed a plan for his eager team of surgeons. The players he'd recruited for more than a decade—led by his star quarterback, Dick Lower—could now make their mark in the transplant world and enter the annals of medicine. By his reckoning, this would be only the ninth human heart transplant in the United States and the sixteenth in the world. It came with the added bonus of helping everyone, including himself, get past the initial resentment of Dr. Christiaan Barnard's borrowing of their work.

Of course, Hume knew MCV was a relative latecomer in the medical race. There would be no pictures of Lower and him on the front of *Time*, *Life*, or the *New York Times*. No one from CBS or NBC was likely to ask them to appear on a morning talk show. And though the White House was only one hundred miles away, they wouldn't hold their breaths for an invitation to the Oval Office. And yet . . .

Hume seemed ready for the lights, cameras, and microphones surely awaiting them. Ready for the media horde, he assigned his second-in-command, Walter Lawrence, to take any calls. "Hume was beside himself," Lawrence recalled. "I couldn't keep a close eye on him because I was at the telephone at the central desk."[2]

At the morning staff meeting, he mapped out the division of labor. He would supervise the removal of the brain-damaged man's heart by a talented surgical fellow, Dr. David Sewell. The second group, headed by Dr. Lower, would be next door, preparing Mr. Klett. After the donor heart was removed and put in a protective saline solution, it would be taken next door. Then Dr. Lower would remove Klett's damaged heart and insert the new one.

Hume covered other details, such as calling in the transplant team of anesthesiologists, perfusionists, and nurses for the long day and night ahead. He also took up the vexing problem of contacting the donor's family to gain permission to remove the donor's heart. Hume asked his underlings to contact the police once again in an effort to find the family.

Hume then turned to the visitor in the room, Dr. Fatteh. He asked the assistant medical examiner to be prepared to help them stay within the bounds of the law. If Bruce Tucker's relatives couldn't be found, Lawrence said, "They had to get approval . . . for declaring him dead."[3]

In Virginia, the medical examiner played a number of roles—performing forensic examinations in murder cases, conducting autopsies, and determining the cause of death in accidents, suicides, and other fatalities. They also advised medical researchers such as the MCV surgeons.

Initially it seemed like they were just covering their bases by bringing in the assistant medical examiner. "We weren't too concerned about it," Lower said of the morning discussion. The consensus opinion was that "the family's going to give permission for this—once they know the person's dead."[4]

Their confidence was bolstered by a growing consensus around the country about the inevitability of making legal reforms to keep up with contemporary medical advances. This was a particularly hot topic at David Hume's alma mater, Harvard. The notion of "brain death" was the subject of a long-running study by a committee of respected ethicists, professors, and surgeons. Their report was due out soon.[5]

In lieu of guidance from the respected panel, Hume and Lower were heartened by the prior tacit approval from Fatteh's boss, Dr. Geoffrey Mann. As luck would have it, Mann was out of town that weekend and they would have to rely on his assistant to work through some of the potentially nuanced issues ahead. For example, the old nineteenth-century statute cited by Dr. Mann required a twenty-four-hour waiting period from the time a patient was declared dead to when the body could be used for research. The legislators of the 1880s had included this restriction to address allegations of body snatching and the desecration of graves. But by 1968, there was a sense among many doctors—including Hume and Lower—that this provision was as outdated as using leeches for bloodletting or diagnosing "humors" as the cause of disease. In what they considered a more progressive view, it made no sense to wait an entire day to declare someone dead who no longer had critical brain functions. Waiting that long, in their view, would render the donated heart useless. This, in turn, would mean certain death for Mr. Klett.[6]

Dr. Fatteh listened intently to the unfolding plan. He understood the general clinical issues; that is, Tucker's head injury and Klett's weakened heart. He also knew of the Harvard advisory group and the growing consensus about brain death. Nonetheless, he wanted to follow the earlier guidance from his boss, Dr. Mann. *Find Mr. Tucker's relatives*, he'd said. *Ask for permission to transplant his heart and kidneys. When you've done so, get back to me.*[7]

The examiner had a list of autopsies to perform that day. He couldn't afford to drop everything to be at Hume's beck and call. Nonetheless, to be on the safe side, he wanted to call Dr. Mann and one other legal expert to seek their guidance. Not that Fatteh was lacking in confidence. He had traveled a long road to Richmond to work for Dr. Mann, who was known as one of the nation's leading practitioners of forensic medicine.

A native of a small village in India, Abdullah Fatteh was a bright young man with an ambitious father who wanted him to study medicine and law. "Coupled with wanderlust and brains, Dr. Fatteh moved to Bombay when he was old enough to get his medical degree," journalist Lisa J. Huriash writes. "He worked in England and Ireland and planned to permanently settle in Canada, but got a job offer first in Virginia." MCV was one of a number of postings he would hold in a long, successful career, including serving as associate chief medical examiner for the state of North Carolina and working in South Florida for the Broward County Medical Examiner's office.[8]

But on that Saturday morning in 1968, Fatteh hoped to lean on the wisdom and experience of Dr. Mann. When he reached his boss's home, he learned that Mann was out of town and unreachable. As a backup, Fatteh called an attorney for the medical school, Thomas D. Jordan. After hearing the general situation, Jordan assured the young physician that he'd given sound advice. Tell them to keep trying to find the donor's family, Jordan said.

Fatteh knew he'd already asked for the family to be contacted and provide permission to donate Bruce Tucker's organs, including his heart.

So, feeling encouraged by the legal counsel, he walked several blocks to his office to start his day's regular duties. The surgeons knew where to find him.

11:30 a.m.

Some ten hours after his first emergency surgery, Bruce Tucker started gasping for breath again. The earlier tracheotomy had afforded some relief, supplying oxygen to his brain and heart. But by late morning, he became "apneic"—suffering from a temporary suspension of breathing. His treating physician, Dr. B. W. Brawley, ordered him to be put on a ventilator. While this afforded some measure of relief, only a few minutes later, Brawley, an associate professor of neurological surgery, deemed Tucker's "prognosis for recovery is nil and death imminent."[9]

Meanwhile, Bruce's family members remained unaware of his whereabouts or his grave condition.

Noon

Before eating lunch, Dr. David Sewell looked over Bruce Tucker's chart. It was just another day at work for the young surgeon. As one of Dr. Lower's protégés, he was familiar with the discussion of brain death. In fact, over the past year, he'd suggested a couple of possible candidates to serve as heart donors. But for one reason or another—such as obesity or old age—they hadn't passed muster.[10]

Now Dr. Lower seemed ready to overcome his past reservations and get on with a transplant. Sewell was proud to be on his team; indeed, he felt indebted to Lower for helping him become a surgeon. Sewell's entry into the surgical fraternity had been a bit circuitous. After graduating from medical school at Tulane University in New Orleans, he'd stayed for another year as a medical resident. After choosing to specialize in the field of ear, nose, and throat medicine (ENT) he found his options for advancement and study were limited at Tulane and elsewhere. His best offer came from MCV's residency program in the specialty. By his second year in Richmond, Sewell was bored. He realized he'd made a huge mistake by choosing to focus on allergies, snoring, and problems with swallowing—some of the typical maladies treated by ENTs.

He caught a huge break when Hume and Lower helped him gain admission into their general surgery program. Buoyed by their support and energized by the challenges in the operating room, Sewell went on to earn a prestigious fellowship in heart surgery at MCV.[11]

It was a unique opportunity to scrub in with a master surgeon and also to participate in his research projects. "I was helping Dr. Lower in the OR when he was operating," Sewell explained, "and when he was not operating, he was in the lab doing heart transplants in dogs. I was really prepared." After conducting a number of canine cardiac transplants, Sewell published a paper on how some dogs rejected their newly transplanted hearts. To study this problem Sewell performed biopsies on the canines' heart tissue in an effort to better understand organ rejection.

He also witnessed Christiaan Barnard watching Lower in his dog laboratory. At the time, Sewell thought Barnard's ambition outpaced his readiness. "He went back to South Africa and tried to do it in dogs, but he couldn't."

The difficulty, he said, was that "the aorta in dogs is hard to sew because of the bleeding. It took a lot of effort and training. . . . The dog aorta is thick and doesn't have the elasticity the human aorta does. A needle and suture can tear it."[12] Human hearts actually are more pliable, Sewell said, which may help explain how Barnard managed to pull off his transplant feat.

By the time he looked over Bruce Tucker's chart that Saturday, Sewell felt up to the task. After lunch, he placed some calls on his boss's behalf. One was to Lower's perfusionist, Lanier Allen, who would assist on Klett's heart operation; another was to an anesthesiologist, Dr. J. G. Campbell.

"We have a prospective donor," he told them.[13]

1:00 p.m.

A staff neurologist, Dr. Hooshang Hooshmand, was brought into Tucker's room to administer an electroencephalogram. He placed electrodes on his scalp and prepared to monitor his brain activity for the next hour. The EEG, as it's known, measures the steady fluctuation of low-level currents between the nerve cells (or neurons) in the brain.[14]

At the time of his exam, Hooshmand would say later, he knew nothing of the doctors' designs on Tucker's heart. He performed one twenty-five-minute-long EEG that "found no clinical evidence of viability and no evidence of cortical activity." He also noticed signs of a lack of blood supply to the eyes, causing what he termed "corneal cloudiness." This, he said, was yet another sign that Tucker was "dead from a neurological standpoint."[15]

Tucker's pulse (94) and his blood pressure (130/100) were high, but acceptable for someone in his condition. His body temperature was 96.5 Fahrenheit—below the standard 98.6 degrees.[16] "At this time," Dr. Fatteh later wrote, "the neurologist also found [Tucker's] heart was beating and that his body temperature, pulse, and blood pressure were all normal for a patient in his condition."

Fatteh later agreed with the staff neurologist's conclusion that Tucker's "brain was dead prior to the time he ran the EEG." Because the brain stem controls breathing, he added, there was "no evidence of being able to breathe spontaneously at all. The respirator was doing all the breathing."[17]

2:00 p.m.

Time was running out for Tucker. Where was his family? Why hadn't anyone claimed him? Didn't anyone care? Were they afraid of paying his medical bill? One doctor who was in the operating room recalled, "I was just told they tried to [find the] family and that nobody would agree that he was part of their family, as if they didn't want to pay for hospitalization or funeral."[18]

Fatteh later described the last-ditch efforts to find the Tucker family. "Hume sought the aid of the Richmond Police in locating [Tucker's] relatives at the address shown on the hospital chart, 109 East Charity Street, Richmond, Virginia."[19]

But once again, the cops struck out. Nobody seemed to know anything about his family's whereabouts. Even if they did know something, given the tensions on the street, would they have told the police? On that Saturday, the *Afro* warned that Second Street downtown had become "a powder keg" after three hundred people took to the streets to protest a shooting by a white security guard who "opened fire on a fleeing shoplifter." The black man managed to avoid the guard's fusillade and was charged with stealing five suits with a total estimated value of $125. Richmond police hung back, one cop explained, because "we didn't want to precipitate an incident."[20]

Community relations suffered in part because the Richmond police were still far from achieving anything close to meaningful representation of the African American populace. Among black patrolmen on the force, only one in forty could expect to be promoted to sergeant.[21]

So after the second failed attempt by the police, Hume called Dr. Fatteh again to get his authorization to begin the transplant operation. Perhaps distracted by his other duties, Fatteh continued to hold back. "Call me when he's pronounced dead."[22]

2:30 p.m.

William Tucker was hard at work when the phone rang. It was a friend who worked about fifteen blocks away, at MCV. "Did you know Bruce is here?" he asked in a hushed tone. "There's something strange going on."

"What are you talking about?"

William set down a pair of shoes on his workbench. His days were long—opening at 6:00 a.m. and closing at 6:00 p.m.—Monday through Saturday. The demand from customers was steady. People needed their shoes.

He was his own boss and ran a neat shop. His workbench was lined with the tools of his cobbler's trade—hammers, scissors, a ruler, various threads and needles, and leather for repairs.

So what was this call about? An operation involving Bruce? As far as he knew, his brother was fine. His friend started to tell him more, but said someone was coming, then hung up.

William reached for the phone book, searching for the hospital's main number. When he finally reached the information desk, he was told Bruce was in an operating room.

Operating? William wanted to know. *On what?* The receptionist blithely suggested he might want to come over to find out. Bruce tried explaining his situation and how he was stuck at work. But the receptionist was no help.

"You'll have to come over," she said.[23]

Around that time, a friend of Bruce Tucker's set out on her own fact-finding mission. Mrs. Evelyn Gregory took the bus from the east side of town down Broad Street and over to MCV hospital. It's not clear how she learned about Bruce's situation, but it may have been the same insider who tipped off William.

Though she visited the hospital in person, Mrs. Gregory also struck out. Either no one knew anything, or they had been instructed not to talk.[24]

Undeterred, she crossed the alley to St. Philip Hospital, where "colored" wards had long been in place. Despite its recent integration, Evelyn Gregory could see the signs of the hospital's second-class status that remained—moldy ceiling tiles, cracks in the linoleum floor, and old benches. The smell of floor wax and disinfectant hung in the air.

She gathered up her courage and approached the front counter. She asked about her missing friend.

But even here, at the old hospital for black Virginians, no one could give her any help.

Walking out, Mrs. Gregory thought, *Bruce, where are you?*[25]

2:45 p.m.

The surgery department's wheels started spinning faster. Hume's dual operating teams were scrubbed in and ready to go. Bruce Tucker, his heart still beating strong, "was taken back into the operating room in preparation for the removal of his heart and both kidneys. He was receiving oxygen to continue the viability of his heart and both kidneys.

"During the same period, he was receiving solutions of dextrose and saline to furnish nourishment to the organs."[26]

3:30 p.m.

Dr. Brawley switched off the ventilator keeping Bruce alive. Glancing at his watch, Brawley marked the end of MCV's artificial life support: *3:30 ½ p.m.* He believed there was no sentient life left to support.

As Bruce lost the ability to breathe on his own, he didn't flail around as he had before noon. After five minutes, a man who only hours before was hanging out with his friends, breathed his last. *Time of Death,* Brawley wrote on his chart, *3:33 p.m.*

In the adjoining room, Richard Lower began opening Joseph Klett's chest to receive its new heart.

3:35 ½ p.m.

William Tucker called MCV again, his heart racing. He went through the same frustrating routine with a receptionist. But this time he learned something new. Bruce had been taken into a "recovery room."

Recovery room? he thought. *What does* that *mean?*

On the eleventh floor of the hospital, where the transplant team was hard at work, any idea of "recovery" had taken on a strange double meaning. The surgeons went to work recovering what *they* wanted. Bruce Tucker's body represented a valuable asset for the transplant team because his heart—still being pumped with oxygen—was being prepared for transplantation. So were his kidneys.

Only one more thing was needed. Hume picked up the phone. "Mr. Tucker's been pronounced dead," he informed Fatteh.

It was what the assistant medical examiner needed to hear. Now, in Fatteh's mind, everything was going by the book. Though he hadn't examined Tucker himself, he felt the right boxes had been checked. Now he was ready to check the final one.

"You can take out his organs," Fatteh told Hume.

Actually, one legal box had been left unchecked: the provision in Virginia's Unclaimed Bodies Act requiring a twenty-four-hour waiting period before a body could be used for research purposes. It's not clear whether the surgeons knew of this provision in the law or if they discussed it. But as subsequent court testimony and oral history accounts would show, the surgeons felt they made good-faith efforts to contact Tucker's relatives.

Nonetheless, whether intentionally or not, no one at MCV thought to check with their front-desk receptionists to see if anyone had been searching for Bruce Tucker. Apparently, nobody at the information desk thought to tell them.

★   ★   ★

Surgically removing a heart requires extensive training and skill. But it actually doesn't take much time. Experienced surgeons say it can be done in less than thirty minutes.

"The way you remove the heart," Dr. Sewell explained years later, is "once you get the pericardium [the double-walled sac that contains the heart and the roots of the great vessels] opened, and the heart exposed, you put a needle to the aorta and attach it to potassium chloride."

The chemical "stops the heart and cools it against warming . . . Then you take the heart out."

Asked what it was like to see and hold Tucker's exposed heart, Dr. Sewell demurred. "I can't really comment," he said. "I didn't think about that . . . I was just thinking about the job I had to do and was trained to do on dogs." He simply "focused on the job at hand."[27]

It took between fifteen and twenty minutes. Once Tucker's heart was taken out of his chest—along with the coronary arteries to reattach it—it was cooled to about 46 degrees Fahrenheit by immersing it in a cold salt solution.[28]

Then Sewell put it in a sterile container and handed it to Hume, who promptly took it to a nurse next door. Sewell made quick work of closing Tucker's chest. It was left to another surgeon, Dr. H. M. Lee, to excise Tucker's left kidney at 4:39 p.m. and his right one seven minutes later, at 4:46 p.m. One kidney was sent to help a patient at Georgetown University, while the other stayed at MCV for research purposes.[29]

Earlier in the day, Lower had talked to Joseph Klett and his wife to let them know a potential donor was at hand. Given the businessman's recent history—with multiple heart attacks and severe blockage of his coronary arteries—the Kletts could see this was his last, best chance to live. So they gave him their approval to proceed with the transplant.

At 3:33 p.m., just after Dr. Brawley pronounced Tucker dead, the second phase of the transplant operation commenced. Klett was kept on a heart-lung machine to maintain his breathing and circulate his blood. It was a crowded operating room, with seven surgeons and many more nurses and support staff looking on.

After opening the chest and making the incision into the pericardium, Lower got his first full view of Klett's heart. It was so damaged that it reminded him of an old soccer ball.[30]

He began the operation, knowing so many things could go wrong. Lower was confident he could succeed, though, especially after he saw the healthy-looking organ in the saline solution. Despite any damage caused by smoking, Bruce Tucker's heart appeared remarkably resilient.

4:30 p.m.[31]

William Tucker made his third call of the afternoon. He was told that Bruce had been moved again to "room number five on the fifth floor of St. Philip Hospital." The information desk wouldn't reveal anything else.

6:00 p.m.

William Tucker took off his work apron, put up his tools, and got his bench ready for the next day. He would drive home, clean up, and then get over to MCV to find Bruce.

Driving across a bridge toward home on the city's south side, the James River swirled below, gorged with spring rain. Most days he could have enjoyed the view. Not now, though, not with Bruce's life seeming to hang in the balance. Reaching his one-story home, he couldn't stop thinking about his family down in Stony Creek, especially Abraham: How would he break the news that his daddy was in the hospital?

William washed up and put on a coat and tie. He wanted to look presentable at the hospital. Then he drove back across the river and found a parking place near St. Philip Hospital. Using his crutches, he made his way into the front lobby.

When he asked for his brother, he was directed to the second floor. Stepping off the elevator, a group of white men approached him. They looked uncomfortable. Finally, one of them spoke up. "I'm very sorry," he said, "but your brother was pronounced dead about four hours ago."

"Dead?" William cried out. "What do you mean?" The tall, proud black man fought back tears. Time seemed to stop. The men's mouths kept moving and making sounds, but William found it hard to follow. Nothing made sense. It was like a bad dream.

An autopsy, one man said.

His body will be released tomorrow about noon, said another.

Released? William thought. *Released from what?*

The last thing he could remember was someone saying, *Then you can make funeral arrangements.*

They left him alone in his grief, grasping his crutches, unsure of what to do next.[32]

★   ★   ★

The lack of information about Bruce Tucker's status and the nature of his death, coupled with the lack of informed consent before the heart transplant, "reflects Bruce Tucker's status as 'socially dead' before he was pronounced physically dead by the medical examiner," medical historian Susan E. Lederer wrote years later. Citing the work of ethnographer David Sudnow, she writes, "Social death" is what happens when a hospital patient "is treated essentially as a corpse, though perhaps still 'clinically' and 'biologically' alive."[33]

Bruce Tucker "entered the hospital without friends or family members. Even worse, in terms of medical decision-making about his 'terminality' as a patient, he entered the hospital with alcohol on his breath and on his clothes."

The profiling of Tucker as a "charity patient" fits a pattern of behavior chronicled by Sudnow and other academic researchers in the late 1960s at public hospitals such as MCV.

"In the case of Bruce Tucker," Lederer writes, "physician concern about his recovery was colored by his race, socio-economic class, and alcohol use."[34]

Bruce Tucker was the medical equivalent of novelist Ralph Ellison's Invisible Man. One passage from the award-winning 1952 novel about the black experience in America seemed to foreshadow the Richmond factory worker's tragic end. "Everywhere I've turned somebody has wanted to sacrifice me for my good," Ellison writes. "Only *they* were the ones who benefited. And now we start on the old sacrifice merry-go-round. At what point do we stop?"[35]

CHAPTER THIRTEEN

The Scream

THE FACTS OF WHAT actually took place on the eleventh floor of MCV hospital slowly began to emerge, albeit in a ponderous, somewhat paranoid way. The institution's leadership was bent on protecting the image of an up-and-coming medical school; this meant standing firmly behind the decisions made by its star surgeons, Drs. Hume and Lower. Thus the first draft of the Klett-Tucker transplant was written by that most unreliable of narrators—the institutional spokesman. Damage control was the order of the day.

A shroud of secrecy fell over the campus as soon as news of the transplant broke in Klett's home, Orange, Virginia. Once the Associated Press posted a bulletin about the local businessman's heart transplant, the press corps in Richmond scrambled to catch up to the story. Much to their chagrin, they found their normal sources had clammed up. It was a near-total news blackout.

"The 11th floor of the Medical College of Virginia Hospital was reportedly where the transplant was performed, and it was the most closely guarded floor in the hospital last night," the *Times-Dispatch* reported.[1] The hospital was under a near lockdown, with no access to the surgery department. "An elevator operator said she was instructed not to make any stops whatsoever on the 11th floor."

"I'm sorry," the female operator told a reporter, "that floor is closed. Maybe the lady at the reception desk can help you."

For those journalists fit enough to climb eleven flights of stairs, it was all for naught. The doors were blocked by campus guards in the stairwells. The blockade was all the more galling as "reporters could see the doctors and nurses in blue surgical gowns moving rapidly across the corridors when police opened and shut the door to let interns and other hospital personnel in and out."[2]

David Hume and Richard Lower "were inaccessible to newsmen," the paper reported. Among those frustrated journalists prowling the halls and climbing the stairs was a young reporter from the *Times-Dispatch* named Jim Seymore. With the regular medical writer, Bev Orndorff, out of town that night, Seymore was taken off his normal police beat and sent over to MCV to see what he could find.

It was a tough assignment. Seymore knew things weren't breaking his way when he talked with one of the familiar hospital police officers named R. M. McNeil. Outside one of the doors to the surgery department, the cop shook his head and said, "It's no use trying to see him [Dr. Lower] tonight. You're just wasting your energy."

Seymore persisted, though, and managed to get the sympathetic sentry to deliver several handwritten notes to the surgeons. The pressure was building from his editors to get something—anything!—that would help his newspaper save face on such a big, breaking story that the wire service had already reported.

Surely some of the paper's many friends in the surgery department would throw him some tidbits of news. That way, the paper could run an article with his byline. Otherwise, out of professional courtesy it would have to cite the Associated Press and leave his name off this big story. This was a matter of pride within the newsroom as well as with the two hundred thousand subscribers of the Sunday *Times-Dispatch*, which boasted on its masthead to have the "Largest Morning Circulation in Virginia."

But every time Seymore or other reporters sent handwritten notes into the surgery department, Officer McNeil returned empty-handed. "No, nothing tonight," he said.[3]

Humiliation lurked around every corner. Seymore approached a pair of student nurses and asked if they knew the location of Hume's office. "Yes," one replied, "but you will never find him there tonight." She added dismissively, "*You* probably won't find him at all."[4]

For an institution whose leaders had long dreamed about being in the national spotlight, MCV's leaders decided on this night of all nights to tamp down expectations. Only minutes before the early deadline for the state edition of the *Times-Dispatch*, the hospital finally released an official statement from Ralph M. Ware Jr., director of development at the medical college. It shed little light on the day's events, though, confirming only that "the transplant operation had been completed. . . . There will be no further bulletins issued until the end of next week."

A few blocks away in the *Times-Dispatch* newsroom, the editors were feeling stymied. They'd been scooped in their own backyard. The next morning's front page seemed to reflect their sour mood, delivered with all of the excitement of a farm report.

"A heart transplant was completed at the Medical College of Virginia yesterday," the article began. "The patient is reported to be in satisfactory condition." After running the hospital's bare bones statement that failed to identify any of the patients, the newspaper continued, "The Associated Press early today, however, said unofficial sources identified the recipient of the heart transplant as Joseph G. Klett, 54, of Orange."

Spokesman Ware said his minimalist release was issued as "a matter of simply a doctor-patient relationship. That is all I can tell you."

The newspaper noted that "the statement was issued approximately four hours after the completion of surgery." It was prepared jointly by the administration and the surgical team leaders—Drs. Hume and Lower.

Undaunted, reporter Seymore kept working the phone. Shortly after midnight, he called Lower's office again and, much to his surprise, heard him pick up. "Dr. Lower, reached at his hospital office at 12:30 a.m., said he was busy and did not have time to talk about the surgery," Seymore wrote. Then the surgeon gave his only quote of the night.

"The team decided that we would not issue any information concerning the patient at this time," he said. "I'm sorry but I'm very busy. You will have to excuse me."

Left holding the phone, the young reporter's mind churned with unanswered questions. Who was Joseph Klett and why was he chosen to receive the new heart? Who was the unnamed donor? How did he die? Why were Hume and Lower and everyone at MCV being so coy? Why hadn't they trumpeted their first transplant? Why all the cloak-and-dagger stuff? Was there something to hide?

Years later, science writer Bev Orndorff described the frustrations his colleague encountered that night and his own struggles the next day after he raced back to Richmond to cover the story. "It was obvious to me from the beginning that the surgeons were unusually closed-mouth about the transplant. . . . Through the weekend, there were more and more indications that the MCV surgeons had clammed up about the case for some suspicious reason."[5]

Adding to his problems was the flood of publicity that followed the first heart transplant in South Africa. "I particularly felt tremendous pressure from some of my editors to find out who the donor heart came from, just as the Cape Town tabloids had learned of the identity of the donor in Barnard's first transplant case," Orndorff explained. "Until then, it had been the usual practice in this country not to identify the donors of transplanted tissue, whether it was corneas or kidneys, and I never pressed—or was pressed—to seek donors' names when I wrote about such cases."

Those informal rules of patient privacy went out the window after the media frenzy of the first transplant. "The heart was different," said Orndorff, "and the precedent for going after the donor's identity in a heart transplant case had already been set in South Africa."[6]

As they dealt with the dearth of news from the medical college, the *Times-Dispatch* editors quoted from old articles about David Hume's kidney transplant program. But it was Lower, not Hume, who got the most local coverage. Lower's picture ran beside the lead story of the day—a minimum-wage boost for French workers—and across the page from "Viet Cong Holding Out in Suburbs of Saigon." He was pensive-looking behind horn-rimmed glasses, with short-cropped hair and wearing a coat and tie. "Dr. Richard R. Lower Pioneered Transplant," the caption said.

The first local news account seemed to raise as many questions as it answered. For example, why had Lower chosen to operate on his patient on that particular day? The only clue came with the news that "Klett had been hospitalized about a month—twice at Charlottesville and later at the Medical College of Virginia Hospital" in Richmond.[7]

"A former purchasing agent at the Virginia Metal Products Co. at Orange, Klett moved to Virginia from New York City about 20 years ago." Little more was said about him, and no information whatsoever was provided about who donated the heart. In their efforts to fill in the gaps in the story, the paper's editors made ample use of Bev Orndorff's many past stories on MCV's kidney and heart research.

They started with Lower's past work with Shumway. "The two first showed that heart transplants were feasible at Stanford in 1959, and the surgical technique they developed has been used in the human heart transplant attempts."

For his part, Hume was called "one of the pioneers in kidney transplants, having done considerable work in this area since joining the MCV staff in 1956."

Despite the generally upbeat tone of the article, readers were cautioned that the transplant patient (who was officially still unnamed) was not out of the woods. Previous heart transplants—including those of Barnard and Shumway—had already shown "that a two-day period immediately following the transplant is the most critical." This was when organ "rejection or acceptance by the patient's body of the transplanted organ is more likely to occur than later."

The editors, whether by design or not, waited until they were deep into the article before saying where MCV ranked on the growing list of heart transplants. "The transplant was the world's 16th. The first was performed by Prof. Christiaan Barnard at Cape Town, South Africa, on Dec. 3, 1967"—a date which would live in MCV infamy.

The paper's account noted Barnard's three-month visit to Richmond from Aug. 1 to Nov. 30, 1966, "to observe and learn about the MCV surgeons' work in the transplant field."

The Klett operation was the ninth in the United States over the past six months; yet, the paper noted ominously, only two patients were still living. MCV spokesman Ware explained the hospital's own position on performing the risky procedure. "On the basis of animal studies in heart transplants, it was understood that MCV surgeons have felt ready to try the procedure for many months," he said.

The spokesman gave no hint of Lower's near attempt in the fall of 1966. "It was also understood that surgeons have had several possible recipients but no available donors at the needed time," Ware said. So even though his name wasn't given, Bruce Tucker was chosen as the best "available donor" at "the needed time."

As the Sunday newspaper coverage spread, Anne and Dick Lower began fielding a steady string of congratulatory phone calls as well as calls from eager reporters from around the country. Lower shunned them because, as Anne explained later, "He was a little worried about the press coverage."[8] He didn't want to have a repeat of the media circus at Stanford that Norm Shumway had endured.

Dave Hume invited the surgical staff and their wives and kids to celebrate the historic achievement out at his farm. The Lowers gladly loaded their four children into the car and headed west into the rolling hills of Goochland County. It was the perfect way to escape the ringing phone.

★　★　★

Even as one family fled the limelight, another was trying to shed light on their loss. William Tucker was caught between rage and confusion as he called the funeral home closest to his family home in Stony Creek. Mack Jones, the owner, offered his condolences and assured him he'd take care of receiving Bruce's body from the state medical examiner's office.

Jones told him to come see him the next day—on Monday—to make funeral arrangements and write an obituary. William agreed. He sat alone in his well-tended home in South Richmond. So many questions kept gnawing at him. With his shoe-repair shop only a matter of blocks away, why hadn't the doctors asked him to come over and talk before they cut Bruce open? And what had they *done* to him in the operation his friend alerted him to?

Finally, William picked up the bag of Bruce's things that the strange men at the hospital had given him. He was stunned to see a business card—*his* card. Bruce kept it on him as a way to refer clients to his brother's shop. "Tucker's Shoe Repair. 2304 E. Main Street," it read, clear as day. *How could those doctors and nurses have missed that?* he thought. It felt like another slap in the face.

There'd been a lot of slaps lately. It had been less than a year since his father, Spencer, had died shortly before his seventieth birthday.[9] Now Bruce was gone.

A familiar anger began to simmer inside. It was as deep as what he felt as a boy when white boys pestered him on his way home from the all-black school in Stony Creek. But he knew he must stay strong now. Even though he was the youngest son, everyone was counting on him to sort things out. If he let himself be consumed by anger, the old haters would win. So would the white doctors at MCV. He resolved to do something about it. He'd read in the *Richmond Afro-American* about a trial lawyer who was making a name for himself standing up for the little guy. He made a mental note to call Doug Wilder as soon as he could.

William woke up early Monday morning and took off for Mack Jones's funeral home in Stony Creek. This took him south on Interstate 95 past Petersburg until he turned onto Route 40 heading east. He watched out for the farm tractors that sometimes crept onto the highway out of fields of soybeans, corn, and peanuts. Besides tobacco in Virginia, peanuts could be a major "cash crop" for black farmers like the Tuckers. The nearby town of Wakefield was known as "the peanut capital of Virginia." Lumber also was a lucrative product.

But even though the Tuckers had been landowners for many years, they never forgot the warnings they heard as children to trod carefully in their white-majority community. Waverly, for example, was the site of one of Virginia's last recorded lynchings. It happened in 1925 when a lumber worker named James Jordan was detained by police at the Gray Lumber Co. After a foreman identified him, Jordan was arrested for "allegedly attacking a married white woman and stealing a pistol belonging to her husband." Word spread of his arrest and alleged misdeed, firing up a mob of hundreds of whites. The angry throng quickly encircled the jail, overpowered the sheriff and his deputies, and dragged Jordan out to lynch him. Later the mob used his corpse for target practice and set him "on fire in full view of passengers on a Norfolk and Western train that pulled into the station during the macabre proceeding."[10]

William Tucker couldn't shake an ominous feeling about how his own brother's life had ended.[11] Stony Creek was as quiet as its name sounded as he drove along Confederate Avenue, crossing the railroad tracks. Turning right on Park Street, he reached the one-story brick building with a long black Cadillac hearse parked out front near a simple sign: "Jones Funeral Home."

It was about 9:00 a.m. when William parked behind the hearse, knowing that soon enough he'd be following it over to Little Bethel Church.[12] He'd done the same thing the previous August when they'd buried his father. Though William was the youngest of the Tucker men, he was the responsible one. With his business background, he was most likely to make sure the bills and taxes got paid on time.

Inside, Mack Jones met him with a pained expression. After offering his condolences, he asked William to sit down. There was something he had to tell him.

Easing himself into a chair, William leaned his crutches against the wall. He wondered why Mack was so upset. Didn't he deal with death every day?

Mack began haltingly. While he was preparing Bruce for burial, he'd noticed something . . . strange . . . something he'd never seen before. He blurted, "William, his heart is missing! So are his kidneys!"[13]

His words were like raindrops that fall too fast for the ground to absorb. It was like when the white men at MCV had told him Bruce was dead. William sat numbly as the undertaker tried to help him understand.

"Bruce must have been the one they were talking about in the paper," Mack said, referring to news of the heart transplant at MCV.

But all William could think of was his mother, Emma. "Does Mama know?" he asked.

"Yes, I drove out to the farm this morning and told her myself."

William hastily got up to leave. His mama should never have to hear such a thing. Neither should his nephew Abraham.

Normally, a funeral should help everyone grieve and find some measure of peace and comfort. But as he drove along Flatfoot Road and topped the rise above Little Bethel Church, it was hard to imagine coming to terms with how the doctors at MCV handled his brother. *What had they done? Wasn't that mutilation? Or worse? How did they think they'd get away with it?* As soon as he got back to Richmond, he planned to call Mr. Wilder.

William slowed on Black Branch Road as he neared the family homestead up in the woods. Leaving the asphalt, he drove as fast as he could along the rising, bumpy road. How many times had he seen Bruce playing in these trees, running freely even when he couldn't? How many times had his brothers played hide-and-seek and chased fireflies here?

Nearing the family's white clapboard house nestled in a stand of trees, William was glad Abraham was probably off at school. He'd hoped to comfort his mother alone, but now he could see folks were already on hand to help her.

The sound of Emma Tucker's loss had sounded like an alarm across the fields. "I remember the day my aunt found out her son's heart was missing," recalled Wilma Malone, a cousin of the Tucker brothers. "It was through Jones Funeral Home. When Mr. Mack Jones told her, the scream she let out is still fresh in my mind. My mother, sister, and I ran to her house to try to comfort her."[14]

Now it was William's turn.

CHAPTER FOURTEEN

"Facts and Circumstances"

ULTIMATELY, THE IDENTITY OF the "donor" in MCV's heart transplant story would not be revealed by its key players. Hume and Lower maintained their public silence, as did the rest of the team of physicians, nurses, and medical technicians. The door guards even kept their lips sealed.

The official silence was maintained for about two days after the operation. This included the follow-up coverage in Monday's *Times-Dispatch*:

MCV Patient Reported "Satisfactory" 16th Heart Transplant

"Unofficial reports listed the heart transplant patient at the Medical College of Virginia as progressing satisfactorily yesterday, but MCV physicians involved with the Saturday operation remained silent about the procedure for the present," Bev Orndorff wrote. "They reiterated yesterday, however, their Saturday night statement that the details of the world's 16th heart transplant, and ninth in this country, will be made 'at the appropriate interval,' meaning some time during the next several days."

Though MCV still had "not confirmed the patient's identity," he was "unofficially identified as 54-year-old Joseph G. Klett of Orange, a former purchasing agent for the Virginia Metal Products Co. there."[1]

The article included more information about Klett's failing health and his life in a small town in Virginia. He'd arrived in Richmond about a month earlier, following hospitalizations in Charlottesville. His heart condition had steadily worsened over the past few years. But following the transplant, neighbors drove his wife, Anna, to Richmond, where she was allowed to talk to him. Her husband looked "wonderful," she was quoted as saying. MCV declined to say how much time they spent together.

The reading public also caught the first glimpse of the celebrated patient. In an old family photo, Joseph Klett stood by a black sedan, looking dignified in a suit and black overcoat. He held a top hat, adding to his serious, professional appearance. In this grainy image, he bore a passing resemblance to FBI director J. Edgar Hoover.

Despite the new details about Klett, much of the article was taken up by MCV's account of what had transpired Saturday evening on the eleventh floor of the hospital. Noting the hospital's lack of access to the news media, Orndorff drolly observed, "the physicians involved with the procedure indicated yesterday they were following the immediate closed-mouth policy for several reasons."

First, they said, this was done "out of respect for the privacy of the patient and the patient's family." Next, they cited "the medical complexities" of the procedure. "The doctors want to monitor the next several critical days for the patient before making a public statement about the operation."

The afternoon *Richmond News Leader* added a fascinating new wrinkle when it raised questions about the surgeons' legal authority to conduct the operation. "The medical examiner's office had not given permission for the transplant operation," the paper reported. "The law which would empower the medical examiner to authorize removal of the heart from a donor in certain circumstances does not become effective until next month." The office "would not discuss whether the family had approved the removal of the heart."[2]

There was no mention of Dr. Fatteh's role in the operation. And, in fact, the new law cited by the *News Leader* was somewhat misleading. This was a separate statute—called the Uniform Anatomical Gift Act—that was passed by the legislature to bring Virginia in line with organ donation laws in forty-two other states. Yet, while the news article may have missed the mark, its underlying question about the medical examiner's role was valid and would not go away.

Up to this point, most of the local news coverage remained upbeat and accentuated the positive. It seemed to play up the story's gee-whiz quality, a life-and-death drama folks could ponder over breakfast or around watercoolers: *Did you hear they put a new heart in a man down at MCV? I wonder if he'll make it?*

Orndorff, caught between his editors' thirst for breaking news and his own sense of fairness and objectivity, took a step back and tried not to get caught up in the hype—even if, by the very nature of the news, he was helping fuel it. "Many surgeons have taken a dim view of the widespread publicity that immediately resulted from the first human heart operations," he wrote. "Several months ago, the American College of Surgeons restated its previous stand urging restraint on immediate publicity following an experimental procedure."

Then he struck a cautionary note about the long recovery ahead for Joseph Klett. "As with other transplanted organs between non-related or non-identical twin persons, there is the potential danger that a recipient's body will reject a transplanted heart." Over the past six years, Hume's team had performed more than 140 kidney transplants, with an overall success rate of 70 percent—or, viewed another way, a failure rate of 30 percent, or about one in three transplants. Adding to the uncertainty in the new field of heart transplantation was a lack of long-term data.

Orndorff mentioned promising research with electrocardiography (EKG) and how it "can be used to help spot an impending rejection crisis."

After putting readers on notice about bumps in the road to recovery, Orndorff then took a side trip to view Lower's recent and potentially controversial work. This included his late-night, experimental procedures proving that hearts taken from corpses—so-called "cadaver hearts"—could be resuscitated within thirty minutes. This may have come as a shock to some Richmonders who'd missed his earlier coverage of animal-human organ experiments. He recalled Lower's work transferring a cadaver heart into a baboon.

Orndorff recalled an interesting comment Lower had made about six months earlier. It came in response to a question about why he was holding off on attempting his first heart transplant.

"We have seriously considered doing the procedure in humans," Lower said, but "because of the fact that we considered it an extremely high risk and untried, unproven procedure in humans, I think we decided it would be reserved only for extreme circumstances in humans."[3]

As he explained his thinking, Lower added that it "should be used only when death of a patient seemed imminent." It should be used to *save* a life, he said, but not to create what he called "cardiac cripples."

Though his self-examination drew scant notice at the time, it showed the surgeon's awareness of the inherent risks that came with bringing heart patients back from the edge of the abyss.

Lower's caution notwithstanding, the Richmond newspapers gleefully got aboard the transplant train. Heart operations around the world became a regular staple, such as:

Heart Transplant Performed in Brazil World's 17th

"A team of 41 specialists simultaneously transplanted the heart and a kidney of a young automobile accident victim into two different patients Sunday. Both patients were reported in good conditions after their operations."[4]

The wave of publicity continued to break, with 101 heart transplants performed around the world in 1968.[5] Houston heart surgeon Denton Cooley achieved his own celebrity status as he transplanted hearts "at a furious rate," Donald McRae observed. Yet, he added that "death stalked every case." Nine out of seventeen transplant patients in 1968 died a month or less after receiving a new heart from Cooley. By contrast Dr. Shumway at Stanford considered the search for an answer to the rejection question and improved postoperative treatment "the two prime battlegrounds in transplantation."[6]

★   ★   ★

MCV's efforts to keep Bruce Tucker's name out of the paper eventually failed because of what Orndorff later called a "fluke." Three days after the transplant, he recalled, "A funeral home director in Southside Virginia phoned in a man's obituary, and at the end of the call, he proudly told our reporter taking the call that this was the person whose heart was used for that big operation in Richmond."[7]

Determined not to get scooped again, the medical writer sprang into action. He was able to draw on the information from the funeral home director, Mack Jones. Orndorff started with the most important fact— the "donor's" name, Bruce Tucker. Then came the list of his survivors. Orndorff employed a valuable research tool of the day to learn more about him: the city directory, a detailed phone and address book with convenient cross-references. He found Bruce's home address, his employer, and other key information. The next morning he broke the story of the man who gave up his heart.

Heart Donor Identified 53-Year-Old Richmond Man

"The identity of the donor was learned late yesterday," Orndorff wrote. "He was Bruce Oliver Tucker, 53, of 109 E. Charity St. here, who suffered fatal brain injuries last Friday evening when he fell from a three-foot-high wall he was sitting on and hit his head on concrete, according to a friend."[8]

Orndorff continued, "Tucker, who was a Negro, died Saturday of 'irreparable' brain injuries, according to one source. He worked at the Schulberg-Kurdle Co. Inc. (Esskay), a packing firm . . . at the firm's egg plant at 1114 E. Cary Street." This was located in the city's Shockoe Bottom neighborhood, a matter of blocks from William's shoe repair shop.

The plant manager said Bruce Tucker had been a long-time employee for "26 or 27 years." He described him as a "good employee who was always punctual." His work involved handling and grading eggs. His accident "occurred sometime after the plant had closed Friday evening," the plant manager said.

This initial report about the heart "donor" was important for a number of reasons. First, it offered firsthand testimony countering any prejudicial notion that Bruce Tucker was some sort of scofflaw brought to the emergency room—a "charity patient" who would leave the taxpayers of Virginia holding the bill for his medical care. Bruce's boss described him as a stand-up guy who paid his bills.

Orndorff's article also provided the first confirmation from a family member that Bruce was involved in the operation. Asked if his brother was the donor, Grover [sic] Tucker replied, "Yes, he's the one."[9]

The article also gave the first hint that trouble was brewing with the family over MCV's actions. "Another brother, William Tucker of Richmond, declined to confirm or deny that Bruce Tucker was the donor, but added, 'If it were done, it was done without authorization.' He declined further comment."

State medical officials—presumably Dr. Geoffrey Mann, the chief medical examiner—appeared to dodge the question by declining any comment "regarding the question of authorization."

How were the Tuckers expected to handle such conflicting and confusing information? Bruce's treatment by MCV had left William shaken.

Now, for some strange reason, the state medical examiner seemed to be avoiding taking any responsibility. Oddly, the office released a brief statement about the state of Bruce's health *before* his fall.

"In response to inquiries earlier," Orndorff wrote, ". . . a spokesman for the chief medical examiner's office here said the donor . . . had been 'previously in good health.' "[10]

Given so much uncertainty, the Tuckers announced that they would delay Bruce's funeral for the time being.

Adding to the family's growing list of grievances, the *Times-Dispatch* appears to have never actually published the obituary that led to Orndorff's scoop. Mack Jones—who eagerly alerted the paper—wound up being used as an unwitting news source.[11]

Bruce Tucker's obituary did run in the *Progress-Index* of Petersburg on Monday, May 27, 1968. This was the same day Jones called the Richmond paper, presumably because that's where Bruce lived. His friends and family in Dinwiddie County—near Petersburg—saw a simple, yet revealing portrait of a local man whose life had been cut short. However, no mention was made of the heart transplant:

BRUCE O. TUCKER

Bruce O. Tucker of Richmond, died May 25, in MCV Hospital, Richmond, after a brief illness.

Mr. Tucker was a native of Dinwiddie County and the son of Mrs. Emma Tucker and the late Spencer Tucker. He was a member of Little Bethel Baptist Church, Dinwiddie.

Surviving are: son, Abraham Tucker, mother, Mrs. Emma Tucker, both of Dinwiddie; five sisters: Miss Carrie Lee Tucker, of Santa Monica, Calif.; Miss Lester Mae Tucker of Richmond; Mrs. Ethel Jennings, Mrs. Pauline Harvey, Mrs. Viola Peters, all of Baltimore; three brothers: Lathan [sic] Tucker, of Dinwiddie; Glover Tucker of Church Road; William Tucker of Richmond; two aunts and one uncle.

Funeral services will be held Tuesday at 2 p.m. in the Little Bethel

Baptist Church. The Rev. W.H. Winston will officiate. Remains rest at
the Jones Funeral Home, Stony Creek.[12]

As the Tuckers prepared to bury their own, Joseph Klett was mount-
ing a recovery and gaining strength. Still, it was hard for anyone to be
sure of the health status of the recipient of Bruce's heart. The hospital
was maintaining its defensive crouch. When it spoke to the press, it
seemed as interested in justifying its policies as it did in explaining how
Mr. Klett was doing.

This statement was typical: "It has been the policy of MCV since the
beginning of the transplant program in 1962 not to release detailed information concerning the recipient until such time the attending physicians think appropriate." This wouldn't change with the heart transplant
or with "any future patients in the transplant program at the Medical
College of Virginia."[13]

As the surgeons and administrators kept fending off press queries,
they tried to explain their policy that said *living* donors could have their
names made public—but only if they were donating organs to their relatives, as often happened in kidney transplants. Another ad hoc standard
now applied to anyone who *died* at MCV in a transplant operation—
presumably, someone like Bruce Tucker.

Such was the labyrinth of issues facing the nation's fledgling system
of transplantation and organ donations in the late 1960s. It was a baffling
place where rules were made on the fly. More often than not, patients'
rights were not paramount. Rather, the authority of doctors and hospitals ruled the day. It would take nearly two decades before the federal
government implemented the patient privacy provisions of the 1996
Health Insurance Portability and Accountability Act (HIPAA).

In 1968, what MCV's leaders hoped would be a glorious victory and
historic event quickly morphed into a public relations monster on the
order of the body-snatching scandals of the 1850s. Those incidents had
required public explanations and press statements of their own. But the

Tucker-Klett saga soon began to emit its own stench. Was this a great victory for Lower and Hume and the whole of MCV? Or was there some sort of problem? Had something gone terribly wrong down at the medical college? Was that why the hospital sounded so uptight? Were they telling the whole story or was there something to hide?

All anyone on the outside knew for sure was that one man had died and another was living because of the gift of a heart. In this new age of intense public scrutiny, MCV struggled to find its footing. How could they tell their story while still controlling the narrative?

Reporters descended on the tiny town of Orange, in Virginia's horse country. They learned that Klett had gloomily told friends three months before the operation, "I'm living now and I have a few days left." He'd been on sick leave from his management post for about eight months, spending most of his time in hospitals. Often he arrived by ambulance.[14]

★   ★   ★

In that heyday of print journalism, nobody at MCV was in any mood to nominate any of the persistent reporters for a Pulitzer Prize, whether they wrote for the Richmond papers, the *Richmond Afro-American*, or the *Washington Post*.

Because he put Bruce Tucker's name in the paper, Bev Orndorff recalled many years later that "I was immediately persona non grata in the surgery department at MCV because of that story. The surgeons were chagrined that I identified the man and seemingly presented him in a highly sympathetic manner . . . They thought I was glorifying [Bruce Tucker]."[15]

It's not clear how releasing the donor's name, along with a slice of his life story, could be seen as an act of glorification. How could anyone expect a fair-minded journalist to portray Tucker as anything but "sympathetic?" Yet, in the heat of the moment, the MCV surgeons and staff failed to notice that the *Times-Dispatch* initially steered clear of one of the story's more controversial angles—that is, its racial undertones.

By contrast the *Washington Post*, which had a news bureau in Richmond, didn't back off from this part of the story. It was a particularly sensitive subject in light of the rioting, arson, and arrests in Washington that followed the assassination of the Reverend Dr. Martin Luther King. Nonetheless, the *Post* ran this headline:

Va. White Got Negro's Heart

It ran below pictures of Lower and Hume. "The donor in Virginia's first heart transplant was identified today as a man, 40, who died Friday night in a fall. He was a Negro."[16]

Even though the *Post* didn't have Tucker's name and misreported his age (he was fifty-four), the paper's editors chose to report his race. After identifying Klett as white, the article noted that this was "the United States' first interracial heart transplant." It also reported that MCV "has done a number of interracial kidney transplants among the 140-plus it has performed in the past six years."

Post reporter Victor Cohn managed to get the previously mum chief medical examiner—Geoffrey Mann—to discuss the question that had dogged Hume and Lower since the first new reports:

Who authorized them to remove Tucker's heart?

"The medical examiner's office here also said today that it did not give permission for the transplant, nor was permission asked," Cohn reported. He added that "a new Virginia law will allow the examiner to authorize a heart removal in some circumstances. That law does not take effect until late June." [17]

Once again, the still-pending Uniform Anatomical Gift Act was being held up as a kind of legal shield by Dr. Mann. Either he didn't yet grasp the role his assistant, Dr. Fatteh, had played in giving the doctors a green light, or he was trying to distance himself from it.

Despite this new twist in the *Post*, the MCV surgeons and their supporters kept griping about the supposedly unfair coverage they were getting in the local paper. In their view, Orndorff had broken an unspoken rule of professional courtesy in Richmond.[18]

MCV proceeded to mount a public relations counteroffensive described with the *Times-Dispatch* headline: "Donation Held Legal, Ethical." There was another twist in this story as well: the Tuckers had retained legal counsel.

"Medical College of Virginia physicians involved with the heart transplant operation last weekend issued a statement late yesterday stating, among other things, that the donor organ was obtained according to 'proper ethical and legal standards,'" Orndorff wrote. "Among the repercussions from the transplant and subsequent news reports has been a question about the authority for removing the organ from the donor. Last night, a lawyer representing Bruce Tucker's family said an investigation was being conducted of the facts and circumstances surrounding Tucker's injury and death.

"Lawrence Douglas Wilder, the lawyer, also said, 'No member of the Bruce O. Tucker family has given any persons any authority to do anything about the person of the decedent or with any of his anatomical components.'"[19]

MCV officials insisted everything had been done aboveboard to protect patient privacy—including that of the Tuckers. Yet at this point, MCV officials still hadn't officially informed them about the removal of their loved one's organs.

Instead, the college seemed intent on portraying itself as a beneficent protector of its patients. It claimed that "it was the desire of the [Klett] family not to become embroiled in publicity." As a result, MCV said, "We attempted to adhere to their wishes."

As to the still-unnamed other patient, the anonymous officials followed the same tack. "The donor organ, which [was] obtained according to proper and legal standards, was also not discussed because it has been the policy of the transplant program at MCV not to make public information on the donation of organs. We will continue to attempt to maintain the anonymity of donor organs."

MCV was caught in a quandary of its own making. On the one hand, it used its privacy policy to justify its lack of transparency with the Tucker family. But as a publicly supported institution, the college's brain trust seemed to sense they needed to shed more light on the situation. They promised to release some details about Joseph Klett's status while still "attempting to maintain restraint about releasing daily details about the patient's condition." There was a practical reason to be circumspect, they noted. "He is currently listening to television and radio."[20]

Klett may well have been an eyewitness to the first salvos being fired by William Tucker's outspoken attorney. "It would be premature at this stage of the investigation of the facts surrounding the injury and death of Bruce O. Tucker to be able to correctly state what did transpire," Doug Wilder said.[21]

His previous employment in the state medical examiner's office would come in handy. Yet, at this point, the lawyer's role was somewhat limited, since he already had a full load of criminal defense cases. But Wilder had been moved by the desperate call from William. He viewed himself as the David in this legal battle, with MCV the Goliath. When Wilder spoke of "this office," for example, he sounded like he was invoking a deep-pocketed law firm that would get to the bottom of things. In reality, his was a one-man operation where he answered his own phone and did his own cleaning. His frugality was well-known.

Still, when he became the voice of the Tucker family, L. Douglas Wilder, Esq., was able to draw on a full range of rhetorical skills honed over the years in Richmond's courtrooms. It was not a place for delicate sensibilities. Black lawyers such as he and Henry Marsh would work themselves to the bone representing mostly black clients before majority-white juries. Stepping up to speak for this powerless black family, Wilder was completely in his element. He would draw on his own rich legacy and experience in overcoming the second-class status into which he was born, but out of which he became that much stronger. His very name seemed to suggest great things to come—"Lawrence" in honor of the influential nineteenth-century poet Paul Laurence Dunbar and "Douglas" after the great orator and abolitionist Frederick Douglass.[22]

"This office will exhaust every conceivable source of remedy for wrongful acts, if any there be," Wilder declared, along with a vow to "pursue that end with dispatch."[23]

★   ★   ★

Bev Orndorff continued to untangle the web of legal issues left in the transplant's wake. Any adult in Virginia, he told readers, "may designate, through a will, how his body, or parts of a body, may be disposed of after death." After citing various "next of kin" scenarios, he noted one legal option that may have applied to the Tucker case. When there's *no* next of kin, the anatomical section of the state health department is notified; they are given the authority to assign the body to a medical school, physicians, or surgeons "to be used for the advancement of medical science." Once again, the 1884 law to promote medical science and protect graves and cemeteries was rearing its head.

Orndorff also explained the concept of "reasonable efforts" to contact next of kin. "Public institutions, such as hospitals, have the responsibility of trying to locate relatives of a patient." But what, he asked, actually constitutes a *reasonable* search for relatives? It was a matter of interpretation, with few clear guidelines. Some health officials close to the case would only discuss it with Orndorff on a background basis to keep their names out of the paper. For example, one unnamed source—most likely Dr. Mann, the chief medical examiner—told him that a hospital is required to use "only reasonable efforts" to locate the closest living relative of a patient.[24]

"In other words," the source said, "if a patient should be brought into a hospital, and is unable to give hospital officials any information about himself, hospital personnel then attempt to locate relatives through such sources as police and telephone directories."

Once that's done, "If a 'reasonable search' is to no avail, the anatomical section is then notified, along with the information of the fruitless search for relatives." Only then may a body be "turned over to medical schools or to physicians and surgeons if there is a need."

Orndorff also set forth the roles and responsibilities of the chief medical examiner's office.

"The State Health Commissioner has designated Dr. Geoffrey T. Mann, the state's chief medical examiner, to carry out the responsibilities spelled out under the state anatomical act. And, in Dr. Mann's absence, other procedures for carrying out the act are listed."[25]

The following week, the mystery surrounding Bruce Tucker's demise struck a chord in the community:

Heart Donor Law Asked by Carwile

The *Times-Dispatch* reported that a city councilman, Howard H. Carwile, "called for a city ordinance to regulate heart transplants."[26] Amid the struggle for power in the city—with the white establishment continuing to oppose increasing black voting power—Councilman Carwile seized on the factory worker's fate to score political points.

The councilman suggested he was "considering a city ordinance to require permission of families involved [in] transplants." His rhetorical hand grenade was his way of exposing the agenda of Richmond Forward— the mostly white business group working in secret to get Richmond to annex parts of surrounding counties. Many in the city's business elite saw annexation as a vehicle for funding Richmond's municipal services by broadening its residential and commercial tax base. Without it, said a respected business leader, Councilman James C. Wheat Jr., "We face . . . increased exodus of our white citizens."[27]

But a new generation of black leaders had a different view of what it would take for Richmond to actually move "forward." In this regard, they suspected Wheat and others in the business elite were issuing what were, in effect, racial dog whistles. Attorney and council member Henry Marsh criticized them for having "a different philosophy because they represent a small segment" of the city's total population. "They don't even know what is happening because they live in their own little world."[28]

This broadside led the white mayor—Morrill Crowe—to take umbrage. "I have picked potatoes," Crowe declared. "I have worked in wheat fields."

Meanwhile, Marsh's colleague, Carwile, joined in the fray, invoking the Tucker transplant to prove his point. First, by charging Wheat and others with "cheap race-baiting" and "trying to inflame the whites against the Negroes."[29]

Then he painted a dystopian portrait that could have been drawn from the pages of H. G. Wells. In this world, the hearts of black residents would be bought and sold by white traders. "The time is coming," Carwile warned, "when Richmond Forward will control who practices law, who gets a contract, and they may cut your heart out and give it to a member of Richmond Forward."[30]

No such city ordinance was ever passed. Clearly, there was a large element of bluster in Carwile's bleak prophecy. Yet, it seemed to capture the local zeitgeist—with the widening gap between the world views of Richmond's black and white citizens. This was especially true when it came to trust in the medical system. Consider the stark difference between the coverage by the mainstream press and what ran in the *Richmond Afro-American*. The *Afro*'s first article on the transplant asked:

Did MCV Get Heart Use Okay?

Beneath a photo of Bruce Tucker, it cited the recent *Washington Post* article questioning the approval process at MCV.

Paper Says No Permission Given in Transplant Here

Afro reporter Barry Barkan wrote, "Virginia's first heart transplant left a cloud of doubt over whether the heart of a black man was pumping blood through the veins of a white recipient. And if a black man's heart was used in Saturday's operation by an MCV team, the question lingered about whether or not permission for the transplant was ever granted by the dead man's family."[31]

He continued, "The confusion surrounding what could be the nation's first inter-racial heart transplant was fed by a veil of secrecy over the operation by the MCV team and the state anatomical board which supplied the heart [to Joseph Klett]." The *Afro* referred to Tucker as "the colored donor."[32]

Other news outlets raised the issue of Tucker's own fault in the accident "when he fell from a three-foot-high wall" (*Times-Dispatch*)[33] or the "hopeless brain damage suffered in a fall" (*Post*).[34] In those early news accounts, many readers may have thought Tucker only had himself to blame for getting hurt; subsequent articles mentioned the use of alcohol, apparently based on the initial account of the ambulance crew.

The *Afro* took a more tolerant tack. It played up Tucker's work history and said he "died Saturday of injuries suffered in a freak accident." It also noted that "Tucker was characterized by friends as a good-natured man who worked steadily on the same job for 30 years."[35]

★ ★ ★

A week after the operation—Saturday, June 1—the heart transplant remained a hot topic, especially at the medical college's commencement exercises. David Hume chose this safe venue and friendly audience to make his first public comments about the operation. "The 146th transplant done at MCV differed from the others," he told the college's annual scientific assembly. The lecture was a highlight of commencement weekend, where alumni and students received an inside look at the latest research on campus.

Hume began with an overview of his kidney transplant program, which had totaled 145 operations before the previous Saturday's events. Joseph Klett marked the "146th transplant in MCV history," he said.[36]

The growing body of research and clinical success meant that "mortality rates are dropping"—from the double-digit rates of the early 1960s to a single-digit rate of 9 percent in 1968. Hume then surprised the assembled graduates, alumni, families, and friends by introducing the man of the hour: Dr. Richard R. Lower.

In his remarks, the heart surgeon played his cards close to his vest. The transplant would not be considered a success until Mr. Klett had been restored to a useful and productive life. He also warned that the threat of rejection "will be with us for many weeks to come."

Even this cautious tone couldn't dampen the enthusiasm at MCV and around the state. Admiration and amazement at the surgeons' feat filled that day's lead editorial in the *Times-Dispatch*.

New Laurels for MCV

"The heart transplant operation at the Medical College of Virginia— altogether successful, so far—is cause for genuine pride on the part of all Virginians," the editorial began. "Ever since MCV became one of the first medical schools in the world to do successful kidney transplants, its reputation has grown.

"And now, with a heart transplant that appears to be doing as well at this stage as anybody could expect, Richmond's fine old medical center is winning new laurels.

"The fact that the donor of the heart was a Negro and the recipient a white man has added interest to the transplant, but there has been no special reaction hereabouts," apparently ignoring the skeptical questions raised in that day's *Richmond Afro-American*.[37]

After reviewing the local contributions to Christiaan Barnard's first transplant, the *Times-Dispatch* editors exalted, "Now that Dr. Lower,

Dr. Hume and other surgical team members have performed what appears to be a successful heart transplant—the first that has been attempted in the Southeast—Richmond's standing as a medical center is rising steadily."[38]

Referring to the news blackout that surrounded the operation, the paper did its own reporter, Orndorff, no favors by only wearing kid gloves with MCV. Coincidentally, the transplant controversy was unfolding at a particularly sensitive point of the medical college's evolution as MCV was merging with its counterpart, the Richmond Professional Institute. On July 1, 1968, they merged into Virginia Commonwealth University, or VCU.

The newspaper was intent on easing any growing pains due to the merger. "There seems to have been unnecessary secrecy at the outset concerning the operation," it said, adding, "It is to the credit of the participating doctors that they were not seeking publicity, but a medical event of this magnitude is of great public interest, and may as well be treated as such.

"At all events, the skill and knowledge evidenced by MCV's surgical team reflects great credit on all concerned. And it is good to feel the institution responsible will become, just one month hence, an integral part of newly created Virginia Commonwealth University."[39]

The newspaper's love letter to MCV reflected a popular sentiment that reached Tucker's hometown. Even as the family was grieving their loss, some of his friends in Stony Creek heard the news. Among them was Wilbard Johnson, who attended Little Bethel Church where Bruce was buried.

"We were all amazed at what just happened," Johnson said. "He was sort of a local hero. He made history."[40]

PART FOUR

Troubles, Trials, and Tribulations

CHAPTER FIFTEEN

Rejection

ON THE FIRST DAY of June 1968, NASA announced America's race to the moon was back on track. It had been more than a year since the tragic capsule fire of Apollo 1.

Front pages around the country heralded the space program's revival. Photos showed a large metal capsule being transported to Florida and captions like the one that ran in Richmond, "Moonship Arrives at Cape Kennedy." The Apollo 7 spaceship, "built to carry America's first three-man crew in orbit," began ground tests at Cape Canaveral.[1]

Though many Americans still cast their eyes toward the skies, 1968 was generally a bummer—filled with riots, killings, and bombings. From civil rights to black power, the women's liberation to the Vietnam War—the nation was suffering from a major identity crisis. The political and social divisions harkened back to the nation's unrest before the Civil War.

Even the avuncular figure known as America's baby doctor, Dr. Benjamin Spock, was hauled into court. He faced federal charges from his personal opposition to the military draft and the deadly toll it was taking on the same generation of children he'd helped raise with his child-rearing guide for new parents, *Baby and Child Care*. The book, published in 1946, would go on to sell in the millions through-out the 1950s and 1960s. The government's case illustrated how—to paraphrase Lincoln—America was a house divided. Whether it was the military or the medical establishment—including the Medical College of Virginia—the old order could not stand.

For all the controversy swirling around him, Dr. Spock looked and acted like a kindly old caregiver—an early, if hyperpoliticized, version of Mr. Rogers. He was tried with other activists, including Yale University's chaplain, William Sloane Coffin Jr., who was a former CIA case officer. But it was the bespectacled doctor and kindly adviser to worried parents who became an early symbol of what later became known as America's culture wars. Conservatives blamed Dr. Spock for "what they considered his permissive child-rearing advice for the sex, drugs and rock-and-roll culture of the '60s," wrote Ian Shapira in the *Washington Post.* "He was denounced by Vice President Spiro Agnew, Chicago Mayor Richard Daley and minister Norman Vincent Peale for encouraging the country's moral decline."[2]

But the towering doctor was unapologetic. "What is the use of physi-cians like myself trying to help parents bring up children, healthy and happy, to have them killed in such number for a cause that is ignoble?"[3]

Surprisingly, though opposed to the war, Spock said he didn't sup-port young men fleeing the draft by going to Canada, nor did he ap-prove of destroying Selective Service files—acts of civil disobedience supported by other activists.

Even the prosecutor, John Wall, a former paratrooper in the Korean War, was impressed by the pediatrician's passion and logic. "I submit to you, you'd be warranted in finding that if he goes down in this case, he goes down like a man, with dignity, worthy of respect."

And down he went, along with Rev. Coffin and two other activists, all sentenced to two years in federal prison. (Their sentences were over-turned later on appeal.)[4]

An editorial cartoon from the *Knoxville Journal* (Tennessee) captured the roiling zeitgeist with a boy getting sent to the corner of his room by a mother who chastises him, ". . . And Quit Referring to Your Father and Me as 'The Establishment!'"[5]

Such tectonic shifts in American society exacted a steep price in blood, treasure, and, in racially divided communities like Richmond, a loss of trust. With school desegregation still in its early stages around much of Virginia, state education officials were warning school boards to prepare to integrate their facilities. Yet parents in nearby New Kent County were holding out hope that the courts would approve a "freedom of choice" plan—despite a recent rejection by the Richmond-based US Fourth Circuit Court of Appeals.[6]

The power struggle between Richmond's white establishment and the city's African American community played out nearly daily in the press. On June 1, 1968, one city councilman staunchly defended the city's employment record and took a thinly veiled shot at blacks: "Anyone who wants to work for a living can get a job Monday morning."[7]

Black candidates for city council, who'd tried for years to gain the respect of their white peers, were not backing down. One candidate accused the white-backed "Richmond Forward" group of "[accentuating] the positive and [covering up] the negative" in the city. He called for an end to the race-baiting that seemed to come out of the Jim Crow playbook, demanding white candidates "quit labeling the unemployed as lazy, shiftless folks who want to stay where they are."[8]

As the candidates argued over the best path forward for all of Richmond—and not just those citizens with friends in high places—another headline provided another stark reminder of how much work remained to be done:

Burning Cross Thrown in Yard in Henrico Residence

"A burning cross was thrown into the backyard of a Henrico County Negro's home last night by several persons who fled the scene in a gray car and yellow panel truck," the *Times-Dispatch* reported. The suburban homeowner, Mrs. Doris Houze, stoically explained how she doused the burning cross with a garden hose after being alerted by the barking of her dog. The five-foot wooden cross was wrapped in torn sheets and an orange bedspread and was tossed over a chain-link fence into her back-yard.

She calmly told the newspaper that she had lived with her husband in the brick, one-story home for some six months without incident, even as several other "Negro families" also moved into the neighborhood, she said.[9]

As Mrs. Houze set about cleaning her backyard, only a few miles away the Medical College of Virginia's leadership was trying to put on a more progressive face. Hundreds of alumni, newly minted MDs, and their families gathered for the 1968 commencement exercises. One alumnus from New York was feted for his donation of a painting from the Italian Renaissance—*St. Cecelia Playing the Viola de Gamba* by Bernardo Strozzi, a painter and engraver of Italy's baroque period in the sixteenth and seventeenth centuries.

"Masterpiece for MCV," the *Times-Dispatch* declared of the gift to be hung in the medical school's research library. The photo was somewhat risqué for a family newspaper—showing a bored-looking woman with an ample bosom holding a viola-like stringed instrument. Art and religion students would have recognized another Italian figure—Barbara Strozzi, a successful singer and composer not related to the painter—sitting in as St. Cecelia, an early Christian martyr and patron saint of music and musicians. It was just the sort of classy gift that the mostly male graduating class would have appreciated—including the saint's ample cleavage.

Much of the attention that day was drawn by Dr. Lower, who delivered his talk on the historic heart transplant. But if the alumni and new doctors had listened closely, some may have picked up a sense of caution as Lower described the prognosis for his patient, Joseph Klett. But even the most perceptive graduates listening to the star surgeon would have been hard-pressed to imagine what was taking place nearby in MCV hospital. Nobody but Lower and his close circle of doctors and nurses knew the extent to which their celebrity patient's health was starting to deteriorate.

This was all the more disappointing because, in the first few days after the transplant, Klett "made an excellent recovery from the operation." Lower later described how he used a powerful steroid—prednisone—to stave off an initial rejection of the new heart that was keeping him alive. At first, Klett had responded well. He sat up in his hospital bed, began to eat a normal diet, and even spent some time alone with his wife, Anna.

Sadly, the respite was short-lived. Klett suffered "a precipitous onset of rejection" between the fifth and sixth days after the operation, starting on Thursday night and into Friday morning. In clinical terms, the decline was "characterized by decreasing electrocardiographic voltage," which is needed to maintain a normal heartbeat. It didn't help that Klett developed a fever and fell into what Lower termed a "malaise," retaining fluids and gaining weight.

Most worrisome of all, the transplant patient experienced "a rapidly decreasing cardiac output" from his transplanted heart.[10]

In a 1969 article, Lower explained in more clinical terms some of the lessons learned from their first heart transplant.

"Advances in surgical [technique] and immunology have ushered in an era of organ transplantation which now includes the heart," the *American Journal of Cardiology* article began. "Despite increasingly effective methods of immunosuppression, rejection remains the major threat to prolonged survival of patients after cardiac transplantation."[11]

He described "two clinical forms of rejection." The first was *acute rejection*, which "if detected sufficiently early, can generally be controlled with increased doses of immune-suppressive drugs." This is what Mr. Klett suffered. The second, *chronic rejection*, "is more difficult to detect clinically, and once established, is usually not responsive to treatment."

Based on this dichotomy, one might assume that Klett's experience—with a form of rejection that was detected—might have made it treatable. Perhaps Lower's team could have staved off rejection by upping his dosages of steroids or other drugs used in those days. But what happened next showed the highly experimental nature of the postoperative care for a heart transplant patient like Klett.

Lower cited the "increasing awareness that the heart is quite as vulnerable to rejection as the kidney and that our [techniques] for detecting cardiac rejection are perhaps less sensitive than those which signal kidney rejection."[12]

Citing but one example, he explained how it was hard to detect changes in Klett's heart rhythm—arrhythmias. This, in turn, made it difficult to spot the onset of the rejection of Tucker's heart. This led to a key finding about the treatment of rejection—immunosuppression.

"It appears that the recipient of a cardiac transplant may require higher doses of immunosuppressive agents since [the recipient's] immunologic responsiveness is perhaps not as depressed as that of the patient with chronic renal failure" of his kidney.[13]

In layman's terms, Lower had learned something subtle about the difference between a kidney transplant and one with a heart. When it came to kidney disease, these patients *already* had lost some of their own natural powers of immunosuppression. So it followed that they required *lower* amounts of antirejection drugs than what would have helped Mr. Klett when his rejection set in. It was a hard lesson in the complexities of the human immune system that had challenged medicine for so long.

Many years later, as Lower reflected on what would become the case of a lifetime, the pain and regret over losing Mr. Klett were palpable. "It was heartbreaking—because he looked fabulous after the heart surgery. We were joking, 'You look so well!' "[14]

No matter what they tried, though, Lower could see his first heart transplant patient slipping away. His worst fears of organ rejection were realized. "I think we made a serious error in judgment in using the protocol they were using in kidney patients with heart [patients] with too low a level of immunosuppression. So everything went great for a few days and the patient suddenly started to collapse."[15]

The first public sign of the tragedy came in a simple, stark headline one day after Lower delivered his cautious lecture on the operation:

Heart Patient Joseph Klett Dies at MCV
Transplant Failure, Cause Unknown, Spokesman Says

The death occurred on Saturday evening, June 1, the paper reported, "almost a week to the hour following the historic operation."[16] The first sign of any problems came when the hospital made a 1:00 p.m. announcement as "physicians expressed concern over Klett's condition." Six hours later they announced his passing.

On the surface, the hospital's statement appeared to share more about Joseph Klett's transplant. However, MCV once again showed itself to be a most unreliable narrator. For example, though the statement claimed his condition "had begun to deteriorate suddenly Friday evening," Lower's subsequent journal article noted that the downturn began at least a day earlier than that.[17]

MCV also said "the exact cause of the transplant failure is not known at the present time"—which was no doubt true, since an autopsy had yet to be performed. But the timing of the release of more news about Klett's passing was kept deliberately vague—"at a time to be determined by the attending physicians."

Was MCV becoming even more cautious in response to Wilder's legal representation of the Tuckers? There's no record of how MCV plotted its media strategy—if, indeed, it was plotted at all. What is clear, however, is that even at this late date, with the passing of the first heart transplant patient, the *Times-Dispatch* was still reporting that "the identity of the heart which Klett received has never been disclosed by the hospital." Bruce Tucker's identity, it was noted, had been revealed by "other sources."[18]

The *Times-Dispatch* also described the accelerating pace of heart transplant operations around the world—and the many patients who never made it home from the hospital. "Since the transplant operation here, there have been four others" in the week after MCV's breakthrough. "Two other transplant recipients died yesterday."

Albert Murphy, fifty-nine, "Canada's first heart transplant," had passed away nearly forty-eight hours after undergoing an operation in Montreal. A second, unnamed patient died at the New York Hospital–Cornell Medical Center in New York City—the same teaching hospital where Lower attended medical school in the early 1950s. The Cornell patient would mark the world's twentieth heart transplant.

Joseph Klett's pastor, the Reverend C. Bernard Troutman of Mt. Nebo Lutheran Church, reportedly expressed surprise that his parishioner's death "came so quickly." The pastor added one more detail about Klett's passage, revealing that the MCV physicians "have been worried since early Thursday."[19] One interview at a time, the true timeline of Virginia's first heart transplant was falling into place.

Klett's lifelong battle against heart disease also was revealed, along with more about his life. "A childhood illness diagnosed as rheumatic fever left him with a condition described as a 'heart murmur.'"[20] Despite this longstanding malady, Joseph Klett moved to Orange County in his midtwenties and—after serving as a shop superintendent at a metals company—managed to work his way up to vice president and general manager of Virginia Metal Products Co. He was active in his church and a member of its governing council.

Joyce Kipps recalled many years later the rather opaque way the first news of the transplant had been delivered from the pulpit by the minister at Mt. Nebo Lutheran. "He said there's been a heart transplant, but he didn't give any name." She added, "But we knew who it was." Seven days later, she remembered hearing the sad news: "He was gone."[21]

The published accounts of Joseph Klett's life and death created a parallel narrative to the story of the man whose heart was now destined for another's man's grave.

Despite their differences in race, upbringing, and social status, Bruce Tucker and Joseph Klett both worked hard and tried to care for their families until breathing their last at age fifty-four. They also shared a traditional American resting place: the graveyard of a country church.

★　★　★

Heart transplants would remain a risky business for many years to come. In 1968, out of 104 procedures, only 10 people survived; the next three years saw equally poor results with a mere 24 survivors of 170 transplants, according to one estimate from the Baylor University Medical Center.[22]

Dr. Peter A. Alivizatos, himself a cardiothoracic transplant pioneer at Baylor, described the widespread sense of surgeons' remorse. "Even the demigod of American surgery, Denton Cooley, was forced to stop, saying, 'The prescription for success in heart transplantation "cut well, tie well, get well," is a naiveté. The problems come after surgery, and they're not surgical problems.'"[23]

What Alivizatos called "the epitaph of this period" was delivered by a pioneering heart surgeon, Dr. Charles Bailey, who developed in 1948 "mitral valvotomies" to repair the valve between the upper and lower chambers of the left side of the heart. Commenting on the heart transplant craze, Bailey caustically observed, "cardiac transplantation is 10 years too early."[24]

Even Lower, whose surgical prowess had inspired Christiaan Barnard and so many others, later had his doubts. He came to believe that the promise of heart transplants was oversold not only by the media, but even by some of his colleagues. Transplantation "was seen as an answer for all patients who were sick with heart disease and it was not."[25]

There were disappointments, to be sure, and a gathering storm cloud of litigation hanging over Dr. Lower and Dr. Hume and their team. Nonetheless, late in the summer of 1968, they did enjoy a break in the gloom. It began with a referral from an MCV alumnus in Indianapolis who wanted to help a local teacher. His name was Louis B. Russell Jr., a black educator who embodied the old saying, "He never met a stranger."

Russell soon would be shaking Dr. Lower's hand and asking for help in staying alive.

CHAPTER SIXTEEN

The Making of a Medical Celebrity

IN THE TROUBLED WAKE of Virginia's first heart transplant, the arrival in August 1968 of a quotable teacher from Indiana with a failing heart provided a much-needed morale boost for MCV and its surgeons. At age forty-three, Louis B. Russell Jr. was living proof of the value of education, marriage, and religious faith in the face of an uncertain future.

Russell, who taught industrial arts in Indianapolis, had used his own youthful indiscretions as a teaching tool to help redirect the lives of the inner-city youth in his junior high shop class. But a series of coronary events had left his heart badly damaged and cast a pall over his otherwise bright, promising life.

At the time, Drs. Lower and Hume and the entire MCV surgery department were smarting from the news coverage of the threatened lawsuit from the Tucker family. The arrival of Louis Russell, a possible candidate for the hospital's second heart transplant, must have felt like a life preserver tossed their way from the public relations gods.

Like Bruce Tucker, Louis Russell was African American. But unlike the many unanswered questions still swirling around the factory worker's treatment, the teacher's tale had the easy appeal of Sidney Poitier in *Lilies of the Field*.

With a character like him, MCV's skittish administrators and public relations staff could sit back and let Russell write his own script and deliver his own lines in a real-life saga that might have been called *From Mean Streets to Homeroom*.

Though he was the son of a Baptist minister, Russell told *People* magazine, "I've lived a pretty rough life. I started smoking and using dope as a kid. I've been in street fights where I said to myself, 'Old Buddy, you are going to be lucky if you get out of this one.' But there was no fear."[1]

Russell's medical morality tale brought more media attention MCV's way. But with the Hoosier educator, it unfolded in a clear, unambiguous fashion. Eventually, it led to hundreds of speaking engagements and made Russell a spokesman for American heart research.

But first he had to survive four hours of experimental heart surgery performed by Dr. Lower. When he woke up, he learned that he owed his life to a black teenager who'd been shot in the back of the head during an argument. Russell was so moved by the deceased youth's sacrifice that he started pondering what he would do with the gift of a new heart.

The Louis Russell heart transplant—MCV's second, the world's thirty-fourth—also gave the hospital its own second chance in the public arena. It began with a statement that MCV had received permission from the family of the seventeen-year-old youth. In addition, the decision to authorize the use of the youth's heart wasn't made by an assistant medical examiner as it had been with Bruce Tucker; instead, Dr. Mann, the chief medical examiner, made the call.[2]

Mann played another role after the operation by being candid about the identity of the donor. Even as MCV said it would "decline to name the donor" of the teacher's new heart, the evening *News Leader* reported that "Chief State Medical Examiner Geoffrey T. Mann identified the donor as Robert Clarence Brown, 17, of Providence Forge who died of a gunshot wound in the head. Dr. Mann said he authorized the use of the victim's heart after he died."

Louis Russell made the 615-mile-long trek to Richmond after a heart specialist in Indianapolis—Dr. Robert Chevalier—told him about the heart transplant program at his alma mater (Chevalier was a 1955 MCV graduate).[3]

Russell expressed few qualms about flying to a city in the South to meet a doctor he'd never met. Russell had survived too much in life to let it end without a fight. The native of Terre Haute, Indiana, had served three years in the Army Air Force in World War II, where he served as a teacher to other black airmen. He helped them overcome their personal struggles against the rampant racism in the nation's military.[4]

After the war, he graduated from Indiana State Teachers College with a BS in industrial education and later received a master's degree from Indiana State. He started by teaching juvenile offenders; then he moved to Indianapolis to educate students who, like him, came from challenging homes.

By the time he was battling his heart ailments, Russell had more than a decade of teaching experience where he developed "a storehouse of mother-wit and good advice for his students."[5]

When he first came to Richmond in July 1968, he didn't know what to expect from the famous surgeon Richard Lower. All he knew for sure was that he was prepared to give up his body for medical research, even if he died in the process. His oldest son, Charles, then a twenty-one-year-old senior in marketing at Indiana University, told the Associated Press that his father "did not intend to have a transplant when he entered MCV a week ago."[6] But given the precarious state of his health, a heart transplant was his only hope.

He'd had to leave his wife, Thelma. She was "a buyer for an Indianapolis department store," H. P. Wasson and Co., where she reportedly was the only department store buyer in the Midwest who was black.[7] Their four children included a nineteen-year-old daughter, Connie, who hoped to follow her father into teaching.

Early on the morning of Saturday, August 24, Louis Russell "was awakened from his sleep at the Medical College of Virginia and was told the 'situation was go' and that there was a donor for a heart available."

As Russell observed later, "I knew that I had to have a new heart or die."[8]

The initial news reports about the "approximately four-hour procedure" went into detail about the transplant, as well as into the tragic circumstances of the donor's demise. "Seventeen-year-old Robert Clarence Brown of Providence Forge . . . died from a gunshot wound in the head shortly after midnight Friday . . . with a small caliber pistol following an argument at a New Kent County restaurant."[9]

After the disappointing results of MCV's first heart transplant, its second one drew more skepticism from the press. The specter of organ rejection loomed larger. "Each person's body is biologically-unique," Bev Orndorff wrote, and "when an organ or tissue from one person is transplanted or grafted to another, the recipient's body recognizes the graft as foreign born." This, in turn, can trigger "the body's defense mechanism . . . just as they are triggered into action when the body is invaded by such foreign substances as bacteria, viruses or other organisms."[10]

Lower was treating Russell with "drugs aimed at reducing the punch of these substances" to allow the transplant graft to "take," he explained. Orndorff wrote "there is still a lot for them to learn about the basic mechanisms of rejection, and how to control it."[11]

Given his ongoing coverage of Lower's work—coupled with his six years of writing about Hume's kidney experiments—Orndorff demonstrated his sound knowledge of transplant medicine. He managed this despite the silent treatment he was still getting from them after his earlier coverage they felt was "glorifying" Bruce Tucker. Orndorff, to his credit, never mentioned the professional shunning to his readers. He also managed to translate Lower's surgical techniques into plain English.

"The actual technique of transplanting a human heart varies somewhat among transplant surgeons at different centers," he explained. "In general, however, most of the recipient's diseased heart is removed, but portions of the heart's upper two chambers are left in place. Also, the sinus node—the heart's pacemaker, which gives rise to the electrical impulses that cause the heart to contract—is generally retained in the donor heart."[12]

Orndorff pointed out that "some tailoring of the donor heart is involved in the procedure as it is sutured into the recipient's heart."

Once the new heart was joined to the proper arteries and vessels, an electric shock was often used "to get it beating in a rhythmic, coordinated fashion," he wrote.[13] It wasn't clear whether this was done with Louis Russell. But given the teacher's vigorous and vocal recovery, sometimes it seemed like he might have been plugged into a wall socket.

By early October, midway through his three-month-long recuperation, Russell began giving interviews, starting with Orndorff. Since he "knew that I had to have a new heart or die," Russell told him, "I was a happy person." He was just "glad" to get it done.[14]

Russell said he'd "felt fine since the operation" and managed to walk around his hospital room only a day after opening his eyes. He was undergoing physical therapy to try to get back some lost muscle tone and strength, riding a stationary bicycle the equivalent of a mile and a half. He was also doing some easy weightlifting. He'd even taken a stroll outside, until he got tired and had to sit down.

Russell had a philosopher's gift for posing penetrating questions about the mysterious ways of the mind, body, and heart. For example, when he opened his eyes after surgery, he asked a nurse, "How old am I?"

"You're still forty-three, Mr. Russell," she said reassuringly.

Russell retold this story for many years to come. He was trying to come to terms with his complex feelings, living with the heart of a youth whose life had been tragically cut short.

"I don't know why I asked that," he recalled later. "I didn't know the donor was seventeen or anything."[15] He wrote the youth's family and stayed in touch for years. He also came to realize that his ordeal afforded many teachable moments for students and parents alike. Louis Russell became known for testifying to the power of positive thinking and living one day at a time.

His joie de vivre was contagious. When he was finally allowed to leave MCV's isolation unit, patients, nurses, and orderlies thronged in the hallways and cheered him on. Louis Russell had won their hearts and minds.

"They were elated," Russell reflected, "and I was too."[16]

★   ★   ★

Over time, Richmonders got to know more about Louis and Thelma Russell. Despite the rise of feminism, most newspapers were still dominated by male editors. As such, they usually pushed feature stories about females back to the "women's pages," or what became derided as the "pink ghetto."[17] This vestige of male-dominated newsrooms was as true in New York City as it was in Richmond, where the *Times-Dispatch* squeezed "women's news" between the business and editorial pages. The old-school treatment was evident in the first story about Thelma Russell headlined "Heart Patient's Wife Confident."

On the front of the "Women and Foods" section, a photo of a woman identified as "Mrs. Louis B. Russell Jr." showed a stylish, shyly smiling woman. She wore a striped scarf and dress, a chic outfit fitting for "a buyer for an Indianapolis department store."[18] Women's page writer Betty Parker Ashton noted Mrs. Russell's unique status as "the only Negro department store buyer in the Midwest." This "slim, gracious and very happy woman," she wrote, had "visited a Richmond department store . . . for lunch with a friend who lives here, making one of her few excursions from the hospital and her husband's side."[19]

Thelma Russell put on a brave face. "It was trying," she said of the operation, "but we believe in God and this has helped me quite a bit." Asked what she said to her husband before the transplant operation, Mrs. Russell said she couldn't remember due to "her nervous excitement" that day. She was the only family member who'd come to Virginia. The hospital's chaplains stayed with her during the operation.

"We knew one of three things would happen," she said. "Medication, resection or transplant." With their abiding trust in medicine and the Almighty, the Russells were fine with following Dr. Lower's advice. (The article didn't raise the vexing questions about the fate of Bruce Tucker or his heart recipient, Joseph Klett; it seems possible that given the dire state of Louis Russell's health that they may have been unaware of the doubts raised by the Tuckers and their pending litigation.)

The women's page reporter kept things light, underscoring the role of a dutiful and stylish wife. She'd returned to Richmond for a week to be "with him whenever he is not taking medication or taking his exercises."

Her children hadn't seen Louis in some time, Thelma Russell said, and were "anxious to see 'Old Dad.'" But their father needed time to recuperate and regain his strength before going home.

Over the ensuing weeks at MCV, Louis Russell managed to carve out time for more interviews, including with one of the few women competing with the male reporters at the evening *News Leader.* Alberta Lindsey knew firsthand about fighting discrimination in the old South: not only did she have to fight to escape the "pink ghetto" assigned to women journalists, she also pushed back against any coddling or discrimination she faced because of her club foot. She'd worked at the paper since 1964, starting as an entry-level clerk answering the phone for the all-male news staff.

"I had two strikes against me," Lindsey later recalled, "I was a woman and I was handicapped."[20] But while her congenital condition may have made her stand out in the newsroom, it never kept her down. After some months spent taking tips and dutifully passing them along to the guys, the soft-spoken clerk took matters into her own hands. Every so often, she kept a telephone tip for herself to pursue a story on her own. This resulted in a number of unsolicited articles that simultaneously impressed and challenged her editors. What should they do with this spunky cub reporter with a wry smile? As they discussed her future, Lindsey happened to overhear her managing editor disparage her request to join the news staff.

"We've got enough women here!" he said in a dismissive reference to the handful of female reporters employed by the Richmond newspapers at the time. Yet Alberta Lindsey soon joined their small ranks and her by-line began appearing alongside those of the guys at the *News Leader*. By 1968, she was covering health news, competing with Bev Orndorff at the morning *Times-Dispatch*.[21] She knew she had to keep scratching and digging, since women reporters still weren't completely accepted or trusted inside or outside the paper's Grace Street offices. This wasn't the case, though, when she met the teacher recuperating at MCV.

"He was a really nice guy," she said of Russell. "He would call me and tell me he was here in Richmond [for routine checkups]. . . ." Though he didn't come right out and invite her over to the hospital, Lindsey recalled, "what was unspoken was that [he was saying] 'I'm here and available.'"

His openness gave her the green light she needed to contact the hospital for an interview. There was no way to circumvent the hospital's gatekeepers. "You couldn't get anyone to talk to you unless you went through MCV."[22] After many calls, her persistence paid off and she visited him in his hospital room.

The teacher and the reporter seemed to click. Nearly fifty years later, Lindsey could still remember his stylish, yet dignified look. He usually wore a dark blazer, white shirt, and a trademark "ribbon-like tie," she said. Russell never tied this in a regular knot, preferring to wear it loosely. It was his signature dash of cool.

When it came to his heart disease, "He just said whatever happened was meant to happen," she recalled. He felt "it was out of his hands and probably out of the doctors' hands as well."[23] His personal faith would later find expression when the Indianapolis police department appointed him as a civilian chaplain.

In her first *News Leader* article about the transplant patient, Lindsey described Thelma Russell sitting beside her husband on a sofa in a "pale green room with red furnishings." Russell wore a beige sweater, along with a white shirt and his signature neckwear. "I have to tell on myself a little," he told Lindsey. "Since the restaurant doesn't open until 8 a.m. and I have to be at physical therapy at 8, I've been skipping breakfast until 10:30." His workouts consisted of chest pulls, kicks, stair climbing, and rides on a stationary bicycle "to regain strength in his weakened muscles."

Amid his busy day, which included occasional walks around downtown Richmond, sometimes Dr. Lower tried to stop by to see him. But, Russell wryly observed, "He has a hard time catching me."[24]

★   ★   ★

By November, MCV's second heart transplant patient had recuperated enough to go home. After his three months in Richmond, he'd become a local favorite. "Louis B. Russell Jr., the recipient in a heart transplant here in August, has pedaled a stationary bicycle more than halfway to his Indianapolis home, about 615 miles from Richmond, during the last seven weeks," Orndorff reported.

He had to reach this goal for Lower to agree to release him from his direct care. Once he did so, "This morning, at approximately 7 a.m., he was scheduled to begin his trip all the way home—this time by airplane."[25]

As Russell bid adieu to MCV and Richmond, he expressed "deeply felt, mixed feelings" about leaving. "I've made so many friends here," he told Orndorff. In fact, he said that if his Hoosier roots weren't so deep, he'd "like to make my home here."[26]

After he returned to Thelma and his kids, his Indianapolis doctors advised him to sit out the remainder of the first semester and not return to the classroom until January. But Russell would have none of it. He couldn't wait to get back to shop class where he savored the smell of sawdust, the grip of a hammer, and the buzz of a jigsaw. He also wanted to fulfill a personal prophecy to get home for Thanksgiving dinner. Through it all, Russell never doubted himself. "When I left for the service, I left saying I was coming back, and this is the same attitude I had when I went into the operating room."[27]

Even after he left Richmond, Louis Russell's uplifting story continued to provide public relations fodder to MCV. Nonetheless, the doubts and questions about the first transplant showed no signs of abating. Doug Wilder made sure of it. From the beginning, he'd found an ally in the *Richmond Afro-American*, whose June 8, 1968, front page announced, "Lawyer Probes Transplant Case."

The story and a photo of Wilder had shared the page with coverage of the assassination of Senator Robert F. Kennedy.

"Did doctors at MCV hospital do all they could to save the life of Bruce O. Tucker?" the *Afro* asked. "Or did they attach top priority to the medical experiment at hand and let the fall victim die so they could use his heart for the historic transplant on the hospital's docket?"

"These are but a few of the searing questions being raised by Lawrence D. Wilder, attorney for Tucker's family as he looks into possible legal action against those who used Tucker's heart without his permission."[28]

The *Afro* provided an alternative view of what the majority-white newspapers were calling a history-making event. "A short time after his death, Tucker's heart was pumping blood through the veins of Joseph G. Klett, a white man from Orange."

The *Afro* took a more skeptical view of the operation and its aftermath. "According to Wilder, the heart was used without the consent of the deceased or of his family. He said shortly after Tucker died a reliable source tipped Bruce's brother, William, about whose heart was used."

After getting the insider's tip, "William Tucker then contacted Wilder." The family "agreed to postpone the funeral to make determinations that were necessary to proceed further."[29]

Wilder cited his past experience working in the state's toxicology lab, where he met chief medical examiner Geoffrey Mann. Describing his early attempts to get to the bottom of things, Wilder said he asked Mann "point blank whether the heart used was indeed that of Bruce O. Tucker." He said he had received "confirmation" from Dr. Mann that Tucker's heart was the one transplanted into the "white man from Orange."

At that point, Wilder told the *Afro* that he was considering "what kinds of legal action can be brought on behalf of the Tucker family." Asked if he planned to investigate whether MCV had done all it could to keep Bruce Tucker alive, Wilder replied, "I think that's on the minds of everybody."[30]

Wilder turned up the heat on MCV by arranging for his client to be interviewed by the *Washington Post*. The article was distributed across the country by the wire services, leading to more dramatic headlines such as "Dead Man's Kin Says Heart Was No Donation."

" 'It was no donation,' says bitter William Tucker, almost three weeks after his brother Bruce's heart was used here in a transplant operation." It was taken from his brother's still living, breathing body after it was deemed "unclaimed" by the Virginia medical examiner's office, "and the day after he was hospitalized with severe brain injuries."[31]

Post reporter Stuart Auerbach's article questioned the legality of the MCV surgeons' statutory claim on the body of the brain-injured man. "William Tucker denies the body was 'unclaimed.' "

In a rebuke of MCV's treatment of the family, "He says he telephoned the hospital three times the day of the transplant asking for his brother, who lived alone in a rooming house.

"He says he talked to the hospital information desk three times. At 2:30 p.m., he says he was told that his brother was in the operating room. At 3:30 p.m., he says he was told his brother was in the recovery room.

"At 4:30 p.m., he says he was told his brother was in Room Number Five on the fifth floor of St. Philip Hospital, a division of the medical college complex."

The article gave the first chronological account of William Tucker's search for his brother. It also poignantly described the impersonal way MCV officials broke the tragic news. "When he visited the hospital at about 7 that evening, he says, he was told that his brother had died at 3:35 p.m.," Auerbach wrote. "He says he was never told that his brother's body had been declared 'unclaimed.' To this day, he says, he has not been told by hospital officials that his brother's heart was removed for the transplant operation."[32]

William Tucker also revealed the telephone call that came from inside the hospital. "He first learned his brother's heart was used from a friend, whom he will not name, who works at the institution."

Ralph Ware, MCV's development director, responded by saying he "strongly denies the hospital did anything medically, ethically or legally wrong in taking Bruce Tucker's heart."

The Post's "calls to the doctors, who are presently out of the country, have been referred to Ware." But the hospital spokesman refused "to discuss with reporters specific questions raised by the Tucker family or the phone calls William Tucker made to the hospital."

Chief Medical Examiner Mann got into the act by defending MCV, saying "the hospital denies receiving the calls from William Tucker." It wasn't clear, however, how Mann, who was out of town on the day of the transplant, could have known anything about William's efforts to locate his brother.

One thing was certain, though. "The Tucker family is considering legal action in this case," the Post reported. The article noted that "William Tucker says he speaks for his 80-year-old mother, Bruce's next of kin, who lives on a family farm in Dinwiddie County. He has hired Lawrence Douglas Wilder, an aggressive young attorney here who once worked for Dr. Mann in the medical examiner's office."

In response to the questions raised about the quality of care provided to Bruce Tucker, reporter Auerbach wrote "the hospital refused to tell newsmen what treatment was given." But MCV's Ware contended that Tucker received "all the medical care anyone could get." Dr. Mann backed his assertion, saying the hospital was "very careful."

Auerbach noted that the state's 1884 law was meant "to provide cadavers for use in medical schools." By 1968, the amended law still required a twenty-four-hour waiting period prior to the release of a body for research or other purposes.

Several days after the *Post*'s coverage, William Tucker pursued his legal right to serve as the administrator of his late brother's estate. He did this in the civil division of the Richmond Circuit Court, known as the chancery court. The legal qualification was necessary, the *Times-Dispatch* reported, because Bruce Tucker "died on May 25 without a will. The brother, William E. Tucker, said yesterday that he was qualifying as administrator for the purpose of filing a suit, but he didn't say whom it would be filed against or why."[33]

Any pall cast over MCV by the threat of litigation was partly dispelled by Louis Russell's continued good health and growing reputation. Over the next year, his saga was shared with a national audience by *Ebony*, the Chicago-based magazine that served as a black cultural counterpoint to *Time, Life, Look,* and other mainstream media. In May 1969, *Ebony* published a six-page spread with the headline, "First Black Man to Survive Heart Transplant: Indiana Teacher Thrills to New Life of Action."

Russell was shown at home, his school, and at his doctor's office undergoing various heart exams. One photograph showed a white nurse checking the wires of an "EKG test." The basic plot could have come from any one of the family shows of TV's golden age. More than a decade before *The Cosby Show*, *Ebony* showed a devoted black husband carrying groceries for his wife and browsing through a photo album with three of his kids.

"Since his operation," a caption explained, "Russell goes through daily household chores he did not possess with his 43-year-old heart."[34]

The junior high school industrial arts teacher was shown standing at a blackboard at Indianapolis Public High School 69. Russell was his typical dapper self, wearing a light sweater with a black border, white shirt, and dark tie. He "throws himself with new zest into his teaching chores" and, on that particular day, was teaching "the correct use of an electric jig saw" to make bookends. His lessons went well beyond his wood shop, the writer said. "Russell not only teaches subject matter but puts equal emphasis on teaching citizenship. The only living black heart transplant recipient uses himself as the living example of schoolboy vices. Fully recovered from the complicated operation, the 43-year-old recipient of a 17-year-old heart warns youths of the dangers of smoking, drinking and otherwise abusing the body at an early age as he did."

Russell explained, "Because I was born on the wrong side of the tracks, too, I can talk their language." The self-described "statistics enthusiast" made some quick calculations and claimed that "during a lifetime the heart is allotted so many billion beats, so for every minute a person smokes and drinks, extra beats are used up."

The tenacious teacher had surprised his doctors with an early return to the classroom, *Ebony* said. Before long, he was on a breakneck schedule of evening and weekend talks at banquets, clubs, and schools. He was on a mission "to tell his story."

Thelma Russell marveled at how far her husband had come. After his first heart attack in 1961 and another one in 1965, Louis would come home from work and go straight to bed after dinner. In the morning he'd pull himself out of bed and "push himself to get to work." Weekends often were spent in bed, where she'd bring him meals.

The transplant changed all that, Thelma Russell said. Louis had gotten healthier by losing about forty pounds. He was now down to about two hundred pounds. By eating mostly healthy foods such as chicken and rice, he hoped to lose another thirty pounds to reach a goal set by his local doctors. He saw them three times a week as they carefully monitored him for signs of organ rejection.

"Louis is a changed man, he looks younger, has lost weight and can accomplish many of the normal activities that were a strain for him be-fore the operation," Thelma marveled. This included fixing leaky faucets in their house and helping their youngest children—Helen, nine, and David, thirteen—with their homework.

Russell, though clearly comfortable in the spotlight, downplayed some of the attention he was getting. "The youngsters at school look to me as something special, which I don't agree with; I'm just a person who had an operation. It just so happens mine was rare."

Even if his transplant operation had been a failure, Russell said, he still would have felt honored to be part of such important research. "These doctors needed a chance to learn and I knew my days were going to be short anyway."

Before the operation, Russell said, he made arrangements to donate his kidneys should anyone need them. It was all he had to offer, he added wryly, because his eyes weren't too good and "of course nobody wanted my heart."

Speaking to various clubs and civic groups, Russell was asked some deep questions, including, "How does it feel to be dead?"

"I don't know," he'd answer, "I was asleep."

To those who wondered if he expected a boost to his normal life ex-pectancy from his much younger heart, he replied, "I don't think so, be-cause my kidney, liver and lungs are forty-three."[35]

Russell's positivity could reap immediate benefits for others. After hearing his testimonial, a woman who'd resisted treatment for a diseased lung decided to go forward with a procedure to treat it. She credited Russell's encouraging words for saving her life.

His colleagues in Indianapolis started a Russell Heart Fund to help him offset his considerable medical expenses (the exact amount wasn't made public). Without this fund, he said, "I would have been deceased by now." He also couldn't have afforded to remain in Richmond as long as he did to recuperate, Russell said, "because in my mind I would have had to come back to work."

Despite its challenges, he observed of his second act in life, "If it were any better, I couldn't stand it." He would come to celebrate three birthdays each year: one for his actual birth in 1926; another for the birthday of his heart donor, Robert Clarence Brown; and another on August 24, the date of his heart transplant.

In 1971, as he marked the third anniversary of his new heart, *Ebony* crowned him the "million-dollar baby" because of his value to medical science. "His achievement . . . is *the* scientific marvel of today, on a parallel with the moon walks."[36] Despite the hyperbole, it was true that Russell had defied the odds. In the more than three years since Barnard's breakthrough, most patients had lived only a few days or months before succumbing due to rejection or other issues. By 1971, out of 170 transplant patients, only twenty-four were still alive. In that sense, Russell's three years and counting of extended life was indeed a marvel.[37]

A photo showed a local doctor pressing his stethoscope against Russell's barrel chest. "Russell, whose donor was a black youth, says there is a theory that black hearts are stronger and last longer than white hearts," the caption said. "Research is presently underway to verify this theory." Ever the optimist, the black educator was ignoring the obvious weakness of his own heart.

But that was Louis Russell, who was a cup-is-half-full kind of guy. Though he wasn't an MD, he enjoyed delivering his own take on organ transplantation. "The only proof they have presently on the life limits of a transplanted heart is my own life dating from the operation," he said. "I am sort of a pioneer paving the way for the other heart transplant recipients coming after me."

Heart disease remained "America's number-one killer," *Ebony* noted, leading to more than 54 percent of all deaths.[38]

Russell would take his new heart's full measure. In 1970 alone, he made more than five hundred speaking appearances before thousands of people. "In less than a year, he logged more than 40,000 miles in Indiana alone."[39] Among many honors, Russell became "a captain on the Indianapolis police force as a lay chaplain" and chairman of the Indiana Heart Fund.

The always-feisty Russell got by on four or five hours of sleep a night. The magazine noted that he "gives his heart an even more dangerous challenge by enjoying some of the old vices that he claims wore out his first heart. He smokes, takes a nip of bourbon every now and then, and, despite the fact he suffers from diabetes, he even enjoys a box of candy occasionally."

Thelma and his doctors cautioned him to ease up on his schedule and get more sleep. He failed to heed their warnings, though, "[pushing] himself beyond the physical limits of one half as young. He seems possessed with a super energy."[40]

He offered his own take on what his doctors had told him. "If you survive a cancer operation for five years, you've recovered," Russell said. "They also say that if you survive a heart transplant for two years, you've recovered. So I'm over that hump now."

Louis Russell may have felt like Superman, but he still relied on a regimen of twenty pills a day to fend off the Kryptonite of heart disease. "All in all," *Ebony* concluded, "life for Russell seems sweeter the second heart around."

Unfortunately, his carpe diem lifestyle brought him to a screeching halt. Until then, more than six years after his MCV transplant, he never failed to make things interesting. There was the day in 1971, for example, when he took his role as a lay chaplain for the Indianapolis police a bit too seriously—wrecking his car while chasing a speeder. "That same year," *People* noted, "he ran, unsuccessfully, for the Indianapolis City Council, and he helped judge the Miss Nude America contest at Naked City, Ind."[41]

The peripatetic educator had to slow down after he developed fluctuations in his heart rhythm in the fall of 1974. Russell blithely dismissed the worrisome development as "my electrical system going haywire, giving off bad vibes." After a pacemaker was implanted, he reported that "everything was cool."

But he finally had to return to Richmond for treatment at MCV. Dr. Lower did allow his most popular patient to make speaking engagements around his adopted state of Virginia. Russell also counseled fellow heart patients.

"I'm not afraid of death," he told *People*. "I've lived yesterday, I'm living today and I'm making plans for tomorrow. How can I be afraid?" After living with his new heart for six years, three months, and three days, Louis Russell, forty-nine, died on November 24, 1974. This time around, he wouldn't make it home for Thanksgiving.

CHAPTER SEVENTEEN

The Defender

WHEN DOCTORS NEEDED LEGAL counsel in Richmond, they called on someone whose name evoked a tenacious defender: Jack Russell. Low-key, with thinning hair and glasses, Russell wasn't a physically impos-ing man. When he rose from his desk at the respected firm of Browder, Russell & Morris, Jack Russell probably didn't remind anyone of Perry Mason or the other alpha males with strong jaws and baritone voices who starred in the TV dramas of the 1960s. So it was easy to underestimate the mild-mannered lawyer who favored bow ties and counted on pretrial preparation and quiet reason—rather than courtroom histrionics—to win over juries.

Despite a busy schedule defending physicians named in medical malpractice suits, Jack Russell also managed to be involved in civic and church activities.[1] Serving in leadership posts at his Methodist church, the Masonic Lodge, and other community groups, "He was almost never home," recalled son John. "He'd come home for dinner, change, and go to some meeting."

His special legal expertise—defending doctors against malpractice charges—grew out of routine defense work he was doing for State Farm Insurance and one particular insurer in Minnesota: the St. Paul Fire and

Marine Insurance Co. By the 1960s, St. Paul "was one of the few insurance companies that offered medical malpractice insurance to doctors," John Russell explained. "Because back then doctors didn't get sued much. Doctors were more revered, and it just wasn't a common practice like it is today."[2]

As he began taking on more medical malpractice cases, Jack Russell found he enjoyed helping doctors who deserved their day in court. He was a Depression-era native of Lee County on the westernmost fringe of Virginia that nestles against Tennessee and Kentucky. The county's independent-minded residents are fond of pointing out they live closer to eight other state capitals—such as Raleigh, North Carolina, and Charleston, West Virginia—than they do to Virginia's capital in distant Richmond.

Nonetheless, the county's historical roots in the Old Dominion run as deep as its coal seams. It was named for "Light Horse" Harry Lee, the legendary cavalry general in the Virginia Light Dragoons who fought with George Washington's Continental Army in the Revolutionary War. Lee, who would serve as Virginia governor in the 1790s, would sire another, even better known, officer destined to become an object of historical debate well into the twenty-first century: General Robert E. Lee.

Despite its historic roots, Lee County soon became reliant on the boom-and-bust economic cycles of its main natural resource: coal. Unless one wanted to eke out a living on a burley tobacco farm, working in the mines was the only option for most mountain people. The best way out was a college education.

That proved to be the case for Jack Russell's father—John H. Russell—who came from a family of eleven and was the first to attend college. He went on to earn his PhD in economics and join the faculty of the University of Richmond, where he became known as an expert in business taxation.[3]

Coming from such working-class roots, Jack Russell, unlike many of his peers, knew life from both sides of Virginia's economic and social divide—from the comfortable elite in Richmond to his hardscrabble neighbors down in the coalfields. After a stint in the navy during World War II, he graduated from Washington and Lee University Law School. He returned home to practice law, but after only a year he realized he wouldn't be able to support his wife or a family there. He went back to Richmond and began practicing law.

Though he left his mountain home, Jack Russell never forgot his family's values of hard work, initiative, and ethics. When it came to winning cases, John explained, "My father was always of the view that . . . the lawyer on the other side might be a better lawyer, but there's no reason that the other lawyer should out-prepare you. That was always his big thing. If he was going to work on a medical malpractice case, he was going to know as much about the medicine involved as the experts and his client."

Jack Russell created his own crash course "to learn medicine. For every case, he would spend a lot of time studying and talking to the doctors involved in the practice, whether it was the experts or the clients." As his legal specialty grew, it helped that he could call on the MCV faculty only a few blocks away from his office.

Soon he began regaling his family with sometimes stomach-turning details about his cases. "He'd come home at dinner and we used to joke how he'd give his 'organ recitals,' and he talked about what he'd learned about this type of medical procedure and the like." A typical malpractice claim would involve "a surgeon [who] had left a sponge in a patient," explained John. "The patient may not have died, however, [he] had developed infections—and wanted to be paid back for his pain and suffering."

In more serious surgical procedures, "Oxygen had been shut off to the brain for a period of time." The case involved the extent of the brain injury caused by such a major error. "The big thing in most medical malpractice cases is everyone knows something went wrong. The question is: was it a mistake, or was it just something that sometimes happens?"[4]

Even when the doctor knew he was not at fault, malpractice lawsuits could be emotionally wrenching events that could lead to personal bankruptcy, professional humiliation, and even suicide. In his role as physician defender, Jack Russell came to understand a key advantage he often had over the patient's counsel: the expertise of his cadre of MCV and other Richmond-area doctors.

"It often came down to expert witnesses," his son John observed, "and that's where he got to know so much of the medical community, especially up at MCV. . . . He would use them as his experts, because they're teachers, they're on the front lines, they're local, and they had the respect of the community and jurors."[5]

As he began winning cases, word spread across Virginia about Jack Russell, the dependable defender of the medical profession. "It got bigger and bigger because the doctors started to get sued [more]," said John Russell.[6]

This was the 1960s, a time when activist lawyers like Ralph Nader started to expose the mistakes of corporate America and make them pay for it. Nader rose to fame after his 1965 bestseller, *Unsafe at Any Speed: The Designed-In Dangers of the American Automobile*. Though it was best known for its exposé of General Motors' ill-conceived rear-engine Corvair, Nader helped jump-start the consumer protection movement to require seat belts and other safety measures.

Yet for every idealist like Nader, the decade spawned another kind of legal figure that Jack Russell came to despise: the celebrity defense attorney. Topping his list was F. Lee Bailey, who rose to national fame by representing Dr. Sam Sheppard, the Ohio doctor whose murder conviction of his wife spawned the TV series, *The Fugitive*. After Bailey won an appeal that overturned the doctor's high-profile conviction, he later represented a string of celebrity clients from Patty Hearst to O. J. Simpson.

Around the Russell dinner table, they called him "Flea Bailey." In Jack's view, the rise of the celebrity defense lawyer marked a paradigm shift in the legal system that bled over into all kinds of cases. It seemed to help those trial lawyers "who could make a plaintiff's case out of anything," recalled John. As Jack Russell defended doctors and corporations alike, he became convinced "that there were a lot of plaintiff lawyers out there trying to make a legal case anytime somebody got hurt for any reason." This ran counter to his belief that "sometimes bad things just happen that aren't necessarily someone else's fault."

The more he saw of this new generation of ambitious, increasingly wealthy, attorneys, the more Jack Russell became convinced of the righteousness of his cause. "My father didn't see this just as a business or a niche for his law practice. He very much believed that people were too quick to sue a doctor and to blame a doctor for things that happened. He became very much down to his core a defender of the medical profession."[7]

Still, Jack Russell was neither naive nor an apologist for bad doctors. He knew physicians were mere mortals who sometimes made mistakes. That's why "he was very quick to settle cases where he knew his client had been negligent."

John explained how his father determined when to fold his hand when it looked like he had a weak case.

"Generally he would go to his friends who, even if he was not necessarily going to use them as an expert, he knew enough that if it was a cardiology-related issue, he'd go to one of his friends at MCV to talk to them about the case. They had enough of a relationship where they [could] say, 'Jack, he shouldn't have done that.'"

Over time, as he learned more about the best practice of medicine, Jack Russell began to decide for himself when mistakes were made or when bad doctors were in the house. "He knew there were some bad ones out there, just like bad lawyers or bad bus drivers."

It was never all about the money, according to his son. Unlike plaintiff's cases—where attorneys could split a large percentage of damage awards that could run into the millions of dollars—working as a defense lawyer was "never going to be so lucrative because it's all based on hours," John Russell said.[8]

"Unlike plaintiff's cases, you're not going to have a million-dollar re-covery in a case," he continued. "You're still only able to make however many hours of work you can bill."[9]

As Jack Russell became closer to Richmond's medical community, he came to admire their role in making the city and, indeed, the entire state a better and healthier place to live. Nonetheless, he knew doctors had their foibles and some—especially surgeons—could have massive egos. One of his favorite jokes went like this: "Somebody's in line at the Pearly Gates waiting to go in. He sees somebody walk by in a long white coat with a stethoscope around his neck and just walk to the front of the line. And he says, 'Just because he's a doctor, what does he think he's doing?'

"'Shh,' someone whispers, 'that's God, and he just *thinks* he's a doctor.'"

Despite encountering the occasional swelled head, Jack Russell "could stand toe to toe with them," observed John. "He respected their egos and they respected his."

So in late May 1968, when the news broke about the historic heart transplant at MCV, it was the talk of the Russell family dinner table.

"He thought it was wonderful," John said. "He was *so* enthusiastic about the fact that MCV was on the global cutting edge of transplants." He already knew about David Hume's kidney transplantation program, "so he was very proud of MCV."

John Russell said he was "fairly certain" his father knew the key play-ers in the May operation, Drs. Hume and Lower. "I'm absolutely certain he knew they were planning it before it was general knowledge. . . . He had either heard it because somebody asked him about it, or someone mentioned it" during his regular "close contact with MCV."[10]

By then, the defense lawyer's stature had grown to the point where he was now teaching a course at the medical college. "He did a seminar for fourth year medical students in how to avoid medical malpractice cases," said John. This included the dos and don'ts of what to put in a pa-tient's medical chart.

Years later, this would become standard practice at many medical schools. But in the late 1960s, Jack Russell's expertise and insights gave Richmond medical students real-world training in coping with the growing concern over getting hauled into court. They left school with some tools for avoiding a lawsuit in the first place. "A lot of his early cases came down to charts, and what was put in there," his son explained. Sometimes the fault was a nurse who put in a medical note something "that sounded so much worse" than she'd meant it to sound. The only option when a patient sued for malpractice was to deal with it; the same thing held true "if a doctor had failed to go back and properly chart something."

Jack Russell wasn't one to toot his own horn, but his son remarked, "If you'd asked him, and he'd been honest, he would have described himself as the number one lawyer for the medical profession in Richmond. That's the way he thought about it: He was the defender of the medical profession in Virginia."[11]

Even as he treated his family to "organ recitals" over dinner, or held forth on the latest medical news, the physician's advocate could never have imagined that he would soon be asked to mount the biggest defense of his life.

★　★　★

America began the 1970s in the same way it had ended the previous decade, with a widening divide of social and political values. After an eight-year-long hiatus, Republicans retook the White House in 1968 by pursuing a Southern strategy that stoked the latent fears of white southerners smarting from federally mandated school desegregation and a rise in black voting power. Richard Nixon donned a law-and-order mantle and became a hard-liner on Vietnam. Surrounded by savvy media handlers such as a young Roger Ailes—who would later head Fox News Channel—Nixon's tough rhetoric seemed to soothe the frayed nerves of many voters who felt America had lost its way.

Any doubts that Nixon's base, "the Silent Majority," may have had of the country's demise were erased the following summer when some four hundred thousand music fans descended on a six-hundred-acre dairy farm in upstate New York for what was billed as "3 Days of Peace & Music" at the Woodstock Music & Art Fair. The sprawling, rain-drenched festival billed as "An Aquarian Exposition" would one day be seen as the zenith of young America's group experiment with sex, drugs, and music. The freedom-loving fans cavorting on Max Yasgur's farm seemed to live in a parallel universe beside the uptight world of people who'd backed "Tricky Dick."

Only a few weeks earlier, on July 20, 1969, the nation experienced a short-lived period of unity after the first moon landing when Neil Armstrong declared through the radio static: "That's one small step for man, one giant leap for mankind."[12]

For every step forward, though, America suffered from a collective malaise that snuffed out so many of the decade's earlier hopes and dreams. Among the reasons was the "generation gap" and racial polarization; the numbing daily body count in Vietnam; and such shocking crimes as the Manson Family's brutal murders of five members of the Hollywood elite.

The Rolling Stones' concert at Altamont Speedway north of San Francisco in December 1969 ended the decade in a dark, deadly way. A Hells Angels bodyguard stabbed to death a youth who was pointing a pistol at Mick Jagger. The violence unfolded in front of the stage and was captured by a documentary film crew as the Stones played "Under My Thumb." But it was their previous song, "Sympathy for the Devil," that seemed to capture the tragic events of the day as well as the decade's darkening zeitgeist.[13]

Songs arose from both sides of the conservative and liberal divide—from "Okie from Muskogee" on the right ("We don't smoke marijuana in Muskogee") to "Ohio" on the left ("Four Dead in Ohio").

★　★　★

In Richmond, Doug Wilder continued to pursue his civil case for William Tucker and his family. In his own way, the recently elected state senator was challenging much of Virginia's legal and political establishment in court and in the statehouse. In early 1970, a mere three weeks into his senate term, he introduced a bill to get rid of the state song, "Carry Me Back to Old Virginia." He shocked his white colleagues by criticizing the nostalgic song penned in 1878 during the era of Jim Crow, with its pining for the old days "where the cotton and corn and 'tatoes grow," and where "There's the old darkey's heart am long's to go." Proclaimed Wilder, "We can ill afford the luxury of coining into song, phrase, or what have you, words which in their very construction recall the memories of our shameful history."

His white colleagues "sat in silence," Wilder later wrote. "You could hear a pin drop in the chamber, the cool reception masked an underlying dismay and even outrage."[14] The senate ignored his plea and let the song stand for many years. For his efforts Wilder was excoriated in the press and received hate mail, including "a tract from the Ku Klux Klan and a report declaring 'Scientists Say Negro Still in Ape Stage.' "[15]

During this period, Wilder also began to speak publicly about his experience as an African American raised only a few blocks away from the state capitol. His stark comments came as the senate was considering a bill that would have made it legal to remove bodily organs for transplantation without permission from the family of the deceased. Since he was representing William Tucker at the time, the proposal gave Wilder a chance to raise some of the same issues he would later use in court. As medical historian Susan Lederer described his address, "Wilder called on traditional wisdom in the African American community about so-called 'night-doctors,' who abducted black children for use in medical experiments."

Wilder painted a grim picture for his white colleagues. For many, this marked the first time they'd ever heard anything about MCV's legacy of grave robbing to obtain fresh cadavers for eager medical students.

His remarks also provided some hints about his thinking about how he would represent the Tucker family when their case came to trial. He would show, in effect, that MCV's past was prologue to Bruce Tucker's treatment. The college's history of grave robbing fueled Wilder's opposition to any law, no matter how well intended, that would make it *easier* for doctors to remove human organs.

Supporters of the measure countered that the organ-sharing bill, the "uniform anatomical gift act," was simply meant to put Virginia in line with the laws of forty-two other states. Wilder remained unmoved. He cautioned against giving the chief medical examiner or his deputy the same sort of blanket authority that had led to the removal of Tucker's organs. The measure, he objected, would allow them to "take an organ from anybody without notifying the next of kin [and] do whatever he wants with it."[16]

Wilder raised the specter of allowing a transplant surgeon to request the medical examiner to provide the organ "without notice to the next of kin of the decedent, provided that there is no objection on the part of such next of kin known" to the authorities. But the "requirement for viability of the organ"—with every minute counting against it—"makes such notice [impractical]."

As he ripped into the bill, it was clear that he had the Tuckers in mind. "How are they going to object when they're not notified?" he asked, adding darkly that nobody wants to "open a butchery."

He brought up the desperate search mounted by his client, William Tucker, when he learned Bruce was in the hospital. "My client ran around the Medical College of Virginia for two days trying to find his brother," Wilder said, adding a day to the search.

The *Times-Dispatch* reported, "Wilder said his client went to the operating room and was told his brother was in the recovery room, was told there he was in the morgue and told that he was 'in Prince George County some place . . . '"[17]

As he unleashed his rhetorical firepower, Wilder drew on his own poignant childhood memories of venturing away from Church Hill near MCV.

"It was unsafe, I was told as a little boy, to even walk around the Medical College." Parents even used the specter of "night doctors" to make their children stay in bed. "'You'd better go to bed,' they'd say, 'or the night doctors will get you.'" His story only served to amuse the white senators.

But for the lawyer-legislator, the pending organ-sharing measure was no laughing matter. He'd seen and heard too much about what can happen to a black man when he gets run over by the wheels of the medical machine. "They don't want dead bodies," he said, they want living, "viable" ones. Despite his objections, the bill passed.

Though Wilder caused ripples of nervous laughter in the senate, his message was relatively tame compared to some social commentary of the day. In an appearance at Carnegie Hall in late 1969, the iconoclastic black comedian Dick Gregory riffed on a variety of hot topics—from Vietnam to urban riots to heart transplants.

"Much of his humor is inescapably racist, but it is a reverse-twist racism in which he drives black paranoia and white prejudice to sublimely ridiculous extremes," observed *New York Times* reviewer McCandlish Phillips. "He states that of all the transplant hearts in the recent spate of surgery, the one that ran the longest was a black heart transferred to a white patient." Gregory didn't say which patient he had in mind when he reached his punch line: "That heart would be goin' yet," he said, "if he'd had a little soul food."

As the laughter died down, Gregory made a serious point when he warned whites in the audience not to assume that "we goin' to be your spare parts." The Carnegie Hall audience applauded, but he interrupted the show of support.

"I'm just against transplants you can *hide*," Gregory explained mischievously. "I'd like to see a white cat get a black *foot* . . . Yeah, next summer, let him take that to the beach with him.

" 'Hey!' they'd be telling him, 'Take off your sneaker and come into the water!' "[18]

Beneath their jokes, black comics such as Dick Gregory and Richard Pryor served a serious purpose by holding up a mirror to traditions that had long troubled African Americans. As Lederer put it, "The controversy over Bruce Tucker's bodily remains reverberated in American popular culture and remained focused on the expropriation of black bodies, rather than on the need for increased minority access to the benefits of American high-tech medicine."[19]

Such questions of medical ethics were part of the wider debate over civil rights throughout the 1960s and into the 1970s. The 1967 Supreme Court decision in *Loving v. Virginia* declaring unconstitutional state bans on interracial marriages (known as "antimiscegenation laws") inspired an interesting corollary in films and novels that "mined the cultural possibilities of medical miscegenation," Lederer wrote. "In the 1969 film *Change of Mind*, the brain of a white lawyer dying of cancer is transplanted into the body of a recently dead black man." The storyline explored organ rejection both in the clinical sense but also in the wider context of American society. In the film, the only place the rebrained black man can seek solace is "in the arms of the widow of the man who furnished the body for brain transplant," according to Lederer.[20]

Similarly, Lawrence L. Goldman's novel *The Heart Merchants* pondered the moral dilemma of a transplant surgeon facing a difficult decision reminiscent of King Solomon. On the cover of the 1970 mass-market paperback promoting itself as "a towering medical novel," the ethical dilemma was boldly spelled out:

One man is old, rich and white. The other is young, poor and black. Which dying man will receive the heart transplant?[21] In a key plot twist, the father of the dead boy providing the donor heart is a racist who crudely states that he won't allow his boy's heart to be put into the body of a black man.

Whether in novels, in film, or on stage, the heart transplant saga continued to cause unease through much of the 1970s. *Los Angeles Times* columnist Sandra Haggerty described an informal poll that showed a deep distrust of leaving life-and-death pronouncements up to white doctors, including this comment: "You notice the heart transplants have all been from blacks to white. I'd like to see a little reciprocation before I get on the bandwagon!"

Another respondent told her: "No way! A brother's likely to go in the hospital with a cold and come out without a heart."[22]

★   ★   ★

The clock was ticking for Doug Wilder to file his lawsuit on behalf of William Tucker. It would be the first legal action in the United States seeking damages involving a heart transplant. Finally, as the second anniversary of the Tucker-Klett heart transplant neared, he felt ready to file the lawsuit. If he'd waited any longer, the two-year statute of limitations under the state's wrongful death law would have precluded filing suit.

Trying to practice criminal law while pursuing a civil lawsuit took a lot of heavy lifting. This was especially true as he prepared to challenge Virginia's medical establishment along with the considerable legal firepower it had at its disposal. This included the Office of the Attorney General, which handled any civil litigation against the state-chartered medical college and hospital.

Wilder later explained the difficulties of working on the Tucker suit while engaged in other time-consuming legal work and legislative duties. Plus, he noted with a chuckle, he was a husband and father with "three children and a wife not working."[23]

On May 22, 1970, Wilder left his law office on Church Hill, ready to do battle. He never forgot his time in actual combat as an army sergeant in Korea who fought Chinese troops in the cold, unforgiving terrain of what became known as Pork Chop Hill. After this epic battle for far outnumbered American troops, he was cited for courage and presented the Bronze Star Medal after helping capture nineteen enemy soldiers.[24] He would summon every ounce of courage as he drove down Church Hill toward the Medical College of Virginia, driven by adrenaline that put him on high alert for the looming conflict in the courtroom.

On the seat beside him was the fruit of nearly two years of legal work, often done at night or on weekends.

Nearing city hall—a stone's throw from the medical school campus— Wilder prepared to file what he knew might well be the biggest legal challenge in the more than century-long history of the venerable medical school. He knew he was taking on a formidable, well-funded foe.[25] Parking in front of city hall, he knew he was going up against the owner of the hospital and the employer of its entire medical staff: the Commonwealth of Virginia.

At times such as this, he remembered what his mother, Beulah, told him as a boy: "Once you have determined what you think is right, once you think where you're heading is the proper direction, don't let anyone dissuade you or turn you back. Not even me."[26]

Taking a deep breath, Beulah Wilder's son gazed up at the towering city hall and walked inside to the Law and Equity Court of the City of Richmond. This was the civil division of the Circuit Court that handled all legal matters of the state.[27] His lawsuit—*Tucker's Administrator v. Dr. Richard R. Lower et al.*—gave the city's deputies plenty of work to do in the days and weeks to come. They fanned out across the medical college campus, as well as to homes in the city and suburbs, serving legal notices to a long list of doctors, nurses, and anyone else who played a role in the operation.

The first three names on the list were Drs. Lowers and Hume and Dr. David H. Sewell, the young surgeon who was asked to remove Tucker's heart. Dr. Abdullah Fatteh, the assistant chief medical examiner who approved the procedure, was also included.

The terms of Wilder's legal engagement were the legal equivalent of his army platoon's charge up Pork Chop Hill in Korea—a wide-reaching, no-holds-barred indictment of everyone and anyone who encountered Bruce O. Tucker during his brief hospital stay. Bruce was admitted to the hospital, in the words of the suit, "as a regular paying patient for the purpose of being treated for a head injury." By admitting the gravely injured patient, Wilder argued, MCV Hospital and the physicians involved in the transplant had the legal responsibility to "diligently, personally and carefully . . . treat and care for Bruce O. Tucker."

Instead, he continued, "While purporting to undertake a decedent's treatment," the doctors and other hospital personnel "embarked upon a systematic and nefarious scheme to [excise] Bruce O. Tucker's heart from his body and transplant it unto the body of another and did in fact terminate the life of Bruce O. Tucker on or about May 25, 1968 for that specified purpose."

Wilder alleged that the assistant medical examiner, Abdullah Fatteh, acted "*in pari delecto*" (a legal term suggesting they were equally at fault) with the surgical team. Dr. Richard Lower, he charged, "led the team of surgeons that [excised] Bruce O. Tucker's heart, willfully, wrongfully, wantonly and intentionally pronounced Bruce O. Tucker dead ahead of his actual death, in violation of law, well knowing that he was not legally qualified to do so."

After identifying the central players, Wilder expanded his field of legal fire by naming nearly two dozen hospital employees for their "carelessness, negligence, unprofessionalism and unskillfulness" in failing to treat Tucker properly.

The hospital's carefully orchestrated plan, Wilder charged, led to "a willful and a gross outrage upon the plaintiff William E. Tucker's rights and sensibilities, and indignity put upon him, and interference with and a prevention of his right to receive the body" of Bruce Tucker, "his brother . . . in the condition in which it was at the time of his decease." The suit also alleged that MCV had prevented William Tucker's "right of burial, greatly wounding his feelings, and causing him great mental distress, anguish and suffering . . ." For enduring the shock and sorrow of his brother's death and burial, Wilder said William Tucker had suffered damages totaling $900,000.[28]

In a second "cause of action" in the lawsuit, Wilder sought another $100,000 for the doctors' and other defendants' failure and neglect "to possess and execute that degree of care, caution, skill, knowledge, and learning" for Bruce Tucker while he was under their care.

The lawsuit alleged "the said body was mutilated, cut and disfigured by the said defendants." Adding to the humiliation, the "mutilated, cut and/or disfigured body, without its parts . . . was delivered" to William Tucker and his funeral home director.

Another key point of the damning indictment of MCV and its star surgeons was how "William E. Tucker was deprived by the defendants . . . of making an informed consent" before his brother's body was cut open for the organ removal.

★   ★   ★

When he opened the next day's *Times-Dispatch*, Wilder knew he had scored a publicity bullseye:

Heart Donor's Brother Files $1 Million Suit

"A brother of the donor in Virginia's first heart transplant operation, two years ago Monday, has filed for $1 million in damages, alleging mental anguish and negligence by those involved in the transplant and his brother's treatment," the front-page article said. "He also contends that his brother suffered a premature death and that the autopsy was unlawful."[29]

After reviewing the history of the transplant, the paper noted that Wilder's litigation "was probably the first known case of its kind"—that is, a civil damage suit involving a heart transplant charging doctors with the "wrongful death" of the donor.[30]

The wide net Wilder had cast was noted, including Dr. Fatteh along with bit players in the operation—"the scrub nurses, the anesthesia team," and "nine other doctors."

The article noted MCV's contention that "the organ was obtained from the State Anatomical Board under proper circumstances and in accordance with existing laws." Additionally, "The Medical College, in what was termed policy, has never released the name of a donor in a heart transplant operation."[31]

Nearly two years after touting its historic accomplishment, MCV was still refusing to give any credit—much less compensation—to Bruce Tucker and his grieving family.

CHAPTER EIGHTEEN

Relative Death

IN THE SPRING OF 1972, David Plageman was a thirty-two-year-old financial professional in Richmond. He enjoyed small-town comforts with his wife and three kids near the Virginia Museum of Fine Arts. It was an easy drive downtown to the city's financial district, where he worked in the Richmond office of Paine Webber.

A graduate of Benedictine High School in Richmond and the Virginia Military Institute, he was steeped in the hierarchical traditions of the Catholic Church and the military. Often it seemed as if the pope was put on a pedestal only slightly above some of the Confederate generals still mounted on their bronze horses on Monument Avenue—Robert E. Lee, Stonewall Jackson, and J. E. B. Stuart. It had been more than a century since Lee surrendered and Abraham Lincoln visited the smoldering ruins of Richmond. Yet the confederate stars and bars still loomed large in some sectors of the local psyche. Somehow, despite all of the blood and carnage and heartbreak of their rebellion, even by the 1970s many Virginians still clung to this as their origin story.

For his part, while the stockbroker was a consummate Virginian, David Plageman had widened his horizons when he was deployed abroad by the US Army. As an army officer in the 1960s, he'd witnessed the lasting legacy of a different war that had split another country—Korea. His broader perspective would come in handy when, in May 1972, Plageman was called for jury duty in a civil case in the Richmond Law and Equity Court. When he first saw the judge assigned to the case, A. Christian Compton, he was reminded of some of the military leaders he admired. "From the moment he walked into the courtroom, I was impressed by him. . . . He was in charge. I liked that."[1]

Plageman noticed something else in Judge Compton's courtroom: the racial divide that still existed in his hometown. On one side, a group of white lawyers huddled and compared notes; on the other, a pair of African American attorneys chatted with a black man whose crutches leaned against the table. Though he had no idea what the case was about, as he sat with other prospective jurors, he immediately sensed a racial component.

And when he was chosen to serve on the seven-man jury, his instincts proved correct. There was not a single black person among them. The subject of the case was murky at first; it seemed to involve the medical college and an old transplant operation, a topic about which he knew little to nothing. He also was unaware that the all-white defense team was allowed to dismiss, or "strike," potential jurors on the basis of race.[2] But though this surprised Plageman, the lawyers and their black client seemed to take it all in stride.

Plageman was the youngest member of the jury that was finally chosen. He was joined by a mechanical engineer, a Western Union clerk, a state tax examiner, a banker, a sales manager, and an accountant.[3] His fellow jurors, he observed later, "were really average people you'd run into every day."

William F. Tompkins Jr., in his midfifties and a sales manager for a real estate firm, was elected to serve as foreman. "If you were a lawyer for the doctors," Plageman said of the homogenous group, "that's probably the perfect jury for you."

Doug Wilder, one of the black lawyers Plageman saw that first day in the courtroom, later explained why he appeared to be unfazed by the all-white jury. "I didn't have any problem with it," he said. "I did it all the time." His experience helped him "to build a very good reputation as a criminal trial lawyer with all white juries."[4]

No matter the obstacles he might face, or the amount of money or power MCV's defense team could muster, Doug Wilder felt confident that once the trial began, he would have the upper hand. After all, wasn't the law on his side?

"When they took his heart from him," Wilder said of Bruce Tucker, "he was *not* dead, according to the law."[5]

Still, this was a *civil*, not criminal, case. Wilder would have to work outside his comfort zone to win the day. Civil law demanded painstaking attention to detail, particularly when it came to finding legal precedents and applying them to this case. This required time to study, analyze, and develop a trial strategy that would hold up in court under the steely-eyed scrutiny of a veteran judge like Christian Compton. But given Wilder's criminal defense work, time was tight. So was money.

"A guy like him is making a living trying criminal cases," explained Theodore J. "Ted" Markow, a retired judge in Richmond Circuit Court who presided over a number of such cases where Wilder was the defense attorney. "When you have a good practice, and he did, it's a very high pressure—four or five cases a day—type of thing."

Someone in Wilder's position has "to make a living—you don't have *time* to sit around and research and all that kind of stuff," said Markow.[6]

One group of lawyers who did have time and money were those assigned to defend MCV on behalf of Virginia's attorney general, Andrew P. Miller. The state's defense team included a young Ted Markow, who was an assistant attorney general. He served with other ambitious lawyers eager to win a high-profile case with national implications. Virginia's legal eagles had ample time and money to conduct a thorough review of case law; interview many witnesses; and travel far and wide researching key cases involving charges of wrongful death against doctors.

Doug Wilder, by contrast, was representing William Tucker on a contingency basis. He stood to earn 25 to 33 percent of any monetary damages awarded by a jury. But any compensation would come only after the trial and a possible appeal by the state. This could take years. Furthermore, Wilder had to delay the start of the trial several times due to a heavy caseload and his duties as a state senator. His only outside assistance came from another successful black lawyer, Harrison Bruce Jr.

Years later, Markow reflected on the imbalance of legal power that he witnessed in Compton's courtroom. "We had an advantage," he said, "because the state was paying attention to it."[7]

This included having a travel budget to prepare their legal arguments. William Crews, another young assistant attorney general at the time, remembered flying to San Francisco to meet lawyers who'd been part of a well-known court battle that later changed California's legal determination of time of death.

The civil case involved a head-on collision on Interstate 680 in the San Ramon Valley, east of the city. The accident took six lives, including those of a wealthy couple, Max and Patricia Schmidt. The Schmidts, along with two of their children, perished at the scene. But before they died, various emergency workers and bystanders reported hearing a woman moaning inside the wreckage. Her agony led to a lawsuit and, ultimately, to a state court decision about when a person should be pronounced dead.

Since Max Schmidt left no will, a nasty legal fight broke out between family members over dividing up the estate. "The sole question presented to the trial was whether there was sufficient evidence that Patricia survived Max during the fifteen to twenty minutes that elapsed between the impact of the collision and the arrival of the highway patrol officers," according to one account.[8]

Teams of neurologists and other physicians provided expert testimony about the impact of the accident on the Schmidts; the focus was on their heart and brain functions. The case led to the passage in 1966 of

California's Uniform Simultaneous Death Act, a law intended to help the courts work through the complexities of accidental death.

Bill Crews, visiting from Virginia, wanted to learn more about the Californians' legal arguments on determining "brain death" and "time of death" they'd used in the Schmidt case. He picked up some useful pointers from the lawyers.

His visit showed how the MCV defense team, which could travel at the state's expense, had a decided advantage over Doug Wilder in terms of pretrial resources and staffing. But their most valuable asset wasn't money or even personnel. Rather, it was the knowledge and experience of their outside counsel, Jack Russell, who became the de facto coach of the entire MCV defense team. He spent months pursuing his own research about heart transplants, head trauma, and other related medical issues. The "organ recitals" at Russell's dinner table reached a crescendo.

"From the very beginning" of the case, recalled son John, "that was a major issue in the trial: How do you define death?" By now, Jack Russell's son was in college, getting updates about his father's trial preparations over holidays and other visits home. His thoughts on the nature of mortality were an eye-opener.

"Up to that point, I'd never thought about it," John Russell said later. Over a full-course meal, his father "explained about measuring the brain activity." He explained the term "flat line" produced by an electroencephalogram. "It means your brain isn't producing anything—and it doesn't come back," Jack Russell informed his family. "You don't put the electric paddles on your brain and get it to start."[9]

By the time dessert was served, Jack Russell may have moved on to how the doctors at the medical college managed to keep a brain-injured patient like Bruce Tucker alive through artificial means until they could remove his heart.

Jack Russell worked long and hard to learn about the latest in organ transplantation and neurological research. He also mastered the latest litigation and court decisions around the country that might help to bolster his case. The burden of protecting Drs. Hume and Lower from not only financial loss, but also from suffering damage to their reputations and professional standing, weighed heavily on him. After Wilder sued the surgeons for malpractice and negligence, Russell understood the impact losing the case might have not only in Virginia, but across the United States. He believed that it might set back medical research if academic surgeons such as Hume and Lower were forced to look over their shoulders as they conducted groundbreaking, if sometimes risky, experiments.

The negligence case against Hume and Lower would test Virginia's legal definition of death itself. "When there is a death caused by the wrongful act of another, you get into the question of what constitutes death. This had never been litigated in the United States before—in that sense of the word."[10]

"The essence of the whole allegation," Jack Russell explained, "was these [surgeons] had 'maliciously and nefariously entered into a scheme to take this man's heart from his body while it was still beating and thereby kill him.' "

Under the state's definition of death at the time of the 1968 operation, Russell knew the surgeons could be held liable for the sort of negligence that Wilder was alleging. With this in mind, he knew he would have to try to get the judge and the jury to approach the case from a different, more enlightened, perspective. That is, when had Bruce Tucker actually *died* in the scientific sense of the term? For by the early 1970s, the concept of life itself, like so many long-held beliefs, was being widely questioned.

★ ★ ★

After Dick Lower was served with legal papers in his office at MCV hospital, he didn't say anything in public. It would take years for him to express his true feelings about Wilder's allegation that he'd "nefariously entered into a scheme" to kill Bruce Tucker.

"Oh, I didn't say anything," Lower recalled. "He was just a flamboyant local lawyer [who] had some notoriety. But even then, we sort of assumed they weren't really too serious. . . . Are they after money? It was two years before the trial, with all the Mickey Mouse things that happen."[11]

At the time, he was still performing heart transplants and caring for patients like Louis Russell, who was still going strong in Indianapolis. But as the legal process dragged for about two years after its 1970 filing, Lower admitted, "It was kind of putting a damper on transplants."[12]

The pretrial proceedings began to weigh on him, raising the specter of a prison sentence. He should have known this was a civil complaint, not a criminal case with a potential of a prison sentence. The only thing at stake was his reputation and possibly a payout by his malpractice insurer to the aggrieved Tucker family. His dark thoughts weren't helped by a letter from his malpractice insurer in late 1971, some six months before the case finally came to trial.

The letter arrived after Wilder also sought damages in federal court in Richmond, a way to build on the lawsuit already brought at the state level. The federal claim doubled the amount of the financial exposure faced by the surgeons from the initial $1 million claim to more than $2 million. Lower learned this in a letter from his malpractice insurer, the St. Paul Fire and Marine Insurance Co.

"The suit is seeking $2,000,000.00 in damages divided into $1,500,000.00 for compensatory damages and $500,000.00 for punitive damages against each and every one of the defendants," wrote a local claims manager.

In this latest legal challenge, Lower had to wrap his brain around the large numbers typed below the company's logo, which promised that St. Paul was *Serving you around the world . . . around the clock.*

The insurer seemed intent on stressing the magnitude of Lower's potential exposure by listing as many zeroes as possible, down to the last cent. The same letter was sent to Dr. Hume.

"It is our duty to advise you," wrote Nelson, "that the compensatory damages you are being sued for [are] in excess of your liability limits. . . . It is also our duty to advise you that punitive damages are not covered under your Professional Liability Policy [malpractice insurance] in the event of a judgment. . . .

"This means you may be responsible for payment of the punitive damages in addition to the compensatory damages that may be awarded against you in excess of your liability limits."

Even as this sunk in, Lower could find some solace in St. Paul's promise to "provide coverage for legal expenses and undertake to defend you for the punitive damages as well as the compensatory damages at no extra to you . . ."

Lower read on: "You do have the right to obtain private counsel at your own expense to advise you on the matters for which you do not have coverage." The letter was filled with other official disclaimers, such as one that warned of the limits of St. Paul's protection as ". . . we will continue to reserve the right to deny liability for punitive damages in the event of a verdict rendered against you. . . ."

After all this bad news, he must have been heartened to see a familiar name on the letter. Wilder's federal lawsuit had been forwarded to Jack B. Russell, Attorney at Law, 1510 Ross Building, Richmond, Virginia, "for purposes of defending the suit." Russell would "be willing to cooperate in any way with any private counsel that you may select to represent you on your uncovered interests."[13]

It was an outrageous turn of events for someone like Lower, whose entire adult life had been dedicated to saving lives. His biographer, Donald McRae, described his darkening mood in *Every Second Counts*: "Lower, struggling to contain his rising anxiety, knew that he was not the only surgeon to have encountered such trouble." In 1968, shortly after the MCV heart transplant, "an esteemed Japanese surgeon, Juro Wada, had carried out his country's first heart transplant." When the eighteen-year-old recipient of the transplanted heart died three months later from an infection, "it was only then that Wada was accused by a fellow physician at Sapporo Medical College of not having done enough to save the donor patient, who was declared brain dead after a swimming accident. Wada was charged with murder."

Though the damning charges were eventually dropped, it led to a thirty-five-year-long ban on heart transplants in Japan and left Wada's career "under a shadow."[14]

Lower's colleagues noticed the sharply different way he dealt with the litigation compared to his more relaxed codefendant David Hume.

"Hume thought that was exciting," recalled Dr. Walter Lawrence, who'd answered the phone in the surgery department on the day of the operation. Hume was unfazed by the legal battle for the same reason he was willing to risk using baboons or chimps for human kidney transplants—he enjoyed the adrenaline high. Similarly, Lawrence said, Hume basked in the pretrial publicity "because he knew this would be an opportunity to sell the idea of brain death being synonymous with death."

If it took a trial to change the law, Hume thought, then so be it. Lower might agree in principle, but he couldn't shake the feeling that he'd been put on a "Most Wanted" poster. During staff meetings, Lower would air his grievances with the loud lament, "But they're claiming we murdered him!"[15]

Anne Lower tried to soothe his worries, but to little avail. In the days before the trial, Dick voiced the same complaint: "I'm being tried for manslaughter!"

She did what she'd been doing since their earlier, simpler days together when he dealt with criticism from animal rights activists and skeptical surgeons at Stanford. She stood by him.

"It didn't scare me," Anne said of the lawsuit, "because I knew the surgeons were on the right track."

Sometimes friends would ask how such a thing could happen. Why would anyone try to tarnish Dick's historic achievement? If only Anne could speak her mind about that "flamboyant" man—Doug Wilder—and his lawsuit.

It was too risky, though. Dick's career came first. "I couldn't say a word. I couldn't say anything. You know, as a doctor's wife, I learned early to keep my mouth shut."[16]

★ ★ ★

The pink and white azaleas bloomed on Capitol Square in the spring of 1972. With the trial nearing, Dick Lower noticed something worrisome on his drive home as he passed Old City Hall where Judge Compton would soon hold court. Someone was burning the midnight oil. "Whenever Lower left the hospital late at night . . . he would look up instinctively at the windows of Judge Christian Compton," McRae wrote. For the anxious surgeon, this marked a "quietly terrifying" reminder of the attention the judge was giving the case.[17]

Was this a good or bad thing for him? There was no way to know.

As he was doing his own legal homework, Ted Markow noticed others getting ready in the Virginia State Law Library.

"In those days before digital records," Markow explained, "that's where the attorney general's staff attorneys did much of their research."

As they looked for one more legal precedent or advance in neurology that might bolster their case, Markow said, "We happened to run into someone doing similar research—Judge Compton."[18]

CHAPTER NINETEEN

Time of Trial

May 16, 1972

THERE WAS A BUZZ of anticipation among the twenty or so spectators who'd arrived early for the opening of the trial. Shifting in the stiff wooden chairs of the old, high-ceilinged courtroom, a small group of doctors—Lower and Hume and colleagues from MCV among them—traded their white coats for dark suits. Friends and family came in a show of support.

Shortly after 10:00 a.m. the bailiff quieted the courtroom and declared, "All rise for the Honorable A. Christian Compton. The Richmond Law and Equity Court is now in session."

At one of the tables up front, one man did his best to comply. With his long, rubber-tipped crutches for leverage, William Tucker could move only so fast. He wore a neat gray suit, white shirt and tie, and shiny black leather shoes. Though he'd never gone to college, the earnest-looking man with horn-rimmed glasses and a trim mustache easily could have been mistaken for one of the two plaintiff's attorneys at the same table.

His chief advocate, Doug Wilder, stood ramrod straight and looked like a coach ready to start the game. He was joined by his cocounsel Harrison Bruce.

At the table on their left, Jack Russell led the opposing defense. The veteran of dozens of malpractice trials looked cool and calm as always, his fingers tapping the legal pads that contained the notes he'd need to execute his well-crafted game plan for the trial ahead. He was joined by an assistant, Tommy Stokes, along with the two younger lawyers from the attorney general's office, Ted Markow and Bill Crews.

Behind them, Dick Lower peered toward the bench, while Anne sat by his side. While Dick looked worried, David Hume looked as relaxed as if he were hosting another faculty bash. Eight other MCV doctors and various staff members would join them as needed through the trial, including David Sewell, who'd just returned from Vietnam after serving as a combat surgeon. Another doctor arriving from out of town was the former assistant medical examiner, Abdullah Fatteh, who now lived in North Carolina, where he'd taken another post in forensic science.

A tall man in a black robe entered and, after quickly scanning his courtroom, settled into a high-backed chair with studied ease. A woman sat at the table below him—resting her hands before she started taking notes on the custom keyboard of her stenotype machine.

Judge A. Christian Compton had the calm demeanor and dignified bearing of someone who was cut out to wear black robes—a man in full command of his courtroom. "He had the perfect temperament to be a judge."[1]

Now in his seventh year on the bench, Chris Compton was the son of a high school principal, a navy veteran, and a former college and semiprofessional basketball player. After nine years at a prestigious Richmond law firm, he was named by Governor Mills E. Godwin Jr. to fill a vacancy in the Richmond Law and Equity Court—the court for handling such civil lawsuits as *Tucker's Administrator v. Lower.*[2]

With his wide forehead, aquiline nose, and strong chin, Compton seemed to come from central casting—a modern-day Atticus Finch ready to tackle a case that already had shaken the confidence of the MCV surgeons and drawn criticism in the African American press. Indeed, before a single word was spoken in his courtroom, Compton made a key, pretrial ruling about the scope of the legal issues that would come before the jury.

Though Doug Wilder had cast the widest net possible in his original lawsuit—naming not only the famous surgeons, but also the entire supporting cast of some twenty other doctors, nurses, and medical technicians—Compton had exercised his judicial authority to narrow the scope of the plaintiff's complaint and, along with it, the number of defendants.

"The case," he later wrote, "evolved into a proceeding against the three surgeons who participated in the heart transplant and an Assistant Medical Examiner who purported to give permission for use of the heart and kidneys when no relatives or next of kin of the donor could be found."[3]

Compton's pretrial ruling about six months before the trial began dismissed some of the most shocking—and potentially lucrative—allegations Wilder made by claiming the transplant team committed an "unlawful invasion of a near-relative's rights with respect to a dead body." His ruling in late 1971 found Wilder's "unlawful invasion" claim fell under a section of Virginia law that was separate from those wrongful death statutes that Judge Compton said *did* apply to the case being brought by Bruce Tucker's brother.

Siding with Jack Russell and the rest of the MCV defense team, Compton based his rejection of the more lucrative claim on a section of the state's legal code that made the claim of an invasion of Bruce Tucker's body "a purely *personal right*" of his brother William. And for that to claim to have applied to the case, it had to be made within a year of the operation—that is, by late May 1969. Compton ruled in favor of a defense pleading that this part of the case should be dismissed.[4]

Wilder objected, but there was little to do but keep working on the part of the lawsuit that the judge allowed to go to trial. Still, the ruling had reduced the size of the pot of any potential payout to William Tucker and the rest of the Tuckers, including Bruce's adolescent son,

Abraham. Before a single witness had been called, the size of any poten-tial damage award in the case had plummeted by 90 percent—from $1 million to $100,000.

"Good morning, members of the jury," Compton said, looking to his right and greeting the seven conservatively dressed men in the jury box. Then he asked Wilder—as the plaintiff bringing the case—if he had an opening statement.

"Thank you, Judge Compton," Wilder said, his voice rising above the steady hum of an air conditioner rattling a bit in the window. Like a lead-ing man used to having eyes upon him, Wilder didn't hurry across the courtroom stage. He took his time approaching the jurors, perhaps not wanting to seem overbearing.

"Good morning, gentlemen," he said in his rich baritone. "One of the things you will determine is *when death comes* . . . The Code of Vir-ginia lays no claim as to when a person is dead," he said, pausing to em-phasize, "and the advancement of medical science should not trample upon God-given rights."

His brown eyes flashed like a prophet's. "What flickering flame and hope he [Bruce Tucker] had was *snuffed out* by those more interested in perfecting medical skills than in saving a life."

He reminded the jury that—whatever evidence they might hear to the contrary—the law was the law in Virginia, without any of the gray areas the defense would try to say existed. No matter what they say, Wilder stressed, the law is clear that "death is not the appearance of death, but the *cessation of life*."

Then, quoting from his lawsuit, he upbraided MCV and its surgeons for making Bruce Tucker the victim of a "systematic and nefarious scheme"—one in which the fifty-four-year-old gravely hurt worker "never had a chance" to make it out alive.[5]

As Wilder took his opening shots, he also subtly studied the jurors' faces—looking for any signs of connection. Could he get them to cross the boundaries of race, class, and culture? Could he get them to empathize with the plight of the wounded brother? He'd done it before with Richmond's mostly white juries and hoped to do it again.

Then it was Jack Russell's turn. He quickly set to work trying to erase the dark intimations and grisly scenes that Wilder had conjured up. He started by reviewing why Bruce Tucker was rushed to the hospital in the first place after falling off the wall behind the Esso. "We expect to show that his brain injury was an absolutely irrevocable condition, that there was no reasonable medical means of reversing his condition."

Once he let that sink in, Russell sought to parry Wilder's opening lunge.

"We will show that the time a person is pronounced dead doesn't indicate the time *death itself* occurred, it does not indicate that that is the moment a person *ceases* to be a person." In fact, he said, the occurrence of death "is a question of medical fact and opinion."

Now he had entered the gray area of the law that Wilder had warned them about. After stating this leitmotif—that "death" itself was a matter of medical opinion—Russell tried to demonstrate how this revised standard applied to Bruce Tucker's MCV experience. After his transfer from the ER to the main hospital, and the multiple tests and treatment for his head injury, through it all, Bruce Tucker was unresponsive, the defense lawyer argued.

So it followed that by midafternoon Saturday, as the surgeons considered taking Tucker's heart, he was actually "dead from a neurological standpoint." And soon enough he was pronounced dead.

After this short review of the facts of the matter, Russell delivered the deepest thrust of his opening argument: Bruce Tucker was never the surgeons' patient. Because of this key fact, Russell said, Wilder was suing the *wrong people*.

Or as the *Times-Dispatch* explained it: "A brother of the donor in Virginia's first heart transplant operation is suing the wrong persons for the alleged 'wrongful death' of his brother, since none of these personnel being sued had anything to do with the care or treatment of the donor prior to his death.

"That was the opening challenge from the defense yesterday in what is believed to be the first wrongful death lawsuit over a heart transplant in the nation, if not the world."[6]

Wilder called his first witness—William Tucker. The cobbler pushed back his chair, pulled himself up, and crossed the wooden floor, the rubber tips of his crutches squeaking against the wax. At the witness stand, he swung himself up in one deft movement. Compton acknowledged him with a friendly nod and readied a pencil to take his own notes—which, as it happened, would be the only surviving record of the trial.[7]

The morning newspaper described William Tucker's wrenching experience "when he got word that his brother had had a fall and was at the hospital. Tucker said he telephoned the hospital three times and went there at 7 p.m. after he got off work" and "was taken to three different people."

The reporter, James N. Woodson, rendered Tucker's testimony in the flat, impartial style of 1960s reporting, with little attention paid to William Tucker's tone of voice or the impression he might have made on the jury. Strictly by the book.

"After he got off work, [he] was taken to three different people and subsequently told that his brother was dead though he hadn't seen him."

Wilder, in his questioning of his client, asked William Tucker to describe how he felt about the hospital's treatment of him and his family—and how MCV officials kept him in the dark about Bruce's condition and whereabouts. "Tucker said hospital officials could have contacted him because his business card, giving his phone number and business address, was in his brother's personal belongings when he (William) picked them up afterward."[8]

Once again the *Times-Dispatch* reporter dropped in this surprising fact without adding any context or offering further explanation, such as where Bruce Tucker's clothes were kept or whether his possessions—

including the business card—should have been inventoried and shared with Hume's surgical team as they struggled to find the family. William Tucker testified that "no one asked him" for permission to take Bruce's heart. Neither did MCV notify him of his brother's injury or "his brother's injury or death prior to their occurrence."

Christian Compton provides a more nuanced view of the still-grieving brother. At times the judge's cursive notes resemble free verse:[9]

> *Brother had identifications*
> *on him with my*
> *number—*

> *Credentials turned over to*
> *me at MCV with my*
> *personal business card*
> *on me—*

Describing William Tucker's lonely search in the hospital ward, Compton writes:

> *on second floor—three men*
> *never saw them since*
> *stayed on second floor*
> *15–20 minutes—I didn't*
> *know where I was—*
> *After 15–20 minutes, they told*
> *me he was dead—*

> *I asked to use the phone*
> *—told me body wouldn't*
> *be released until 12 noon*
> *on Sunday—*

After William Tucker left the stand, Wilder called other witnesses to give the jury a sense of the family's confusion and grief. This included the funeral home director, Mack Jones, who went to MCV to gather Bruce's remains. After that he called Bruce Tucker's only son, Abraham.

Once again, there was little about the young man's testimony in the newspaper's account, with Judge Compton's notes filling the gaps . . . how Abraham's "father contributed" to his son's support and his attendance at Dinwiddie High School . . . and his birthday, which showed he would have been younger—age fourteen—than previously reported at the time of his father's passing.

Much of the rest of the first day of testimony was taken up by Wilder's examination of the two key figures who emerged after the transplant—the forensic doctors who sent out mixed messages about who gave permission to the surgeons to take Tucker's heart: chief medical examiner Geoffrey T. Mann, and his former assistant medical examiner Abdullah Fatteh.

Mann, in one of his more surprising revelations, explained that his second-in-command was not actually a full-fledged forensics doctor at the time he was asked to work on the Tucker case; rather, he was doing a postgraduate fellowship in forensic pathology at the time he was put on the hot seat by Hume and had to make such critical decisions by himself.

Under questioning by Wilder—who'd worked for Mann as a toxicologist before attending law school—Mann explained the series of events over the weekend. He'd been taking a three-day vacation, so he delegated his young protégé to "act as my agent" while he was gone. He defended his decision, contending that despite Fatteh's job title at the time, "Fatteh was not an assistant." Furthermore, he said, "Fatteh was licensed as [a] medical examiner in my view and was a licensed assistant in my view."[10]

Then he sought to explain how his office worked, and how he wore "two hats"—one as medical examiner, the other as administrator "of the use of unclaimed bodies for scientific studies."

This latter role was at play during the decision-making about how to handle Bruce Tucker's body, Mann told the jury. Harkening back to the days of the 1884 law to promote medical science and protect graveyards, Mann gave a thumbnail sketch of Virginia's medical history.

This legal authority, Mann explained, lets him supply various body parts and whole bodies for scientific uses at medical schools across Virginia. The fact that a heart was involved in the historic transplant made "no difference to us," he insisted. "It was just another organ as far as we were concerned . . . We had supplied other tissues for years."[11]

It was Dr. Fatteh's time to take the stand. Wilder tried to probe his thought process when he gave Hume and his team the green light to remove Tucker's heart and kidneys. Starting with the surprise call on Saturday morning, Fatteh related his advice to get in touch with Tucker's family to seek their permission. Then came the mid-afternoon call from Hume, and the continued failure by police to locate the family . . . and the final okay when the doctors turned off the heart-lung machine keeping Bruce Tucker alive.

Judge Compton's notes fill in some of the gaps in the news coverage of the day's events. Besides trying to reach Mann—"I needed his advice," Fatteh said—he testified that he reached out to a lawyer who advised MCV regarding transplants.

"I made another phone call to Thom. D. Jordan that a.m.," Fatteh said. "He was at home—I asked his advice."[12]

Fatteh said Jordan's advice lined up with what he'd already told the transplant team. After getting this reassurance, Fatteh said, he "carried on with my work" performing autopsies "all the daylight hours" at the hospital morgue.

Under questioning from Wilder, he said he "was not aware that the decedent's brother was trying to contact" Bruce Tucker.

"Hume didn't tell me who the treating physicians were—I didn't ask him," Fatteh said. "I didn't ask him who pronounced him dead—when Dr. Hume calls and says [Tucker] was pronounced dead, I have no reason to question."[13]

Fatteh, who was left minding the morgue, explained, "I relied on [the] professional caliber of colleagues."

Wilder "worked him over pretty good" and managed to score points with the jury on the trial's opening day, Plageman recalled.

After court adjourned, the juror mulled over Fatteh's testimony. Why had he authorized the transplant while William Tucker was busily searching for his brother? Why hadn't he or anyone checked Bruce's possessions and found William's business card? Didn't they owe the family that much?

The assistant medical examiner "really didn't have much defense," Plageman recalled. "He sat there . . . very much taken aback. I think he knew he was wrong."[14]

CHAPTER TWENTY

Friends in High Places

OVER THE NEXT FEW days, juror David Plageman was impressed by the depth and passion of the arguments made by each side. He wasn't the only one. As word spread around town about the brash black lawyer taking on MCV, the courtroom's limited seating began to fill before the bailiff announced at 10:00 a.m. sharp, "All rise!"

"Doug Wilder knew he had an audience, and he performed," Plageman recalled later of the growing public interest in the case. The stockbroker described the "flamboyancy" of Wilder's courtroom antics and his often scathing questions and remarks that held the jury's attention.[1]

On the other side of the courtroom, the defense team led by Jack Russell was "all business."

Beyond the personalities and theatrics, what stood out most to the young juror was the quality and credentials of the defense experts called to the stand. "I was impressed they could get the type of witnesses to appear on their behalf . . . ," Plageman said, "men from the Northeast medical schools, even California. These were top people in the profession in this country that commanded a lot of respect."[2]

They came from the upper strata of the groves of academe: Harvard, Yale, and Stanford, and closer to home, the University of Virginia and

MCV. They were leaders in the fields of organ transplantation and brain research. And, for good measure, one was a leading medical ethicist—Dr. Joseph Fletcher—who was asked to discuss some of the more difficult and disturbing aspects of the case.

Fletcher was more than up to the task. Though he was introduced as a philosopher and theologian teaching ethics to medical students at the University of Virginia, his own career had more twists and turns than a spy thriller. Since the 1930s, he'd been a social activist, Episcopal priest, and a spokesman for the United Mine Workers and other union members. His left-leaning pacifism and political activities had even drawn the ire of the angry anti-communist Senator Joseph McCarthy.

While teaching at Harvard in the 1950s, he began to explore the intersection of medicine and ethics—helping him become known as "the father of modern biomedical ethics." In 1966, he published *Situation Ethics: The New Morality*.

The Tucker trial—with its core questions of human intelligence and mortality—was the perfect forum for a man of Fletcher's keen intellect and varied experience. His nuanced thinking would help sway not only the jury, but also help turn the tide of the case by impressing the trial judge.

The gathering of academic and medical glitterati in Richmond wasn't really Jack Russell's idea, though. It was the brainstorm of David Hume, who invited many of his longtime friends and professional colleagues ostensibly to attend a professional conference on the latest trends in transplantation. Leaving nothing to chance, Hume even managed to cover the cost of his colleagues' travel and stay at Richmond's classic John Marshall Hotel covered by a major drug company, the Roerig division of Pfizer Pharmaceuticals.[3]

Russell later said he first became aware of Hume's brilliant strategy when he got a phone call "not long before the trial" while "we were getting our witnesses lined up." The conference began on Monday, May 22—after the trial was well underway, entering its second week.

While Russell may have somehow hustled to invite the experts to testify, it seems more likely that any planning was done well before the transplantation conference and trial ran their parallel courses. Supporting this theory was William Crews, the assistant attorney general who traveled to California in an effort to glean more about "time of death" in the tragic car crash.

"Dave Hume had called a conference of international transplant surgeons at the same time" as the trial, Crews said. "So every transplant surgeon probably in the world that was known, they were in Richmond during the course of the trial."

The brilliant doctors and thinkers came to circle their wagons around two respected medical innovators—Lower and Hume—whom they viewed as victims who were under attack for standing up for their beliefs. According to Crews's account, this explains why Hume "decided to have everybody in town in case [Russell] thought witnesses were needed. That's what he told me."

Asked about how Hume orchestrated his conference with the trial, neither defense lawyer—Crews or Markow—could say for certain how far in advance Hume planned his symposium. It was "probably after the trial date was set," Crews said.[4]

The question of the setting of the trial date concurrent with the arrival of the team of experts comes into clearer focus when one considers the legal niceties of the Virginia General Assembly. With Senator Wilder tied up with his governing duties, he could not be compelled to appear in court during the legislature's regular session from January through the end of March. By setting the trial date in mid-May, Compton managed to meet the scheduling needs of both parties: Wilder would have a full month (in April) to prepare for the case; and Hume had ample time to arrange the conference and help the defense team choose its best witnesses.

Russell offered his own version of meeting Hume's high-profile friends—starting with a phone call to his law office early in the trial. It seems like it would have come after the fourth day—Friday, May 19—as the conference speakers started arriving.

"I was called by David and told to come down to the John Marshall Hotel." The doctors and professors were in town for what Hume called "The First International Symposium on Organ Transplantation." And, Hume informed his attorney, "They all want to meet you."[5]

Since Russell needed a break from reviewing his trial notes, he agreed to walk up West Franklin Street to the stately hotel. With its old-fashioned "Hotel John Marshall" sign on top, the sixteen-story-tall brick complex was a traditional meeting place for politicians, lawyers, and even reporters. Now the doctors were taking over for the weekend.

Passing through its revolving door, he was quickly greeted by Hume and surrounded by well-wishers. It was a humbling feeling to be welcomed by such an esteemed group of surgeons and professors. The best-known experts in the transplant world were there, everyone but Norm Shumway.

"He's on some island down in the Pacific somewhere," Hume told Russell. "If you want him, I'll get him!" Hume had taken up flying and was ready to retrieve Shumway.

There was no need, Russell said. Shaking hands at this gathering of doctors, he could see they'd come because of the high esteem in which they held Hume and Lower. There was William Sweet, chief of neuro-surgery at Massachusetts General Hospital and chairman of the Harvard Ad Hoc Committee on the Definition of Death; William Collins, MCV's former chief of neurosurgery who held the same post at Yale; Dr. Edwin Benson, a colleague of Shumway's at Stanford; and Virginia's celebrity author and philosopher, Joseph Fletcher.

"There were a few we didn't take because we really didn't need that many," Russell said later of his final witness list. "But it was a great experience."

It also added to Russell's confidence that he was ready to "convince the jury that neurological or brain death was a very valid concept." Once the handshakes and greetings were over, they got down to the serious business at hand, preparing their testimony. "They appreciated the fact that a lot was riding on [the jury's verdict] because . . . if that jury had decided against us it would have dampened transplant surgery in this country for many years."[6]

The doctors and professors couldn't have known it at the time, but they were making their plans at the same hotel where the lawyer for the plaintiff, Doug Wilder, once worked as a waiter in the 1940s. In those days of segregation, no blacks were allowed to eat, drink, or sleep at the hotel.

When the trial resumed for its second day, the first doctors called to the stand were the local ones who'd been involved in the transplant operation. First up was Dr. Hooshang Hooshmand, the "consulting neurologist" at MCV who conducted the electroencephalogram (EEG) on Bruce Tucker. Despite Wilder's often pointed questions, the neurologist stood firm in defending his diagnosis and his ethics.

When he conducted a twenty-five-minute-long EEG, Hooshmand explained, "There was no evidence of cerebral activity." This came as no surprise, he said, because he'd also tested Tucker's reflexes and made other observations such as the "cloudiness" of the corneas of his eyes. "I knew he was dead," Hooshmand told Wilder. The EEG simply "confirmed my diagnosis."

How had he become part of the transplant team? asked Wilder. Hooshmand countered that he was *not* part of the team, rebutting any suggestion that he gave a home-cooked diagnosis.

"Nobody told me he [Tucker] was a candidate," the neurologist said. He only learned about this after the operation. Hooshmand, who'd emigrated from Tehran to the United States about a decade earlier, seemed unfazed by Wilder's hint of a conspiracy at MCV.

"Bruce O. Tucker was dead," Hooshmand repeated. Because of the mechanical respirator, "his heart was kept alive. But Bruce O. Tucker was not there. . . ." His heart was kept "beating so long as the respirator provides oxygen."

After failing to dispute the doctor's story, Wilder shifted to a more philosophical line of query.

"When you define death," he asked, "how do you take into account the legal, moral, or ethical considerations?"

"I consider three types of death in my own definition," Hooshmand replied. "Clinical death, that is the total cessation of brain function. Then I consider biological death—meaning the death of cells, organs or any other part of the body; and I also think of theological death, which can be various things to various religions. But to me, it means when the soul leaves the body."

Judge Compton's notes capture the interaction between Doug Wilder, raised in the Baptist tradition, and Hooshmand, a native of Iran.

I am Muslim.
You are Christian.
Other Jew
Soul leaving body.

Yet, having said this, Hooshmand said his role in the hospital was strictly clinical. On this basis, he couldn't pinpoint the time when Bruce Tucker's soul may have left his body.[7]

After exploring such philosophical issues, the following morning Wilder took a more down-to-earth tack. He homed in on what became one of his most persuasive arguments against the doctors and MCV staff: *Why* hadn't they tried harder to find Bruce Tucker's kin before taking his heart?

The first state official called to the stand, lawyer Thomas D. Jordan, seemed to bolster Wilder's argument by recalling only the briefest of conversations with Abdullah Fatteh on the day of the transplant. The testimony of Jordan, the administrative assistant for the Office of the Chief Medical Examiner of the Commonwealth of Virginia, wasn't reported by the *Times-Dispatch* or other news outlets covering the trial.

Judge Compton's handwritten notes provide the only record of the lawyer's advice to Fatteh:

> *I knew all the Sat. that a person dying but not yet dead was being considered for a transplant.*

When he called Jordan at his home, Fatteh didn't mention anything about a "transplant" candidate, the lawyer testified. Instead, Fatteh asked him about the state's "Unclaimed Body" law for medical research. Jordan's counsel, according to Compton, was as follows:

> *If no . . . next of kin or family*
> *Body could be used for Scientific Study*
> *I never talk him anything about a transplant.*

Jordan noted how unusual it was to invoke the unclaimed-body law, saying there were:

> *About two bodies used each year for scientific study in Virginia . . .*

And:

> *If it's to be used for study we will send state hearse.*

The lawyer's testimony provided more evidence of how Fatteh was largely flying solo on the day of the transplant. It also bolstered Wilder's suggestions to the jury about the lack of oversight of the MCV surgeons. Jordan said he was never consulted again after the phone call came out of the blue.

Don't recall conversing further with Fatteh that weekend.

On the third day, the jury finally heard from the two main actors, Richard Lower and David Hume. As he eased into his own questioning of his clients, Russell underscored two main points: first, that both doctors tried hard to find the Tucker family; and second, neither transplant surgeon was responsible for Bruce Tucker's treatment for his head injury. That responsibility fell to a staff physician, Dr. B. W. Brawley.

Gently guided by Russell, Lower stressed how his entire attention was laser-focused on his dying patient, Joseph Klett. As for Bruce Tucker, he was seen as a potential organ donor who was not under his care. But, Lower stressed, "We agreed we should make an effort to locate the family."

For that reason, an assistant checked Tucker's chart and "determined first there was no indication that any family [member] had come with him to the hospital." After that, he suggested the police should be called to visit Bruce Tucker's home address.

Now it was Wilder's turn.

"Did you, Dr. Lower, check Bruce Tucker's valuables for a wallet to see if it might contain some identification of his next of kin?"

"No," he replied, "they were locked up somewhere" by the hospital staff. And since there was no mention of relatives "on the [Tucker's medical record] sheet, I assumed the emergency room people would have put it on [if they had found any next of kin]." This was the typical protocol, Lower testified, one he'd seen before in "many, many cases from the emergency room."

Wilder fixed his gaze on the wary doctor. "So, if I understand your testimony today, sir, you never checked yourself to see if this man who was about to be deprived of his most precious organ—his very *heart*—might *possibly* have had some loved ones looking for him, who might have liked to be consulted before you started carving it out of his chest?"

Lower tried to stay calm. Wilder was wrong. *He* hadn't removed

Tucker's heart, something the lawyer surely knew from his pretrial depositions. That part of the operation was supervised by Hume and performed by the junior surgeon, Sewell.

Wilder seemed intent on confusing the jury, or so it seemed to someone who wasn't used to being spoken to in this manner. Lower was accustomed to being treated as *the authority figure,* the equivalent to a ship's captain steering everyone in the right direction in the operating room. In a surgeon's high-pressure world, order was key. Now Wilder seemed intent on starting a mutiny.

There was something in the lawyer's attitude, his voice, and his expression that got under Lower's skin. Wasn't it bad enough that Wilder, who everyone he knew called "flamboyant," had already tarnished his reputation? In fact, he'd hurt everyone who happened to be working in the operating rooms that day. Now he was sneering and calling him a murderer! How dare he?[8]

Looking on from the defense table, Jack Russell kept a close eye on the normally stoic surgeon, hoping he wouldn't take Wilder's bait. Like other doctors Russell had seen take the stand, Lower was used to playing the godlike role of a man in a white lab coat that he sometimes joked about. Now with so much power and prestige at stake, it was hard to have the tables turned and be treated like a regular person.

Fortunately for Lower, his defender had seen enough doctors squirm on the stand to see this coming. He'd prepared his clients for the worst and, despite his obvious discomfort, Lower was keeping his cool.

Lower calmly described how he hadn't wanted to operate on Klett unless "there was reasonable assurance that a donor heart was available." Comfortably back in his captain's role, Lower sounded relaxed and less defensive. He told the jury about the businessman's failing condition and how his prognosis for recovery was "nil." Which explained why he desperately needed a new heart.

During this testimony, Lower made a clinical point that had yet to come out in public. Klett's failing heart was causing other key organs to shut down, the surgeon said. "Specifically the lungs and the liver."

So it followed that it was only natural to consider "Tucker's possible candidacy as a donor in the Klett case." The implication was that the decision was made without any sort of premeditation, ill will, or malicious intent Wilder had suggested in his lawsuit. After all, Lower told the jury, he didn't even see the brain-injured patient until midafternoon. This was after Dr. Hooshmand conducted the EEG and pronounced that Bruce Tucker "was dead from a neurological standpoint."

Nonetheless, Wilder kept pressing for answers about the fateful moments before both men's chests were opened in the side-by-side operating rooms. Had Fatteh consented to using Tucker's heart by then? And had Tucker been officially pronounced dead?

"Neither," Lower said with regained authority. "But we were getting ready. If Dr. Fatteh had *not* given permission, there would not have been an operation."

After the assistant medical examiner finally approved the taking of Tucker's heart, Wilder asked Lower, "When did you decide to transplant his heart?"

"When I saw the scarring of Klett's heart was sufficiently extensive that it could not be corrected, somewhere around four thirty p.m.," he coolly replied.

Russell rose to cross-examine his client. "Was there any reason for you to seriously question the granting of permission from Dr. Fatteh after the attending physician pronounced Mr. Tucker dead?"

"There was no reason," Lower said, "providing no family had been found." Then he reiterated how the clock was ticking. Once Bruce Tucker's brain functions completely halted, his heart would quickly start deteriorating and become unusable.[9]

When Hume took the stand, he stayed on script about the sensitive issue of searching for Tucker's kin. "We were extremely anxious to locate the family," he asserted, as shown by the second request on Saturday afternoon for police officers to swing by Bruce's boardinghouse.

Little more of Hume's testimony was reported. The surgeon focused on Bruce Tucker's struggle to breathe due to the pressure caused by his swelling brain. "The patient had a cessation of breathing," Hume testified, "and had a drill hole put in to relieve the pressure."

Compton added this on another part of Hume's lengthy testimony:

police no help
aware that family [was] called before procedure
followed here
was same as follow in past w/
respect to other donors

Not in any way responsible for care and
treatment of Bruce O. Tucker at
MCV—nor was anybody under me—
nothing special done with regard to organ
transplant
than in any other.

Compton also documented how Bruce Tucker was treated once he was viewed as a potential organ donor patient, despite the lack of family contact or consent. This explained why, Hume testified, Tucker's medical chart left out some critical information after Drs. Sewell and Hume removed his heart.

Time left out in any other patient—in chart as
to beginning or ending of operation.
Tuckers only name without time of op.

So it was that even in the hospital's own record keeping, Bruce Tucker remained, in the words of medical historians, "socially dead."[10]

This strange lack of a complete medical record, Hume said matter-of-factly, was because—from the surgeons' perspective—the heart removal

Was not strictly speaking an operation.

After hearing from the surgeons, neither side chose to return to the question of the ineffectual efforts to find William Tucker or family members. No Richmond policemen or officials were called to testify—including the officers sent to knock on the rooming house door. Wilder may have thought that asking white patrolmen to take the stand could backfire, adding more fuel for his critics as a "flamboyant" black lawyer willing to challenge the police department.

For his part, Russell followed suit—perhaps not wishing to open a can of worms about the white cops' efforts to find a black man's family.

Another key character took the stand: Dr. David Sewell. After leaving Richmond, the young surgeon had joined the army and was eventually assigned to the Third Field Hospital in Saigon. In this later stage of the war, Sewell observed later, "I didn't really see any combat."[11] By the spring of 1972, he was back in the States at Fort Ord, California, near San Francisco.

"When I got notification of the trial and [made] arrangements to get back to Richmond . . . I didn't know what to think."

Was he nervous about testifying about the key role that he played in removing Tucker's heart? "I guess I was, but on the other hand," he said, "it was just part of my job. I didn't think we had anything to hide."[12]

His only pretrial preparation came when Jack Russell took him for a long walk near MCV "and asked me what went on. He didn't coach me at all." For example, Sewell said, he first learned of William Tucker's frantic search for his brother when he was waiting to take the stand. And

Sewell, unlike Dr. Lower, said he never felt resentful about the questioning by Doug Wilder.

"I have a lot of respect" for Wilder, said Sewell, who later became a medical professor in cardiac and thoracic surgery at East Tennessee State University. "He was doing his job. I don't think he did anything bad."[13]

★   ★   ★

As news of the trial spread around Richmond, David Plageman started fielding questions from coworkers, friends, and acquaintances after they learned he was on the jury. Until then, "Doug Wilder" was hardly a household name, at least among his mostly white friends and colleagues.

As they read the news about the trial, people started questioning him. "Who's this black guy from Church Hill?" they asked. "Who does he think he is suing these renowned, famous surgeons?"

Despite the public skepticism, such questions weren't being asked by the jurors. They stuck to hearing the testimony and following the judge's instructions, according to Plageman. When it came to Wilder, the prevailing view was essentially, "Yeah, he's performing," but he's also advocating for his client, William Tucker. They also knew he stood to gain financially if he won the case.

"We weren't questioning his legal talents," Plageman said.

Nonetheless, emotions were still running high over civil rights in Richmond and throughout Virginia. A federal judge was issuing rulings to improve public schools in an effort to reverse the racist legacy of Virginia's "Massive Resistance" policy. Advocated by US senator Harry F. Byrd Sr., a former governor who coined the term, "Massive Resistance" became Virginia's official policy in 1956; it was an effort to block the desegregation of public schools mandated by the US Supreme Court in its 1954 ruling in *Brown v. Board of Education of Topeka, Kansas*. A number of Virginia school systems, including Norfolk and Charlottesville, shut down and only reopened by court order. By the early 1970s, many white

Virginians still shared Senator Byrd's "reflexive disdain for federal government intrusion into state affairs."[14]

"That was the attitude of the time," Plageman said. "There was still a feeling of segregation of black and white."

Against this volatile backdrop, Jack Russell trod carefully, focusing on the broader implications of the case for all of American medicine. Soon he would bring in the big guns assembled down the street and ready to testify. But first he skirmished with Wilder over how much leeway the jury should be given in considering the latest in medical and scientific opinion in reaching their verdict.

The *Times-Dispatch* summarized this key clash on the fourth day of the trial: "Is the death of a person a matter of medical judgment, left to the physician to determine, or is it a legal question?" It was, in its own way, an updated version of the nineteenth-century controversies over body snatching, or what historian Michael Sappol called "the hue and cry [that] disrupts the secret ritual of the medical cult."[15]

Jack Russell and his defense team asked Compton to dismiss William Tucker's lawsuit over wrongful death. The jury was sent out as the judge heard from both sides. Russell began by arguing that, after three days of testimony, no evidence had been introduced that showed the MCV's doctors had failed to meet "an accepted standard of care for the treatment of injuries such as those sustained by Bruce O. Tucker." He suggested to Compton that "the court should not submit speculation by a lay jury a question so clearly one for expert medical testimony, and where expert medical testimony is uncontradicted."[16]

Russell also said Wilder had not proven any sort of malpractice by the surgeons and other medical personnel. Indeed, he said the plaintiff's attorney had failed to show that the surgeons had a physician-patient relationship with Tucker. But even if there had been one, Russell repeated his assertion that no one had proved there had been any departure "from an accepted standard of care" for Bruce Tucker.

Russell asked the judge to consider how complicated the case could be for a jury of regular citizens not trained in medicine. He contrasted what the "laypeople" of the jury—as bright and responsible as they may be in their daily life and work—could be expected to comprehend. This was especially true when compared to the insights of doctors and academics who'd testified or would take the stand soon, said Russell. Only they, he implied, could be expected to grasp the complex clinical issues presented in the case.

With this in mind, Russell tried to convince the judge that the seven-man jury should not be "allowed to speculate" about the events surrounding the 1968 transplant. This was even more true in light of Wilder's attempts to sway the jury by making such dark assertions about the surgeons' motives and characters.

Considering the serious charges of wrongful death that Compton had allowed to proceed, Russell argued "evidence that removal of the heart terminates life would have to allow the jury to disregard all the medical evidence in the case" that his brain, not his heart, was what meant he was alive.

He circled back to Dr. Hooshmand's neurological exam—Tucker's flat-lining on the EEG—which he said "unequivocally" proved "that Bruce O. Tucker's life ended at one o'clock on May 25, 1968." After that, "His heart was not removed from his body until nearly an hour after he was pronounced dead."

Case closed, or so Russell hoped. Compton, for his part, neatly summarizes the lawyer's talking points:

Jury would have to disregard
Medical testimony to
Determine when
Tucker died.

Looking up from his notes, Compton asked, "Are you saying the question of death is a medical question and not a legal definition?"

"Yes," Russell said.

Compton, for his part, sounded doubtful about ceding such legal authority. "You are aware the courts have had occasion to rule on this," he said, "mostly where you have simultaneous deaths and a question of survivorship—where one preceded the other."

Over at the defense table, Bill Crews nodded appreciatively. The judge clearly had done his homework and read his legal brief about the 1964 car accident that led to California's Uniform Simultaneous Death Act.

Any sense of victory was short-lived, though. For Compton was not about to challenge a long-standing tradition of Virginia judges not dabbling in the legislative process. Instead, he ruled that the traditional definition of death was the only permissible interpretation of the law. "The courts in 1958 followed *Black's Law* [*Dictionary*]," he said, "which differs from the medical definition you have testified to in this case."

Russell tried to dissuade Compton from applying an outdated definition from the 1950s and the days of Dwight Eisenhower's heart attacks. "The cases are clearly distinguishable," he countered. "It would be highly unusual to resort to a *legal* dictionary to answer a *medical* question."

"I think you're right," the judge conceded. "The dictionary definition is not controlling, but we can take cognizance of the rulings of other appellate courts."

"It's a matter for medical opinion," Russell repeated, "and not a definition from a legal dictionary."

If only he could get the judge to throw out the old dictionary definition. But Compton wouldn't budge on his conventional view of death. He felt obliged to adhere to a definition drawn from a legal dictionary that had not been revised to include a loss of brain function. *Black's* defined death as "the cessation of life; the ceasing to exist; defined by physicians as a total stoppage of blood, and a cessation of the animal and vital functions thereon, such as respiration, pulse, etc."

Russell pressed on, though. He argued that three words from the dictionary definition—"defined by physicians"—were key. "Whoever compiled that dictionary recognized that this had to be a medical opinion."

Russell concluded by noting the legislature's passage in 1968 of the Uniform Anatomical Gift Act, which had taken effect shortly after the Tucker transplant. The organ donation law held that a physician determines the death of a patient. With this in mind, Russell said that granting this power to doctors "was the intent of the General Assembly of Virginia" and was the new "public policy in the state."

Now it was Wilder's turn. He would try to rebut Russell's effort to get Judge Compton to allow the jury to consider a broader interpretation of Virginia law. Approaching the bench, he knew he'd soon be battling the collective brainpower of the all-star lineup of academics ready to back the defense.

Wilder knew that his best option was to appeal to the common sense of the judge and jury alike, asking them to follow the laws that applied when Bruce was rushed into the emergency room in May 1968. Considering subsequent laws or novel legal theories was something for academics to discuss at conferences. It was not the proper direction for a judge to take in Virginia's tradition-bound court system.[17]

"Mr. Russell would have you believe there was legal authority [to donate Tucker's heart] because this was the tenor of thinking, but this has *never* been the law," Wilder argued to Compton. He freely acknowledged the need to update the state's organ donor law because, when it came to the growing field of organ donations, "The medical examiner had no authority to donate the organs at all."

The reason for that was simple, Wilder said. Harkening back to 1884, when the legislature passed the law that regulated the use of unclaimed bodies, no one could have imagined a future where surgeons might be able to remove a human kidney or liver—much less a *heart*— to put into another person.

Continuing to draw on the original law, Wilder reminded Compton of its basic requirement to honor a twenty-four-hour waiting period before anatomy professors or other researchers could open up anyone's body for its parts. And it was *this* rule, he argued, that was simply ignored by the MCV surgeons and their ally, Fatteh.

In reply, Compton asked Wilder to address the defense's contention that the surgeons and MCV staff did *not* mistreat Bruce Tucker and cause his wrongful death. What about Russell's assertion that Tucker actually was dead before his heart was harvested and put to good use to save another man's life?

"Is Russell right in arguing that Virginia's courts should not close their eyes to reality?" challenged Compton.

Wilder, always fast on his feet, alluded to Hooshmand's findings with the EEG measuring brain activity. "Significantly, Dr. Hooshmand *never pronounced the patient dead,*" Wilder replied. In the hours that followed in the operating rooms, he said, the law simply didn't have any provision for allowing the doctors to take such freedoms. There was nothing in the law that allowed them to act on the basis of their consensus opinion that Tucker was "neurologically dead." Thus it followed that the law should never have been circumvented. If it had been followed, he added, there would have been no reason to pressure Bruce Tucker's attending physician, Dr. Brawley, to declare Tucker dead or to apply any pressure on Fatteh to allow his heart and kidneys to be taken.

Returning to his original accusation that the MCV doctors engaged in a "systemic and nefarious scheme" to kill Tucker by taking his heart, Wilder said "that was malpractice"—made worse by how "efforts to contact the next of kin fell short of what the norm would be." He urged Compton to apply the law and not, as Russell would have him do, bend it in a way that would exonerate MCV. As a result, the Tucker family would be left empty-handed.

His voice rising with indignation, Wilder declared, "All of these allegations call for a higher standard of professional care. If they were going to do *anything* to Bruce O. Tucker, they should do *everything* they could to help him."

The key to the case, he proclaimed, "is whether their efforts did *thwart* the efforts of others to aid, assist, resuscitate and revive Bruce O. Tucker!"[18]

When the defense returned to press its arguments again, Ted Markow asked Compton to dismiss Fatteh as a defendant. But while Compton seemed more than willing to send home the many doctors, nurses, and medical technicians who were hauled into court, he was equally adamant that the assistant medical examiner should stay.

After this mixed ruling, Markow kept pressing Compton to adjust his thinking about modern medicine, specifically brain death. "I would say *Black's* dictionary definition is certainly not wrong, it just doesn't go far enough," Markow argued. "In this case we have ample evidence to say Bruce Tucker was dead, but what you (the court) come up with is [legal] precedent and will be precedent in determining the course physicians take in the future of heart transplants."

The point was duly noted.

Shaping a Verdict

ULTIMATELY IT WASN'T WILDER'S in-your-face questioning of the men in white coats that turned the tide of the trial in the doctors' favor. Rather, it was the clear, confident voices of authority who took the stand that did the trick. But as the second week of the trial began, Judge Compton issued an opinion that, at first, seemed to strike a blow to the defense strategy and its elite witnesses waiting in the wings.

The judge's opinion came in response to a defense motion to strike all the evidence that had been presented up to that point of the trial. Compton ruled against them and, more important, he signaled that he would not allow the jury to consider the concept of brain death in its deliberations.

In his thirteen-page opinion, Compton reviewed the facts of the case. The question before the jury, he wrote, was whether Bruce Tucker's "death occurred as the direct result of the acts of the defendants."

Or had Tucker died, as the defense contended, as a result of the brain injury suffered in his initial fall?

The judge ruled that Wilder had presented enough evidence for a jury to find "that had the respirator not been cut off and had his heart and kidneys not been removed, Tucker could have lived at least a day or probably longer." This meant that the jury could consider how the doctors' actions had deprived Bruce's mother, son, brothers, sisters, cousins, and friends the opportunity to say their final goodbyes. Whether he could have spoken to them, or even heard them, was impossible to say.

But as Compton set out the trial's overarching issues, he also tried to set some markers to help the jury reach a verdict. First, *timing* was key. "If the jury concludes [Tucker's life] was terminated at a time earlier than it would ordinarily have ended had all reasonable efforts been continued to prolong his life, then it will be allowed to assess damages."

Those could be set in terms of financial losses such as Bruce Tucker's loss of child support sent to his mother each month. They also could take into account what Compton called the "sorrow and mental anguish caused by his death."[1]

The breadth of his ruling showed Compton's intense preparation for the case, whether it was staying late at the Virginia State Law Library or simply taking time to think about its ramifications. This was evident as Compton readily acknowledged Russell's well-crafted arguments about brain death. He also seemed impressed by Dr. Hooshmand's testimony concerning "neurological death."

Yet the judge also acknowledged Wilder's arguments on William Tucker's behalf, noting that Hooshmand "also found that the decedent's heart was beating and that his body temperature, pulse, and blood pressure were all normal for a patient in his condition." Thus, the judge let the jury know that they might draw different conclusions from the same set of evidence.

Compton also tried to dissect the two main definitions of death. The more contemporary one, as advocated by Jack Russell and the defense, was "clinical or neurological death . . . total cessation of function of the central nervous system or brain." The second, traditional definition argued by Wilder was the linchpin of Virginia law; it "defined biological death of an organ or a part of the body or a cell."

ABOVE: Chris Baker lived and worked in the Egyptian Building, where he brought stolen bodies for use in MCV's anatomy classes. He was on the hospital's payroll well into the twentieth century, living with his wife and son in the basement. SPECIAL COLLECTIONS AND ARCHIVES, TOMPKINS-McCAW LIBRARY, VIRGINIA COMMONWEALTH UNIVERSITY

ABOVE: Jean Harris, the first African American student admitted to MCV's School of Medicine, graduated in 1955. She went on to become the first black member of a Virginia governor's cabinet in 1978. SPECIAL COLLECTIONS AND ARCHIVES, TOMPKINS-McCAW LIBRARY, VIRGINIA COMMONWEALTH UNIVERSITY

ABOVE: Richard Lower was lured from Stanford to MCV in 1965 in the hope of winning the heart transplant race. *RICHMOND TIMES-DISPATCH*

ABOVE: Transplant surgeon David Hume was recruited from Harvard in the mid-1950s to raise MCV's stature. *RICHMOND TIMES-DISPATCH*

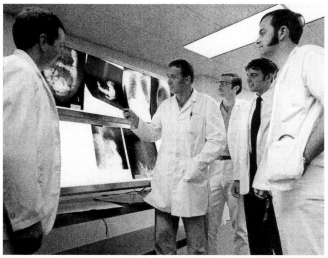

LEFT: Hume, a popular yet forceful figure, examining X-rays with residents ca. 1969–71. SPECIAL COLLECTIONS AND ARCHIVES, TOMPKINS-McCAW LIBRARY, VIRGINIA COMMONWEALTH UNIVERSITY

RIGHT: Dr. Lower (left) in a lab operating on a dog's heart ca. 1966–67. SPECIAL COLLECTIONS AND ARCHIVES, TOMPKINS-McCAW LIBRARY, VIRGINIA COMMONWEALTH UNIVERSITY

BELOW: Lower with fellow heart researcher, Richard J. Cleveland, in the lab in 1966. SPECIAL COLLECTIONS, TOMPKINS-McCAW LIBRARY, VIRGINIA COMMONWEALTH UNIVERSITY

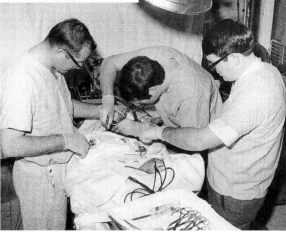

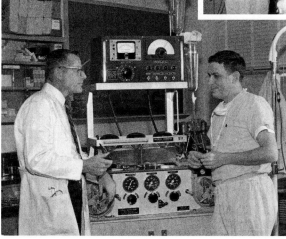

RIGHT: Dr. Hunter McGuire praised Hume's brilliance, but said the surgical chief could be a "completely unconventional, undisciplined brat," who "loved bad boys and recruited them." SPECIAL COLLECTIONS AND ARCHIVES, TOMPKINS-McCAW LIBRARY, VIRGINIA COMMONWEALTH UNIVERSITY

53-Year-Old Richmond Man

Heart Donor Identified

The Medical College of Virginia's heart transplant patient was listed as satisfactory yesterday afternoon; meanwhile, the identity of the donor was learned late yesterday.

He was Bruce Oliver Tucker, 53, of 109 E. Charity St. here, who suffered fatal brain injuries last Friday evening when he fell from a three-foot high wall he was sitting on and hit his head on concrete, according to a friend. The accident occurred between 11th and 12th Sts. on East Cary Street.

Tucker, who was a Negro, died Satruday at MCV of "irreparable" brain injuries, according to one source. He worked at the Schluderberg-Kurdie Co., Inc., (Esskay) a packing firm. More specifically, he worked at the firm's egg plant at 1114 E. Cary St.

J. O. Bowles, manager of the Esskay egg plant, said Tucker had worked there for "26 or 27" years, and described him as a

Bruce O. Tucker
Dinwiddie Native

"good employe who was always punctual." Eggs are candled and graded at the Cary Street Esskay plant.

Bowles said he was not at work last week due to illness, but understood that Tucker's accident occurred sometime after the plant had closed Friday evening.

A brother of the donor, Grover Tucker of Dinwiddie, when asked if his brother were the donor, said "Yes, he's the one."

Another brother, William Tucker of Richmond, declined to confirm or deny that Bruce Tucker was the donor, but added, "If it were done, it was done without authorization." He declined further comment.

State medical officials could not be reached for comment

Continued on Page 2, Col. 3

LEFT: MCV Hospital where Bruce Tucker was brought to its emergency entrance (bottom left). SPECIAL COLLECTIONS AND ARCHIVES, TOMPKINS-McCAW LIBRARY, VIRGINIA COMMONWEALTH UNIVERSITY

ABOVE: St. Philip Hospital, the formerly segregated facility where William Tucker finally learned the fate of his brother. SPECIAL COLLECTIONS AND ARCHIVES, TOMPKINS-McCAW LIBRARY, VIRGINIA COMMONWEALTH UNIVERSITY

LEFT: An aerial view of the MCV campus in 1996 shows its expansion near Interstate 95 in downtown Richmond. SPECIAL COLLECTIONS AND ARCHIVES, TOMPKINS-McCAW LIBRARY, VIRGINIA COMMONWEALTH UNIVERSITY

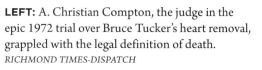

LEFT: A. Christian Compton, the judge in the epic 1972 trial over Bruce Tucker's heart removal, grappled with the legal definition of death. *RICHMOND TIMES-DISPATCH*

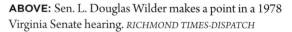

ABOVE: Sen. L. Douglas Wilder makes a point in a 1978 Virginia Senate hearing. *RICHMOND TIMES-DISPATCH*

ABOVE: Businessman Joseph Klett had a long history of heart disease before Dr. Lower began treating him. *RICHMOND TIMES-DISPATCH*

ABOVE: Geoffrey Mann, Virginia's chief medical examiner in the 1960s, studies a skull. He left his assistant in charge before MCV's surgeons decided to try their first human heart transplant. *RICHMOND TIMES-DISPATCH*

RIGHT: Thelma and Louis Russell became the faces of MCV's heart transplant program in the summer of 1968. *RICHMOND TIMES-DISPATCH*

LEFT: Packing for home. Thelma Russell helps Louis prepare to return to Indianapolis after a long recuperation from his heart transplant. *RICHMOND TIMES-DISPATCH*

ABOVE: L. Douglas Wilder exults at his 1990 inauguration after becoming the nation's first elected African American governor. *RICHMOND TIMES-DISPATCH*

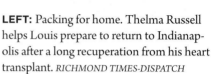

ABOVE: Beverly "Bev" Orndorff, science and medical writer at the *Richmond Times-Dispatch,* got the cold shoulder from MCV's heart surgeons and staff after revealing Bruce Tucker's identity. *RICHMOND TIMES-DISPATCH*

LEFT: VCU archaeologists prepare to remove skeletal material from an abandoned well during a massive construction project in 1994. SPECIAL COLLECTIONS AND ARCHIVES, TOMPKINS-McCAW LIBRARY, VIRGINIA COMMON-WEALTH UNIVERSITY

RIGHT: Interior of abandoned well shows bricks, bones, and artifacts that dated back to MCV's origins before the Civil War. SPECIAL COLLECTIONS AND ARCHIVES, TOMPKINS-McCAW LIBRARY, VIRGINIA COMMONWEALTH UNIVERSITY

ABOVE: The original foundation of the Egyptian Building was laid bare during construction of a new medical sciences building in 1994. SPECIAL COLLECTIONS AND ARCHIVES, TOMPKINS-McCAW LIBRARY, VIRGINIA COMMONWEALTH UNIVERSITY

ABOVE: A mural at VCU School of Medicine shows a grave robber with a body in his wheelbarrow (center). Note the corpse's arm, a shovel, and a wolf howling at the crescent moon. The macabre 1930s artwork remains in the McGlothlin Medical Education Center. JAY PAUL

LEFT: Anne Lower beaming at the family's Montana ranch where they moved in 1989 after Dick left MCV. He ended his career serving as a physician volunteer at a Richmond health clinic for low-income patients. I. N. SPORN

RIGHT: Gentleman farmer. Dick Lower looking content in a cowboy hat and smoking a corncob pipe at his Montana cattle ranch. I. N. SPORN

As he considered the competing definitions, Compton "described [clinical] death as a continuing thing since tissue and organs live *after*[2] the brain dies." From this vantage point, Tucker's "brain was dead prior to the time he ran the EEG," and he had been artificially kept alive by a respirator. Dr. Hooshmand believed it was "very likely" that Bruce Tucker's condition was "irreversible" from the moment he was admitted to MCV.

Despite Hooshmand's testimony, Compton said he must deny Russell's effort to dismiss the evidence because Wilder had made what in legal terms is called a "prima facie" case. That is, his evidence was accepted as true until proven otherwise; Wilder could seek financial compensation for William Tucker under the Virginia Death by Wrongful Act statutes.

In another key part of his ruling, Compton noted that a major "function of the court" is "to determine the state of the law" with regard to applying "legal precedent and principle." So, despite Russell's efforts to widen the scope of what the jury could take up before reaching a verdict, Compton demurred. "This court adopts the legal concept of death and rejects the invitation offered by the defendants to employ a medical concept of neurological death in establishing a rule of law."

Compton's ruling did open the window a tiny bit for the defense, however. To date, he said, none of the applicable cases around the United States had ever involved organ transplants. Which was why he warned that "to employ a different standard in this field would create chaos in other fields of law." The reason, he explained, was that "certainly it cannot be successfully argued that there should be one concept of death which applies to one type of litigation, while an entirely different standard applies in other areas."

Seated behind Jack Russell's defense table, the Lowers and Hume heard Compton announce what sounded like bad news for their side. "The court adopts what it believes to be the legal definition of the word 'death' contemplated by the Virginia statute sued upon and will instruct the jury accordingly."

In another part of the ruling, Compton focused on Dr. Fatteh's actions in approving the transplant. The judge noted that Tucker "was unable to consent" for the loss of his heart and kidneys—a no-no under Virginia law where "a surgeon must obtain the consent of the patient, if he is competent to give it, or someone legally authorized to give it for him, before operating on him." Without such prior consent, Compton said, "A surgical operation on the body of a person is a technical battery or trespass. . . ."

Following this line of thinking, he wrote that the surgeons "acted upon Dr. Fatteh's permission, which he had authority under the law only if the body was unclaimed." It was up to the jury to decide how to apply the law "relating to the use of dead bodies," adding, "Not only does the body have to be a dead one, but it must be unclaimed."

David Plageman listened closely along with the six other jurors trying to follow the judge's legal road map. "In this case," Compton said, "the jury must determine whether proper care was used [in] . . . notifying or seeking Tucker's relatives to determine the fact whether the body was 'unclaimed' so as to authorize Fatteh to give permission and, in turn, the jury should consider whether the other defendants had proper authority to use the body 'for the advancement of medical science.'"

Russell also listened intently, looking for any openings that could help his defense. But the judge's face was hard to read. It didn't help that the old courtroom was starting to get stuffy.

"Bailiff," Compton said, "could you please turn up the air conditioner?"

Now it was Russell's turn to call on his team of experts. "Your Honor," he said, "the defense calls as its next witness Dr. Donald Becker."

Becker, chairman of MCV's neurosurgery department, was called to the stand in an effort to add to Hooshmand's testimony about brain death.

"The brain is responsible for consciousness," Becker said, "and for perceiving what is going on in the outside world. This is human life as we know it. It is centered in the brain."

In cross-examination, Wilder tried to turn one of the defense's key documents, the new Harvard report on brain death, against them. Addressing Becker, he said, "Isn't it true, sir, that the recent guidelines of the Harvard University Ad Hoc Committee on Brain Death, calls for *retesting* a patient twenty-four hours following any tests that [show] a patient's brain has 'died'?"

"Well . . . that may be true," Becker replied, "but although I agree with much of the Harvard report, that's one part of it I simply disagree with. They effectively lumped all cases of brain injury together when they did this. It was four years ago, and there's been a lot of research since then to refute some of their findings—and that twenty-four-hour rule, I would submit is one of them."

Judge Compton took note of the exchange:

Brain no longer functioning
no longer a living
human being

human life no longer
exists when in a coma
when brain cells are destroyed,
they can't recover
or reproduce themselves

no way that brain function
can be restored once
it is destroyed in
the central nervous
system—

Brain totally & irreversibly dead
At time of [Hooshmand's] exam—
Nothing that could have been done.

Then Dr. Israel Penn, a transplant surgeon from the University of Colorado, took the stand. He discussed the importance of transplant surgeons keeping an "arm's-length rule of thumb" on treating any possible organ donors.

He was followed by Dr. Edward Stinson of Stanford University, where he'd performed twenty-two heart transplants with Lower's old friend Norm Shumway.

Stinson reviewed the recent history of the changing medical protocols developed in response to the new technologies, surgeries, and drugs that keep patients alive; some of them were used on patients who had sustained severe head trauma like Bruce Tucker's. Compton wrote:

Generally accepted practice
As to when to stop
A respirator
With total loss of brain function . . .

Death if true in brain caused by lack of oxygen
Once death has occurred its irreversible.

The next morning—the trial's sixth day—Dr. William Collins, the former chairman of MCV's neurosurgery department and now a professor of neurology at Yale University, took the stand. After reviewing the medical charts on Bruce Tucker, the Yale professor said he agreed with the conclusions of his peers.

"Did the removal of the heart from the body of Bruce O. Tucker while it was still viable have any effect on the death of Bruce Tucker?" asked Russell.

"No, the patient was dead before that," Collins replied.

"Was there anything medically that could have been done to save the life of Bruce O. Tucker?"

"No," Collins said, "everything that could have been done had been done for him."

He shared some of the tough calls he'd made himself in recent years as he'd had to shut off mechanical respirators when there was nothing more to be done. But, he added, he "usually waited until the heart stopped beating (after the respirator was shut off) to pronounce them dead."

This remained a sensitive topic, Collins said. Despite the increasing acceptance of the concept of "brain death," the Yale professor said he still used the traditional definition of "cessation of heartbeat" to declare a patient's death. "I'm still aware we are in an evolving state on this."

Perhaps unwittingly, Collins had given Wilder an opening, since the MCV doctors had not waited for Bruce's heart to stop beating before they ended his life support.

Of those experts who came to Richmond to back the MCV surgeons, perhaps none had more of an impact on the case than Joseph Fletcher. Compton seemed particularly fascinated by the former social activist who'd become a leading expert in medical ethics. Compton started his notes on Fletcher's testimony by writing he was:

Concerned with human
Beings and death.

Fletcher didn't seem to harbor many doubts about mortality.

I don't take simplistic view that death is always the enemy.

Fletcher also didn't seem worried that science could be seen as the culprit in cases such as this. "Has modern medicine made the issue of understanding life and death more complicated?" Russell asked.

"No," Fletcher said, "if anything, modern neurological science has simplified it. We need no longer to refer to pulsation (and other vital signs) but we can go directly to the center of vitality, the brain."

Compton listened closely to the ethicist's thinking.[3] "We need no longer to infer that death occurred from the cessation of life," he said, because "life" itself "isn't a biological function." In fact, he asserted, "There is no way to define 'life.' "

Fletcher continued, "There is some disagreement as to the time of death and there are fairly simplistic opinions expressed outside of medical circles, but death occurs when brain function has ceased."

Drawing on his experience teaching medical students at the University of Virginia, he argued that "from an ethical and philosophical point of view and from the point of view of teaching medical ethics, a person is a 'rationality.' "

Fletcher even touched upon a topic that would one day become the third rail of American politics. "Laws don't assign personal status to fetal life. There must be some capacity to communicate, some sense of time, some memory and sense of the past. The parts of the anatomy determine whether there is a person and brain function is of first priority. . . .

"The heart of the matter lies in brain function and neurologic capacity," he asserted. "Once brain function is gone, then there is not a person. One who is being artificially supported is not a person when there has been complete loss permanently of brain function."

Fletcher ended with a comment that could have made William Tucker cringe. "The analogy was drawn to a chicken being killed or being beheaded. The brain is lopped off and the chicken rushes about with hyperactive energy and all other functions remain viable but the chicken is 'out of his mind.' "

On the next day—the trial's seventh—the small courtroom was packed. All thirty-nine seats were filled. Another dozen or so spectators were allowed to stand along the walls. The word on the street was this might be the final day, with closing arguments and a possible verdict that could set the course not only for MCV but also for organ transplants across the nation.

Dick and Anne Lower made their way to the front, smiling as casually as possible at friends and colleagues who came in a show of support. Though Dick tried to mask his anxiety, no one, not even Jack Russell, had been able to completely erase his conviction that Wilder's "murder" charge might be taken literally. David Hume, on the other hand, walked into the chambers laughing and joking as though he didn't have a care in the world.

Amid the crush of doctors, wives, and other supporters, a lone black man made his way into the courtroom. For William Tucker, the weeklong trial had taken its toll, emotionally and financially. To attend the proceedings, he'd had to close his business, costing him a sizable amount of income. But he'd wanted to hear for himself what these doctors had to say about how they'd treated Bruce. As he listened to them speak each day, though, he felt frustrated to hear the MCV doctors say that what happened to Bruce wasn't *their* fault. And then the big shots from other cities came in to say they probably would have done the same things to Bruce. Day after day, he sat at the table next to his lawyer, listening to the men in coats and ties who had more college degrees than he could ever imagine. All William wanted to know was what happened to his brother. For all their talk about life and death, these learned men never told him they were sorry for what happened to Bruce.

The final defense witness was Dr. William Sweet, chief of neurology at Massachusetts General Hospital in Boston. He also was a member of the prestigious Harvard Medical School Ad Hoc Committee on Brain Death. "Dr. Sweet said he examined Tucker's charts and records and had concluded that Tucker died by the time a neurologist examined him several hours before the transplant operation."[4]

There was more talk of "no blood flowing " in the vessels behind Bruce's eyes and how this had been an accepted criterion for pronouncing death for many decades. Once again, there were no words of consolation or regret about what had happened. Still worse for William Tucker and Doug Wilder was a bombshell dropped by Judge Compton. Only the day before, he had ruled that he would stick with the traditional definition of death under Virginia law. This had been a favorable sign for the plaintiffs, who could seek damages for how this law was broken.

But on the last day of the trial, Judge Compton made a surprising reversal. This came in the form of new instructions for the jury to follow as they deliberated to reach a verdict. One instruction in particular showed the impact the outside experts had made on Compton's thinking.

"The court instructs the jury that you shall determine the time of death in this case by using the following definition of the nature of death. *Death is a cessation of life. It is the ceasing to exist....*"[5]

After ticking off the traditional signs of death—no circulation, pulse, or breathing—he dropped in the new definition that Jack Russell had been advocating:

"... the time of complete and irreversible loss of all function of the brain, and, whether or not the aforesaid functions were spontaneous or were being maintained artificially or mechanically."

As soon as he heard the words "loss of all function of the brain," Russell knew the legal grounds of the case had shifted his way. His clients knew it, too.

"The words sank into Dick Lower's own brain," wrote biographer McRae. "He looked straight ahead but, on the inside, he was doing a little cartwheel...." He was feeling like "a kid again"—the weight of the past few years starting to lift. "Compton's implicit advice to the jury was plain: they should exonerate Richard Lower."[6]

To the spectators in the gallery, though, the outcome of the case probably still seemed uncertain. In another key instruction to the jury, Compton said that if they believed "from a preponderance of the evidence" that Tucker wasn't dead when the surgeons began removing his heart, and that taking the heart was the main cause of his death, they should return a verdict against the surgeons responsible for that part of the operation, Hume and Sewell.

To reach a verdict against the two other doctors looking on—Lower and Fatteh—Compton told the jury they must find "by clear and convincing evidence" that they had pursued, with intent, a common plan to commit a wrongful act to remove Tucker's heart *before*[7] he died.

With the jury primed to deliberate, Compton called for closing arguments. Wilder was up first. He started by reviewing the events on the eleventh floor of MCV hospital four years earlier. The mechanical respirator keeping Bruce Tucker alive should have stayed on, he said, at least until Bruce's brother, mother, son, and other relatives had a chance to say their goodbyes. But the doctors pulled the plug, Wilder alleged, because they wanted to take one man's heart in order to give it to another. You've heard these surgeons trying to distance themselves from Bruce, but they had every motive and opportunity to take his life-giving organ, he said.

Then Wilder took aim with the full-throated force of his rhetorical firepower. "The machine was cut off because he was unfortunate enough to come into the hospital at a time when a heart was needed!" he thundered.

"Now, you heard Mr. Russell describe these esteemed surgeons as men of science, dedicated to prolonging life. But the time is not too far from us when men of science made lampshades of human skin!"

There were audible gasps among the spectators. Wilder, undeterred, continued to compare Lower and Hume with the medical monsters of the Third Reich. "Men of science," he said, had devised ways of shortening human life by building gas chambers in Nazi Germany.

Wilder's shocking point was plain: *Don't let our own "men of science" make the same mistakes in modern-day Richmond, Virginia. They should pay for causing the Tuckers such suffering and grief.*

When Jack Russell stood to offer his rebuttal, he began turning down the emotional thermostat. Standing before the seven men in the jury box, he asked them to focus on "only one question" when they made their deliberations on the verdict: "Was Bruce O. Tucker dead at the time when surgeons removed his heart?"

He appealed to their sense of reason and justice, asking them to avoid getting sidetracked by emotion.

"All other issues are purely collateral," Russell said. "All the other matters are nothing but red herrings, often brought in to distract you from the main issue."

He also reminded them of the wider implications of their verdict. "A decision that Bruce O. Tucker was not dead before the heart was removed would put a stop to the transplant operations because viable organs are needed" to keep them going around the United States. A ruling against the MCV surgeons would be a ruling against medical progress, Russell said. People would die.

★ ★ ★

Back in the jury room, the seven men left with deciding these weighty issues began by taking up Judge Compton's new, open-ended instruction. Allowing the concept of brain death to enter into their deliberations changed everything. The jury already had discussed brain death "pretty early" in the trial, according to Plageman. But until Judge Compton gave them the green light to include the relatively new concept in their deliberations, the jurors thought they could only consider the older definition of dying in Virginia. As they began deliberating, the jurors agreed that the all-star team of doctors and ethicists had persuaded them that Virginia law was outdated. This made it fairly easy to reach a verdict favorable to the three surgeons—Lower, Hume, and Sewell—according to Plageman.

Still, there was a lingering sense that Doug Wilder was right about one thing: William Tucker and his family deserved *something* for their ordeal at the hands of MCV. "That was *negligence*," Plageman said years later.[8] Most of the jurors blamed the assistant medical examiner, Fatteh, who'd been singled out by Judge Compton. "All of us agreed that there was negligence there," Plageman said. "So the foreman, Mr. Tompkins, said, 'Let's go back in and get clear with Judge Compton about this.'"

They returned to the courtroom to pose their question. As the jury filed back in, Compton felt a special appreciation for the thoughtful and diligent way these men had conducted themselves during what had been a challenging and highly technical case. They had digested a steady, sometimes arcane, diet of facts and perspectives from many different sources—medical, legal, and even philosophical. In many ways, they'd taken a weeklong crash course. Now they were facing a tough final exam.

"Judge, we got a question to ask you," Tompkins said. "To what degree and to what extent can we hold Dr. Fatteh and the hospital responsible for this—as we perceive it . . . this possible negligence on their part?"

Compton listened carefully and took their point. But he quickly informed them that he'd already ruled that the statute of limitations for negligence had expired after one year; that's why he'd thrown out the part of Wilder's initial suit seeking $900,000 in damages. The jurors were crestfallen. Because of the law, they couldn't award the Tuckers any money to compensate them for their pain and suffering.

Returning to the jury room, the seven men knew their work was done. With no way to penalize the junior medical examiner or the hospital, they were left to reach a verdict that was favorable not only to the surgeons, but also to Fatteh and the Medical College of Virginia.

"I had the feeling—and I think that was the feeling within the jury, that, you know, that's really not justice," Plageman recalled. "The hospital should have been responsible—should have done a better job than that."

Early in the case, he noticed how "the medical examiner had a real problem" with the rush to remove Bruce's heart. Dr. Fatteh should have slowed things down because he was the gatekeeper in the approval process. Instead, Plageman said, "Fatteh was the guy who said, 'Do it!'"[9]

Without the judge's ruling on emotional distress and negligence, the juror added, "MCV would have to come up with a lot of money."

After less than an hour of deliberations, Judge Compton asked, "Have you reached a verdict?"

"We have, Your Honor," replied foreman Tompkins.

William Tucker leaned forward, gripping the table. Anne Lower squeezed Dick's hand. Hume leaned in, too, awaiting his fate.

"Bailiff, would you please read the verdict?"

Taking a single sheet of notebook paper, he read aloud, " 'We, the jury, on the issue joined, find for the defendants.' "

A collective sigh of relief could be heard behind Jack Russell and the defense team. At the plaintiff's table, William Tucker shook his head.

With a bang of his gavel, Compton declared, "Court is adjourned."

As the doctors thanked their defense team, Wilder tucked his legal pads and papers into his briefcase. Then he followed William Tucker on his crutches slowly negotiating the two flights of stairs down to the lobby. Emerging in the late-spring day, sunlight splashed in their faces. The sweet smell of budding flowers filled the air.

But this moment was anything but sweet as they faced a pack of reporters waiting outside. "It's awfully difficult to fly in the face of the system," Wilder told them. "Doctors are presumed to be doers of good and people picture their white coats with no potential for wrong."[10]

Squelching his anger, he proclaimed that "medical history is replete with instances of malpractice, though the proof required is so often impossible to come by. The closed fraternity rules out any exposure of any of its flanks."

Though Wilder was simmering inside, it would take more than four decades for him to admit his true feelings. At the time, Wilder and co-counsel, Harrison Bruce, who joined the impromptu press conference, both sounded like good sports. This came through in the next day's *Times-Dispatch*. "Wilder said he wanted to indicate that neither he, his associate in the case, Harrison Bruce Jr., or William Tucker did not highly respect the medical profession."[11]

Wilder insisted, "We have not sought to demean men of science and the medical profession, but to portray what is and what should be."[12] He announced plans to appeal the verdict to the Virginia Supreme Court.

Harrison Bruce added, "Even if we didn't accomplish anything from a financial standpoint, we have set some guidelines for future medical conduct and I'm quite sure this type of conduct wouldn't happen again."

Two years earlier, Wilder had made his sweeping assertions about how the transplant surgeons had "embarked upon a systematic and nefarious scheme to [excise] Bruce O. Tucker's heart from his body." Bruce Tucker, he alleged, "was mutilated, cut, and disfigured" with the approval granted by Fatteh. This, he charged, had deprived William E. Tucker "of making an informed consent" about the treatment of his brother.

But now Wilder's colleague downplayed any perceived insults or disrespect directed toward the MCV surgeons. "We never questioned ability or professional standards," Harrison Bruce said. "But the manner in which Bruce Tucker's case was handled did not, in my opinion, come up to the type of conduct you would expect."

Hume later stopped by the press conference to comment. "I think this is an issue that had to be decided," he said, "and I think it will have an influence on the medical community for a long time to come."[13]

Lower, for his part, escorted Anne to their car, then walked back to MCV. Safely in his office, he called Norm Shumway at Stanford to tell him the good news.[14] Dick was feeling "elation, absolute elation," Anne observed later.

That night, they stayed home with the kids. "We had no time to have a party," Anne said. "That wasn't Dick's nature. He wasn't a party animal." Besides, she added, he needed to get some rest. A heart operation was scheduled for the next morning.[15]

Yet the next day, Lower found time to grant an interview to the

Times-Dispatch.[16] He sounded much more relaxed as he broke his long silence with the newspaper. The headline of Bev Orndorff's article reflected a newfound belief in the legal system:

Doctor Finds Trial Reinforces His Faith

After praising the "laymen's judgment" of the jury, Lower said, "I hope I would feel the same way if the jury had come to a different conclusion—although (he added with a slight laugh) I might not have."

The story circled back to better days at MCV. This included the fact that Louis B. Russell, recipient of the second of the five hearts transplanted by Lower at that point in time, was now the world's longest-surviving heart transplant patient.

Following that morning's surgery, Lower was still wearing "a green surgical scrub suit and cap," Orndorff wrote. The usually reserved doctor was in a rare, expansive mood. He talked about how one of his sons had been doing research for his high school debate team. The main topic was "America's jurisprudence system and whether it—including the jury system—should be changed," Lower said.

Before his trial, he continued, "I used to think the jury system was outmoded and came into being at a time when there was conflict between classes of people and it (the jury system) was established to prevent oppression of one class by another."

As Judge Compton urged the jury to exercise its own judgment, Lower conceded, he wasn't sure it was up to the challenge, especially with so many "technical questions that have to be understood."

But now he could see he was wrong, Lower said. He told Orndorff that he'd been moving toward this conclusion "regardless of the way this . . . decision came out." He called the jurors "thoughtful people" with "reasonable" educations. "They really were equipped to deal with questions like this. They are not beyond the comprehension of what we regard as laymen."

The trial, he said, "renewed my faith" in the legal system by demonstrating that "thoughtful people can come to grips with questions like this (concerning the determination of death) and arrive at thoughtful conclusions—not to agree or disagree with me, but to come to thoughtful conclusions."

As to the concept of being judged by a jury of your peers, he said, "I think, in essence, we are peers in that sense."[17]

The interview ended the long news blackout MCV's surgery department had imposed on Orndorff after he supposedly tried to "humanize" Bruce Tucker. Now that he was talking again, Dick Lower sounded like a fervent advocate of the First Amendment. The news coverage, he now believed, had sparked "very thoughtful" questions about difficult issues of life and death.

"It helped people to know about these questions; that they are not totally abstract questions, but are related to the everyday practice of medicine, and that they influence the way in which medicine is practiced."

As for the future of heart transplants, the jury—in another sense— was still out. His favorable verdict, he said, "doesn't represent any final legal authority." Rather, Lower said it showed "that in a court of law, this question was wrestled with and a decision was rendered more in keeping with our body of knowledge." The jury had done well in grappling with vexing "questions about the time of death, and diagnosis of death."

Lower ended by saying that it was "helpful to know that the view of the profession was upheld in this circumstance, and this will permit transplantation to continue."[18]

Even as Lower expressed his admiration for the legal system, William Tucker's attorney kept his own feelings to himself. It was a position he maintained for more than four decades. When Governor Wilder was first approached in 2017 to discuss the trial, he rejected several offers to discuss the story of Bruce Tucker, William Tucker, and the heart transplant trial. He had briefly touched on the saga in in his 2015 memoir,

Son of Virginia, such as how MCV, after failing to find Tucker's relatives, "went ahead with the transplant of Bruce's organs, making the assumption that Bruce was a derelict."[19]

Wilder's memoir also raised the issues of class and race that he'd navigated before the all-white jury and judge in 1972. And he stressed that the Tuckers were hardworking citizens of Richmond, not "derelicts." Wilder observed, "His brother William was known in the community, and he had a shoe repair shop right down the street from the hospital. The racial component was also clear. Bruce's race and socioeconomic circumstances made him vulnerable for organ removal, demonstrated by the simple fact that doctors declared him derelict without making much of an effort to find his family."[20]

Wilder sought to find something positive in the verdict. For example, he wrote that "prior to the Tucker trial, the predominant view of death was a cessation of all vital organs." The jury's verdict prompted the Virginia General Assembly to adopt a new law to help others avoid the sad fate of the Tuckers. "Even so," Wilder wrote, "poor old Bruce Tucker and his brother William got a raw deal. But they rewrote a new definition of death for the nation."[21]

Beyond his written account, Wilder hesitated to discuss the case, perhaps because it might open old wounds. He agreed to an interview for this book only after it was made clear that its intent was to delve deeper into Bruce Tucker's story.[22]

Looking dapper in a dark tweed coat and brown slacks, with his trademark cowboy boots, Wilder appeared relaxed. The self-described "son of Virginia" exuded Southern charm, humor, and hospitality. But as he began revisiting the events of 1968 to 1973, it quickly became evident that even after nearly a half century the trial's outcome still rankled him. Old suspicions smoldered like campfire coals, ready to burst into flame.

As he recalled Hume's first international transplantation conference in Richmond, for example, Wilder remarked on the advantage this gave

MCV's defense team. "It was interesting how they set the trial for the case . . . they were having a convention of neurosurgeons worldwide at MCV, and *everybody* was there. . . . And so it was convenient they set the trial for that time."

But it wasn't just the influence of "all these people who came in from around the world to testify" that rankled him the most. It was Christian Compton's last-minute change of the jury instructions.

Wilder explained why the Establishment wanted to protect the stellar reputation of the Medical College of Virginia—and by extension, of the entire Commonwealth. MCV was too important to the power brokers in government, medicine, and business to lose a lawsuit that cast into doubt the triumph of the 1968 heart transplant.[23]

"Do you understand what this does to the system?" he asked rhetorically.

Harkening back to the days of the grave robbers, body snatchers, and "night doctors," Wilder began connecting the dots of Virginia's often hidden history. William Tucker's lawsuit, he believed, had inadvertently disturbed the old ghosts of the medical school's past. This had a ripple effect that exposed parts of its troubling present.

"Not only would they be accused of doing what had been the thing feared through rumors" for many years, he said, "but look what it does as far as race is concerned—look what it does as far as class!"

Wilder remained convinced that the law on the books should have guided the jury's verdict, not the more expansive interpretation allowed by Compton.

After more than four decades, Wilder maintained that when Bruce Tucker was rushed by ambulance to MCV, it was "a godsend" to Hume to fulfill his dream of finally putting Lower's skills to their best use. He alone could put MCV on the heart transplant map. Thus, in Wilder's view, the doctors "were ready to pounce."

Even after all he'd accomplished over his long career—including his groundbreaking election in 1989 as America's first-elected African

American governor—the trial's outcome and Bruce Tucker's treatment still bothered him.

"I don't know—I'm not a surgeon but when you see modern science . . . and [something] couldn't have been done for him?" he asked. "And there was nothing wrong with his heart," repeating, "nothing wrong with it!"

Despite his initial pledge to appeal the verdict, this proved to be impractical. William Tucker "didn't have the resources to pursue it, and I didn't [either]. I carried it as far as I could carry it."

His second lawsuit in federal court floundered and was ultimately dismissed by US district judge Robert R. Merhige Jr.—himself a controversial figure for enforcing the federal government's orders to integrate Richmond schools by busing students.[24]

Beyond the courtroom drama, the medical science, and Wilder's suspicions of undue influence, one image stood out more than any other: the look on William Tucker's face when the verdict was read on May 25, 1972.

"He was very bitter about it," Wilder recalled with a trace of sadness. "He had a deep, resonant voice, and he really felt it was racial discrimination, and he didn't hide it at all."

CHAPTER TWENTY-TWO

The Unresolved Case of Bruce Tucker

IN THE MONTHS AFTER the trial, a number of its key players were tapped by lawmakers to try to bring Virginia's time-of-death law up-to-date with the more nuanced views that had helped sway the jury. These advisers included David Hume, who was approached by one of the young lawyers from the attorney general's office on the MCV defense team, Bill Crews. "Dave Hume was quite a character," he said, recollecting the period in early 1973 when a new law was being drafted for consideration by the general assembly. "I asked him to review it and call me and tell me what you think."

It didn't take long for the outspoken surgeon to reply. "Bill," Hume said, "I've reviewed that, and think I can make it a lot shorter."

Playing along, Crews asked him how. Simple, Hume replied, presumably with tongue firmly in cheek. "A person's dead when a doctor says they're dead."

"Dave," Crews said, "we've been there and that's not going to work."

Indeed, it would take lots of heavy lifting to move the needle on what had been a fairly dormant law on the books in Virginia. This involved collaborative work between lawyers and doctors on both sides of the issue—including Doug Wilder and Judge Compton.

The collaboration paid off, though, when Virginia became one of only three states in the nation to embrace new legal statutes that would, in Compton's words, "establish criteria for determining the time of death of a human being." At the time, he added, "This type of legislation has been called unique in the common law world"[1] with only Kansas and Maryland making similar changes to their state codes.

In a 1974 article written for his alma mater—Washington and Lee University Law School—Compton noted that Virginia legislators had managed to avoid some of the "severe criticism" heard in the Kansas legislature when it took up the sensitive issue of brain death. Remarkably, this unfolded at a time when states were debating the divisive issue of abortion before the 1973 US Supreme Court decision in *Roe v. Wade*.

Considering the toxic track record of that issue, Compton's upbeat account of the relatively calm waters that greeted Virginia's legislative new legal definition of death seems all the more remarkable.

"The statute began its legislative course in the house of delegates of the general assembly about eight months after the judgment in Tucker," he wrote. "Its patron was a surgeon whose legislative district included the City of Richmond." That surgeon, Dr. William F. Reid, was the first African American elected to the Virginia General Assembly since Reconstruction.[2] His 1967 election to the house of delegates was followed by Doug Wilder's successful run for the state senate in 1969. Though Compton didn't note it, Delegate Reid's sponsorship of the bill no doubt helped soothe any lingering objections from black constituents who'd heard about Bruce Tucker's tragic fate, or anyone who might recall Senator Wilder's warnings about MCV's dark legacy of grave-robbing "night doctors."

Despite the potential for controversy, the new section of the Code of Virginia "related to definition of death" moved calmly toward passage by the legislature. This included two public hearings at the committee level where "no one spoke in opposition to the bill at either hearing."[3]

Behind the scenes, there was some grumbling by Old Dominion physicians who opposed *any* kind of legislative remedy to the growing problem—preferring instead to make determining time-of-death solely a matter "to be decided by the medical profession."[4]

The Virginia doctors weren't alone in their reluctance to cede their authority, which was steeped in the traditional reliance on the "gods in white coats" that even their defenders sometimes joked about. Despite "a crucial need for more definitive general rules to eliminate existing uncertainty in the determination of the time of death," Compton wrote, "other responsible voices within the medical profession advocate a prolongation of this uncertainty, but for slightly different reasons." Among them was Dr. Henry K. Beecher, chairman of the Harvard Ad Hoc Committee, who felt more research was needed before establishing a new definition. Saying it was "too soon for legislation," Beecher advised his colleagues "to risk their necks, go ahead and carry out what they believe to be right."[5]

Nonetheless, Virginia's measure passed in February 1973 without a single dissenting vote—93–0 in the house of delegates and 39–0 in the senate. It was signed into law by Republican governor Linwood Holton.

The measure started by including the traditional line of thought. "A person shall be medically and legally dead if . . . in the opinion of a physician . . . based on the ordinary standards of medical practice, there is the absence of spontaneous respiratory and spontaneous cardiac function . . ."

Then it incorporated the more contemporary viewpoint that "[when] . . . in the opinion of a consulting physician, who shall be duly licensed and a specialist in the field of neurology, neurosurgery, or electroencephalography, when . . . there is *the absence of spontaneous brain functions*[6] and spontaneous respiratory . . . and considering the absence of the aforesaid brain functions . . . further attempts at resuscitation or continued supportive maintenance would not be successful in restoring such spontaneous functions and . . . *death shall be deemed to have occurred at the time when these conditions first coincide.*"

Now Virginia physicians could—in effect—choose either definition when certifying a patient's death "for all purposes in the Commonwealth, including the trial of civil and criminal cases."

Compton, while acknowledging the law was imperfect and would need updating, sounded relieved that the state had decreed that it would not try to resolve such Solomon-like disputes on a "case to case basis." So, he concluded, moving into a more informed future, "It is essential that there be a continuance of the present trend of telling the time of human death by statute."[7]

To Wilder, the passage of the 1973 law represented a form of redemption, not only for him, but also for the memory of Bruce Tucker and his family. "I think the underlying theme of the Tucker case [is] that it ultimately led to a redefinition of death in America—brain death supplanting the cessation of all vital organs."[8]

And yet, Wilder added, "It doesn't change the fact that when they took his heart from him he was *not* dead according to the law. So they broke the law and never would admit it, and that's what bothered me more than anything else."

★ ★ ★

The impact of Bruce Tucker's byzantine case is still debated among medical ethicists, especially those who specialize in organ transplantation. And while Governor Wilder and others view this as settled law, the case of Bruce Tucker remains an open book. Two leading transplant ethicists—Robert M. Veatch and Lainie F. Ross—explain why:

"The Tucker case was to become the first widely publicized controversy about the question of when a person is dead," they write in their 2015 book, *Transplantation Ethics*. "Many interpret the case as establishing a brain-oriented definition of death for the state of Virginia, but it could equally be viewed as the first case where a ventilator is discon-nected for the purpose of causing the death of the patient, by traditional heart criteria, in order to procure organs for transplant."[9]

Noting the racial overtones of the case, the ethicists comment, "The doctors were exonerated, but it is unclear whether the court held that the doctors had the authority to turn off the ventilator on a still-living patient in these circumstances or whether it held that Tucker was already dead based on brain criteria."

Veatch and Ross—who've served multiple terms on the ethics com-mittee of the national United Network for Organ Sharing—concede the shifting, conflicting interpretations of the law that the MCV surgeons tried to negotiate. Still, they conclude, "The case leaves many questions unanswered in addition to the issues related to the lack of consent for procuring organs. Why, for example, should a single, flat-line EEG read-ing be taken as evidence of the irreversible loss of brain function?"[10]

Noting the outsize influence of the 1968 Harvard Ad Hoc Commit-tee on the Richmond jury's final verdict, they point out that "a single flat EEG reading would not be sufficient by Harvard committee standards or any set of criteria published since then."

And, they ask, "If Tucker was believed to be dead based on brain function loss sometime before 3:30 p.m., why was the respirator turned off at that time? Unless one feels a need to pronounce death based on heart function loss, it makes no sense to turn off the respirator on a man who is a candidate for organ procurement. Based on brain function loss, he would already be dead before the respirator was stopped."[11]

With so many unresolved questions, the case of Bruce Tucker "shows how confusing the early days were for pronouncing the deaths of severely brain-injured patients who were potential sources of organs for transplant."

The drama that unfolded at the Medical College of Virginia during the heyday of heart transplants points to the limits of human behavior and understanding in something as personal and delicate as a human life. Or as the ethicists put it, "It reveals that we needed to do a great deal of work to understand precisely what it means to be dead in a context where someone envisions medical use of a body and when that use is only acceptable once the individual is considered deceased."[12]

As they explore the latest terminology and thinking about the difficult subject of "death" in the twenty-first century—a big tent with a variety of philosophical and theological stakes and stakeholders—the ethicists caution that no amount of scientific progress will ever make this easy.

"The task of defining death is not a trivial exercise in coining the meaning of a term," they write. "Rather, it is an attempt to reach an understanding of the philosophical nature of the human being and what it is that is essentially significant to humans that is lost at the time of death."[13]

So even after nearly five decades, the hard questions that confronted Hume, Lower, the rest of their transplant team in late May 1968, the decisions made by the harried assistant medical examiner, and the shock and grief that gripped William Tucker, his mother, and the entire family—still haunt the medical college

"The public policy discussion of how to define death began in earnest in the late 1960s, not long before surgeons were confronted by Bruce Tucker's case," the ethicists write. "Now, a half century later, we are still unclear about exactly what it means to be dead."[14]

Yet it's incumbent upon the living to keep trying.

CHAPTER TWENTY-THREE

Down in the Well

Tuesday, April 26, 1994
Virginia Commonwealth University

CHRIS EGGHART WAS WORKING late at VCU's Archaeological Research Center, trying to finish a report before the day was over. He was surprised when the phone rang, but since he was the only one in the office, he had to answer.

The caller seemed highly agitated, so much so that it was hard to even make out his name—Captain *Columbo*? . . . Is this a joke? His Jersey accent and rapid-fire speech made him hard to follow. Apparently, earlier that day there'd been some sort of strange discovery over on the medical school campus. It had something to do with "bones . . . skulls . . . medical examiner . . . construction workers . . ." Beyond that it was hard for the young archaeologist to understand exactly what this "Captain Columbo" was talking about.

As Egghart tried to process the urgent information, including the captain's actual name, all he knew for sure was that the caller was distressed and had contacted the university's archaeology office because it was the place to go when it came to handling skulls and bones.

"The medical examiner has cleared it as a crime scene," the captain offered.

"Can you meet me on site?" Egghart asked, trying to picture the scene.

"Yes," the voice on the other end replied.

"Good, I'll be right over."

Egghart's office was full of boxes, maps, and random artifacts. He grabbed a hard hat, camera, and a notebook. Then he took his gear outside and stowed it in the center's only available vehicle—a beat-up 1972 Dodge van that bore the faded markings of its original owner, the C&P Telephone Co. He set out along the commercial district of the ever-expanding campus to the medical school about a mile away.

He found a parking spot on East Marshall Street beside the Egyptian Building where an adjacent construction site had been cordoned off with a chain-link fence. Two policemen—one uniformed, one plainclothes— were waiting near the entrance. The older of the pair—a short, dark-haired man in a brown polyester suit—waved Egghart over. As he neared them, he noticed how the plainclothes officer had pulled back his coat, displaying the grip of his 10 mm Smith & Wesson revolver in a shoulder holster that nudged his belly.

Whether it was his name or his accent, something about VCU's top cop reminded Egghart of the detective played by Peter Falk in *Columbo*. He felt like he was in a scene from the show, just playing along.

"What do you got for me, Captain . . . ?"

"Captain Palumbo," said the older cop with the revolver. VCU police chief C. J. Palumbo clearly wasn't playing around and beckoned the archaeologist to follow him. Egghart's eyes widened as he took in the depth and magnitude of the medical school site that stretched for half a block below them. Huge backhoes, bulldozers, and other excavation equipment had scooped out a yawning pit that began near the steps of the exotic Egyptian Building with its flared "battered walls"— thinner at the top than the bottom, making it look larger than its four stories. Other historic buildings were nearby, he noticed, including the Monumental Church, which had risen from the ashes of the 1811 fire

at the Richmond Theatre. It took place shortly after one of the last per-
formances of Edgar Allan Poe's biological mother, Eliza, before she
succumbed to tuberculosis. History—like the wooden and metal
shards being unearthed by the earth-moving equipment—seemed to
ooze out of this prime real estate. Egghart had a slightly dizzying sense
about the unfolding view. It was hard to imagine what might be lurking
below.

Chief Palumbo led him down a zigzag earth-and-gravel ramp extend-
ing about twenty-five feet below street level. He stopped in front of the
strange find—a mucky pit surrounded by a curving assortment of crum-
bling orange bricks. Egghart immediately recognized the arc-shaped feature as the only archaeological remains one might expect so deep in the
ground: an abandoned well.

Palumbo shifted from one foot to another. He cleared his throat.
"What do you make of it, Egghart?"

"Well, Chief, " he replied, "you have a well here, that's for sure—and
it's very old. These bricks were handmade. Nothing like we see today."

"So . . . what about that . . . ?" Chief Palumbo said, indicating a skull
with one eye orbit intact. Though he was packing heat, he sounded a little nervous.

"Hmm," Egghart said, pondering something else in the antique
well—a large bone, possibly a femur, poking out of the mud. As a young
archaeologist, Egghart had seen plenty of burial sites. They were part
and parcel of what kept VCU's small archaeology center afloat. It survived on project funding from the state highway department and devel-
opers who couldn't build until their sites had been properly cleared of
historical relics, including human remains.

This find, though, was in a league of its own. When no longer in active use, old wells had often been used for disposal of trash and household waste. Over time, the well shaft would fill up, leaving behind a
stratified material record that could be a gold mine for researchers. The
organic preservation that's typically found in wells only adds to their

scientific value—which was why Egghart was intrigued by the sight of the brick-lined shaft.

And yet, a well filled with human remains was more than he'd bargained for. *What's going on here?* he asked himself. This much was clear: the jumble of bones meant that there were multiple remains. *Was this a mass grave? For whom? Massacre victims? Civil War dead? The plague?* The possibilities were as mystifying as they were intriguing.

Egghart began snapping pictures on his sturdy Nikon FE2, partly to stave off his own uneasiness.

"Let me get started," he told the chief. "This could take a while."

Chief Palumbo nodded. "I'll keep an officer posted," he said, pointing to the entrance. "I'm outta here."

Egghart started turning over the dark, wet muck. He carefully exposed more skeletal material while looking for any artifacts that might provide clues about when the first bodies had been dropped into the well. Several more long bones appeared; the top of another cranium; a disarticulated mandible with worn or missing teeth.[1] Personal items were also in the mix—shoes, metal instruments, shards of glass, ceramic jars.

The archaeologist also recognized another potential clue to the unfolding mystery: a spongy substance that stuck to the bricks like dark glue. This "muck and yuck," as he described it later, contained patches of human skin and hair.

"We had no idea how much further it went below the remaining brick," he recalled.[2] But the excavation was deep enough to make it evident that there was more where this came from. The only question was how much more?

As shadows started creeping across the pit beyond the Egyptian Building, Egghart knew he had to wrap up. After snapping a few more pictures, he reluctantly grabbed his gear and trudged back up the ramp. Who had been so callously left behind, he wondered, and why?

Over the next couple of days, the archaeologists and staff members worked hard to prepare the site for further study—starting by removing earth around the brick lining in search of the original "builder's trench" that might help them assign a date to its actual construction. By doing so, they exposed as much of the skeletal material as they could without moving it.

While the exact contents had yet to be determined, "It was clear we'd found an important archaeological site," recalled Daniel Mouer, who founded VCU's Archaeological Research Center in 1978. He knew they must follow Virginia's burial laws—including the violation of sepulcher statute—making it "a felony to remove human remains from a grave without a court order or appropriate permit."[3]

Mouer began working through the permitting process for the vulnerable site with the assistance of the state's Department of Historic Resources. He also began developing a research plan to conduct a proper investigation.

"Archaeology is all about context," Mouer later explained. When the construction workers unearthed the skulls, "the context was being totally destroyed." His goal was to halt construction until further notice—no matter the impact on the university's ambitious building plans. He knew this might take time, but it was the only way to do justice to a discovery that one of the nation's top forensic anthropologists[4]—Dr. Douglas W. Owsley of the Smithsonian's National Museum of Natural History—called "very exciting" with the potential of helping to "tell you about the history of medicine and the development of surgery."[5]

Over the next few days, Mouer and his team sought to "read the dirt," as they put it. It was how he'd handled scores of other historic preservation projects—burial sites, excavations, pits, hearths. "Whatever it is," he explained, "you have to be able to see it, clean it, photograph and map it. That's the first thing, and that's what we'd started doing" in the first few days after the eerie find. Their work posed a number of tough issues, such as the presence of actual human flesh. The skin was organic material preserved by its "anaerobic" setting—that is, the muck was undisturbed by oxygen. A well-known example of what archaeologists call "composted flesh" can be found in the bogs of England, where archaeologists have found late Stone Age bodies largely intact, along with their clothing.

As they kept scouring and mapping what became known as the East Marshall Street Well, the VCU archaeologists opened a window not only into medicine's past, but into the very heart of Virginia history. In its own way, the site tapped into the troubled waters of slavery that had poisoned the young nation and led to the Civil War. Some of the bodies may have been dropped into the well before the first shots were fired at Fort Sumter and Richmond became the capital of the Confederacy.

But such troubling questions about what Toni Morrison once called "the tenacity of racism"[6] would have to wait for another day and a more detailed analysis. Mouer and Egghart were on the front lines of science, reading the dirt and protecting the site's integrity. Though the top of the well had been smashed—exposing the skull and bones that had rattled the equipment operators—much of it was left unscathed. For a few days it was an archaeologist's dream. Then it became Mouer's worst nightmare.

The first signs of trouble came a few days after the start of their reclamation work. On Saturday morning, Mouer was called by a medical college administrator who informed him that he had until Monday—only two days hence—to wrap up their site work. In the meantime, the administrator said that nothing new should be done.[7]

The veteran archaeologist knew he should tread lightly as he was already on thin ice with the top of the university's leadership. His research center received little in the way of direct funding from VCU, relying on grants from other entities such as the state highway department. He was painfully aware of the fact that his tiny center was just a blip on the radar for the university's growth-minded leadership. At times, Mouer later recalled, the archaeology center had been a source of irritation for his bosses.[8]

He loved archaeology, which he'd studied after returning from a combat tour in Vietnam. Mouer became a free spirit, enjoying the art and music scene around VCU in the 1970s. By the time Captain Palumbo called his office, the archaeologist had already experienced run-ins with the university's leadership when historic sites got in the way of their ambitious growth plans. Such conflicts were probably inevitable given that the university's leader—President Eugene Trani—was determined to change VCU's reputation as a second-rate commuter school where kids came to dress in black, smoke dope, and major in art. Over his nearly twenty-year tenure, the former history professor would be credited for lifting VCU's academic standing by starting a College of Engineering, adding life sciences programs, helping start a Biotechnology Research Park, and spinning off the hospital to create a more effective VCU Health program.

By April 1994, Trani was only in his fourth year at the helm. There was much work to do to reach his overarching goal of raising VCU's state and national profile. Part of that drive was to expand the School of Medicine and add other research space with a spanking new $23.5 million Medical Sciences Building.

Like any developer eager to start a big project, Trani's patience had its limits, especially after he learned that a team of archaeologists, *his* archaeologists, were single-handedly holding up a major building project. The same striving for professional glory that had driven the medical school in the 1950s to recruit David Hume from Harvard and bring Richard Lower from Stanford in the 1960s was repeating itself.

That very week Trani had appeared on the front of the *Times-Dispatch* under the headline "MCV, Corporation discussing deal."[9] Time waits for no one these days, Trani said amid reports he was engaged in talks about a large-scale private-public venture with the large hospital corporation, HCA.

"MCV can't be an island in the future," Trani declared. "Joint ventures are the only way we're going to survive."

Given his striving for growth, Trani's mood couldn't have been helped by the sight of heavy equipment ground to a halt along with their idled operators. With the clock ticking, he knew the cost of his beloved project was rising by the day. Finally, Trani had seen enough.

Sunday, May 1, 1994

Chris Egghart had returned to work in the well over the weekend. His boss, Mouer, hadn't shared the disturbing news from the MCV administrator about the possible impending end to their site work. Though it was Sunday, Egghart wanted to keep marking key finds—no matter how difficult and gut-wrenching they might be. This was science and it really mattered. That is, until a figure appeared on the wooden rampart above.

Looking down at them was the unmistakable face of the university president, Eugene Trani. Though he was casually dressed in khakis and a short-sleeve shirt, the college president wasn't out for a Sunday stroll. He summoned Mouer up from the well with his index finger.

Grabbing a rag to clean his hands, Mouer glanced at his colleagues with the look of a kid getting called into the principal's office. He was in trouble again.

"Do you know who I am?" he asked the nervous archaeologist.

"Yes," Mouer replied, adjusting his hard hat. Deep in his memory, he could hear the staccato gunfire and deafening booms of enemy mortars as someone shouted, "Incoming!"

Flashing back on Vietnam made it hard to pay attention. "This is *not* going to be my problem," Trani ordered. "Get rid of this!"

They had until Monday, he said.

Mouer took a deep breath and stood by his president in the quiet broken only by the squishing of rubber boots below.

"So are we *clear* about this?" Trani said.

"Yes," Mouer said resignedly.

His mission completed, Trani did an about-face and walked away.

Mouer trudged down into the well to join his stunned and dismayed colleagues who found him "shaken."[10]

Despite his frayed nerves from the dressing-down, Mouer had the presence of mind to ask everyone to keep things quiet. So far they'd managed to keep a low profile, avoiding reporters and cameras so they could do their work discreetly. The less publicity the better, Mouer said. "We don't want Patricia Cornwell coming down and sniffing around" for new material, he added, alluding to the popular crime writer. Early in her career Cornwell had worked at the nearby office of the chief medical examiner Dr. Marcella Fierro. She had become the model for Cornwell's protagonist, Kay Scarpetta.

But while Scarpetta may have been able to work her way out of such a jam, there didn't seem to be any easy escape route for the overmatched VCU archaeologists.

"When the head of the university tells you to do something," Egghart explained later, "you have no choice."

The wheels were set in motion to restart the bulldozers and backhoes and continue carving out the base of the medical school masterpiece. Adding to the pain for the idealistic archaeologists was knowing how close they'd come to adding to the depth of knowledge about MCV's origin story—no matter how shocking or brutal it might be. Beyond that, the well held the potential to shed new light on life and death in antebellum Richmond. "We never did get a chance to do a proper excavation," Mouer said.[11]

The next day, Monday, they worked hard, combing through the backfill. The result was a pile of material that local magazine writer Tina Griego called "a macabre treasure hunt"—more skulls, bones, and other human remains interspersed with medical waste from the earliest days of the school.[12] The sight of more human remains spooked some of the nearby construction workers gazing into the pit. One man exclaimed in Spanish, "¡Mira! Mira!" ("Look! Look!")

As his devoted team tried to salvage what they could, Mouer tried to mask his disappointment. This was no way to treat an archaeological treasure, he felt, especially one where people had been treated like trash. "We lost a huge opportunity to recognize them as once-living persons," he said. "Human beings whose mortal remains ended up in the well."

Added Egghart: "And now it seemed their stories would end there, too."

Finally the order came: they had one more hour, then they must abandon the well site. Any remaining bones or relics would have to be sacrificed in the name of progress. No one knew exactly how much was left behind.

"We were told to leave it," Egghart recalled. "We're digging it, and we can see it in plain view. But we didn't remove it."

Then it was over. As soon as Mouer's team dejectedly abandoned the well, the diesel engines roared back to life. It didn't take long for the bulldozers to grade the remaining dirt into a flat surface, burying its secrets once again.

Some university officials sought to reassure them that they would preserve any human remains or relics left behind. But the archaeologists weren't so sure: heavy equipment was just as likely to crush anything below. Progress was no friend to history.

After the dust settled, the final tally of the recovered remains was put at fifty-three humans in all. The majority were adults older than fifteen, with an estimated nine children who were fourteen years of age or younger. There was one newborn identified on the basis of two tiny ribs. Most were thought to be African American: eighteen skulls could be definitely identified as having African American ancestry, with two consistent with European ancestry, according to the report prepared by Owsley at the Smithsonian.[13]

A separate report issued many years later by VCU shed more light on the historical origins of the remains in the well. In 1860, after a $30,000 appropriation by the legislature established MCV as a state-owned college, the medical school faculty had chosen to build a new

hospital. The new facility was favored over adding to the College Building (later renamed the Egyptian Building). The 1860 hospital construction, started on the eve of the Civil War, hit a number of early snags as
workers began digging a foundation near the College Building—a pre-
cursor to the aborted archaeological dig of 1994.[14]

The 1860 project "required the demolition of a stable and privies
located on the spot of the proposed hospital. Workers also had to con-
struct a culvert to facilitate drainage on a plot of land that was once bi-
sected by a stream." Among MCV's work-related bills at the time, two
were of particular interest: on October 20, 1860, the college paid a
worker $151.62 for "digging and bricking up sink [well] under col-
lege." A month after the old well was closed, the college dean's account
book recorded a transaction for "rope used in digging sink." By early
1861, another bill shows the purchase of "rope & wheel-wells for dissecting room." Altogether, "This evidence indicates that MCV sealed
one well and dug another during the construction of the hospital."[15]

In the report, VCU's medical archivist Jodi L. Koste notes that while
it's "difficult to prove conclusively that the well closed in October of
1860 was the same one uncovered" in 1994, the evidence "would suggest that it was sealed prior to the opening of the new clinical facility" in
April 1861.

Since that time, Koste writes, "The college has undertaken five
major building projects" on the same grounds. While most of the other
expansions didn't turn up such "bone pits," the record shows "workers
did uncover a large refuse well under the basement of the Egyptian
Building" during its 1939 renovation. A former administrator "confirmed that this well has once been used to dispose of cadavers and other
anatomical specimens in the late 19th and 20th centuries."[16]

Taken together, these facts suggest that "the well discovered in April
of 1994 may well have been used by various demonstrators of anatomy
to dispose of human remains" between 1848 and 1860.

The relics and remains that Mouer and his team managed to recover and document were sent to the Smithsonian in Washington, DC. The cache included "animal bones, building debris, broken ceramics, leather, fabric, medical implements, and a large quantity of human bones," Owsley reported. In all, "423 artifacts and faunal [animal] bones were non-systematically retrieved by VCU archaeologists."[17]

Owsley and his team of forensic anthropologists conducted a detailed analysis as they sought to understand how the bodies were used to teach anatomy in the early days of the Medical College of Virginia. As they studied the remains, they made a number of interesting discoveries, such as a man who suffered a small-bore gunshot wound which ultimately proved fatal; his skull showed signs of suffering "endocranial pressure from swelling."[18]

According to the Smithsonian study, "strong African affinities are expressed" in the analysis of the shape of the skulls, "while others more closely align with American Blacks." Owsley concluded that these "VCU crania with African ancestry" indicate these were the remains of people born in Africa as well as in the United States. "These results reveal a potential biological means of evaluating nineteenth-century diversity, more specifically the diversity of the population subject to use in medical teaching and training."[19]

The forensic anthropologist also noted that "the remains from the VCU well represent a compelling narrative of the nineteenth-century South. As Americans continue to move toward eliminating the disparities in society, it is important to document and understand this tangible evidence of the past. In doing so, history can be made complete where written records fail to fully inform."[20]

★   ★   ★

After more than twenty years, the issue of what was found in the well—along with what was left behind—began to resurface. A new generation of VCU leaders and professors were joined by interested citizens as they posed tough questions about the earlier treatment of the window into the past. In 2016, the university formed a study group that included "surrogate descendants" of those discarded and forgotten Africans and African Americans. The "Descendant Community" group quickly began to advocate ways to study and memorialize the people who'd been exploited, and ultimately dumped, by MCV in years past.

Among the first findings of what became the Family Representative Council of the East Marshall Street Well Project was an admission of errors made in 1994, as they described the "dehumanizing practices surrounding the well during the 19th century and the 1990s."[21]

Using New York City's African Burial Ground National Monument as a model, the Richmond group envisioned taking a similarly careful and comprehensive approach to VCU's site. They suggested conducting more research to understand the condition of the remains; genetic testing to help establish ancestry ties; and the creation of memorial sites around the area of the Hermes A. Kontos Medical Sciences Building "to pay respect to those who have contributed their remains for the benefit of scientific learning."[22] This memorialization and research effort was led by Trani's successor at VCU, President Michael Rao.

In late 2018, some forty people gathered in the Kontos Medical Sciences Building auditorium, not far from where the skeletal remains had first been spotted by the construction workers, police, and archaeologists. In hushed, reverential tones, a woman in a flowing brown-and-white robe chanted before the group, "The ancestors are traveling their journey, the journey to return home . . . the earth is a place we visit, and the other world is home."

Janine Bell, a noted African American folklorist, continued, "In ritual bring their walks into our lives . . . reflect light with love that in this moment is in our hearts . . . as we make this a sacred space."

She tapped a bell and spoke of life, health, and strength "as we pay homage to our ancestors from Africa—the cradle of civilization." She honored "those who rest in the earth in America," including those "who completed their life in a dry well."

Other speakers struck similarly somber notes about the need to confront the hard truths hidden in the sacred ground below.

"We honor those who were dishonored," said Richmond councilwoman Ellen F. Robertson. "The well and our ancestors discovered in that place rose up and said to us that our history has to be visited and recognized, and the dignity and honor that all men created by God deserve. . . . We are here to say the voices of the graves have been heard. . . . We are remorseful and beg forgiveness [and pledge] to do whatever we can do to restore and bring them the dignity they deserve."[23]

Such invocations to honor the "voices of the graves" also could be made far from the medical school campus. An hour's drive south of Richmond, in a small country cemetery in Dinwiddie County, the grave of Bruce Tucker can be found near those of his parents. The Stony Creek community remains home to many of Bruce's old friends, and the Tucker family retains a farmhouse and property in the rolling, wooded hills. Yet, to date, no one has reached out to Bruce Tucker's descendants "to restore and bring them the dignity they deserve."

The Soul of Medicine

AFTER THE 1972 TRIAL, Dr. Richard Lower continued his lifelong mission of repairing the human heart. One of his patients was the attorney whom he credited for so ably defending him, Jack Russell.

"Dick Lower did a triple bypass on my father at MCV," said Russell's son, John. "The fact of the matter is that Dick Lower was one of the best heart surgeons in the world." When his father died at age ninety-two, John was told by another heart surgeon that some thirty years after the triple bypass, Lower's sutures were still holding tight.

From 1968 to his retirement in 1989, Lower conducted 393 heart transplants.[1] Yet his early ardor for the procedure cooled as he struggled to win the battle with the human body's immune defenses and the frequent rejection of transplanted organs. By the 1980s, he began to use what was hailed as a "miracle" antirejection drug—cyclosporine. He also developed a biopsy technique to monitor rejection.[2] These and other innovations dramatically improved his patients' survival rates.

Today, according to the noted cardiologist and author Dr. Sandeep Jauhar, "About 85 percent of patients live for at least a year after the procedure. The median long-term survival is probably greater than 12 years, and it's about 14 years if the patient survives the first year."[3]

But by the mid-1970s, Lower was having some doubts about the role he'd played in the heart transplant craze. He shared his views with the *Washington Post* upon the tenth anniversary of the first human heart transplant by the curious visitor from South Africa—Dr. Christiaan Barnard.[4]

Lower wasn't alone in his change of heart. With a decade's worth of hindsight, the *Post* noted widespread agreement among surgeons that "what was hailed as the dawn of the transplant age was really just the beginning of a long, slow, step-by-step period of experimentation with human subjects following experiments with dogs and primates."[5]

Lower believed there had been "a degree of optimism, even in the profession, that was not justified." In the late 1960s, transplantation was seen "as an answer for all patients who were sick with heart disease, and it was not. It was hoped survival would be better. It was hoped that matching donor and recipient types would be the answer to the rejection problem, and it wasn't."

Lower didn't completely dismiss the value of heart transplants, which he was still performing. "For the few patients who make it through and live comfortably for a significant period of time," they had been worthwhile, he said. Yet even after nearly a decade's worth of operations, the survival rate was low: Of the eighteen of his patients who had received new hearts since his first transplant in May 1968, only four were still living. Two-thirds lived for seventy days or less.

"It is certainly not a highly successful form of treatment," Lower reflected. "It's quite properly reserved for patients in relatively terminal stages of their disease. You have a choice when you reach that stage of saying, 'Let nature take its course,' or trying an experimental procedure."

★　★　★

In 1989, Dick Lower abruptly walked away from the Medical College of Virginia after nearly twenty-five years on the faculty. He made his decision after the college brought in a new chief of surgery who he didn't like. Lower also was dealing with a muscular condition that was starting to affect his hands and his ability to stay at the top of his surgical game, according to Anne. He surprised everyone by leaving Richmond to move to Montana to his longtime getaway—Big Hole Ranch—where he raised cattle and enjoyed hunting and fishing.

"Dick said he was a lucky man," Anne recalled. "He used to say, 'Most guys can't do that. I was an academic surgeon for twenty-five years, then I managed a ranch for five years out in Montana, then I had ten years as a volunteer at an inner-city clinic in health care.'"

Some of his colleagues thought the esteemed surgeon seemed happiest when he returned to practicing medicine as a volunteer at CrossOver, a free clinic for low-income residents of Richmond, including many newly arrived Spanish-speaking immigrants. Since his early days treating Native Americans in the West, his life seemed to have come full circle.

★   ★   ★

By contrast, Dr. David Hume never had the chance to open a new chapter in his eventful life. He died on May 19, 1973, when the light plane he was piloting alone crashed into a mountainside shortly after takeoff near Los Angeles. He'd traveled to California to pick up his plane, a twin-engine Aero Commander 560F, which had undergone repairs on its autopilot system.

Initial reports said the plane plummeted into rough terrain a few miles outside the Van Nuys Airport because it lost power. But a subsequent accident report by the National Transportation Safety Board cited the difficult flying conditions and "very limited" visibility due to fog. The report noted a local pilot working with Hume on his plane "attempted to dissuade him from making the trip" due to the low visibility along with the doctor's "unfamiliarity with the Valley area" and his lack of proficiency in instrument-based flying.

Hume, fifty-five, left behind his wife, Martha, and four children.

After the shocking news of the accident, the tributes to Hume began rolling in. A *Richmond News Leader* editorial praised "the essential magnetism of David Hume . . . A dynamo of inexhaustible energy, he attempted to cram into a given day 10 times more than he possibly could accomplish—frequently drawing his only sustenance from a peanut-butter sandwich."

On a more serious note, the editorial cited the "many thousands of people throughout the world who owe their lives to his surgical research and techniques" and the "many hundreds of others who learned at his side, and who drew their life's inspiration from his."[6]

His funeral drew an overflow crowd at St. Stephen's Episcopal Church in Richmond. Dr. Francis C. "Frannie" Moore, his mentor at Boston's Peter Bent Brigham Hospital, described Hume as "a restless genius" who "carried out the first of a long series of organ transplants that truly changed the face of surgery and medicine throughout the world."

But it was his widow, Martha—who'd reluctantly left New England in the mid-1950s to drive south in a blue station wagon with their young family and their pets—who best captured Hume's Icarus-like spirit.

"He often said that he did not want to live so long as to be infirmed in any way," she reflected later. He wanted to be "living as high and fast as he could."[7]

★   ★   ★

L. Douglas Wilder kept practicing law even as he spread his wings in the rarified air of Virginia politics. As the state tried to move on from its segregationist past, Senator Wilder rode the winds of change. His stock began to rise in the 1980s with a resurgent Democratic Party. Doug Wilder was always his own man, challenging the conventional wisdom of party elders. Among his most notable efforts, Wilder pushed for the creation of a state holiday for Martin Luther King. After more than a decade, he finally reached his goal in 1984. Nonetheless, in a perversely Southern way, the Virginia legislature tried to dilute the observance by pairing the civil rights leader with the ongoing commemorations for Confederate generals Robert E. Lee and Stonewall Jackson. This "insane turn of events," as Wilder described it, led to one of the strangest-sounding state holidays in American history: "Lee-Jackson-King Day."[8]

Because of his experience in Richmond's mostly white courtrooms, including William Tucker's lawsuit against MCV, Wilder was uniquely prepared to survive the crucible of Virginia's racially charged politics. He managed to keep his eye on the leadership prize even while facing white voters in restaurants and sitting in homes where Confederate flags were prominently displayed.

A tough and wily campaigner, Wilder surprised political pundits in 1985 by eking out a win as lieutenant governor and followed that four years later by winning a tight race for governor. His historic triumph in 1989 marked the first election of an African American as governor in the nation's history.

During the swearing-in ceremony on the steps of the state capitol— under the bronze gazes of the segregationist governor and senator Harry F. Byrd Sr. and the rebel general Stonewall Jackson—the grandson of slaves spoke eloquently of his hopes and dreams for all Virginians. The grief and disappointment he'd seen etched in William Tucker's face when they lost their lawsuit nearly two decades earlier was replaced by tears and joy of black Virginians and white supporters who never thought they'd live to see this day.

Wilder could have been addressing William Tucker and his still-uncompensated family when he said in his inaugural speech, "In every period of my life, there have been many more deserving and justly entitled to the fruits that wholesome opportunities present. And yet, for many, those chances never came, and the bell of fulfillment never tolled for them."

★　★　★

Judge A. Christian Compton's career also flourished. Two years after the Tucker trial, he was selected as a justice of the Supreme Court of

Virginia, where he served from 1974 until 2000. He became a senior justice until his death in 2006 at age seventy-six.

Over the years, Compton wrote and spoke at length about the implications of the 1972 transplant case. Such scholarly work made him a popular guest at legal forums on the issue of brain death and related issues at the intersection of law, medicine, and ethics. Over the years, Justice Compton also developed a friendship with the doctor who had been so nervous in his courtroom, Dr. Richard Lower. In November 1989—around the time Wilder was elected governor—Anne Lower wrote a letter to the judge from Montana on custom stationery from Big Hole Ranch.[9]

"Dear Chris," she wrote, "As you may know, Dick retired from MCV. In the process of cleaning out his office and deciding what to keep and what to send to the Archives, he became very wistful in recalling the trial of 1972 that established brain death. He mentioned a real wish to have parts of the records for his personal library."

Anne asked Justice Compton to help Dick "pursue this wish." As she did so, she made an interesting point about the *timing* of her query—which she noted was made only after Wilder's gubernatorial campaign was over. She seemed to want to assuage any possible concern on Compton's part of somehow alienating the newly elected governor.

"I have deliberately waited until the recent election had passed to begin pursuing this bit of history," she wrote. "I assure you, there are no political overtones."

Her wish list to Compton included: "Dick's testimony; Dr. Sweet's testimony and Mr. Wilder's cross-examination; Mr. Russell's examination; Mr. Wilder's summation; your charge to the jury."

After offering to pay for material and for typing the transcript, she concluded, "I will be most interested to learn your opinion of how I can put together this fascinating chapter in Dick's life."

Compton waited until after Wilder's January 1990 inauguration as governor, and the end of that year's session of the Virginia Supreme Court, before answering her request for court documents. In a letter dated March 13, 1990, he delivered some bad news about Anne's research project. "Because the case was not appealed," he wrote, "an official verbatim transcript of the testimony was never prepared." He promised to see what he could get by contacting other key players, including Jack Russell and the court reporter.

Compton also made some unique observations on the historic case. After recalling the "memorandum opinion I wrote midway [in] the trial" after Wilder presented his evidence, he wrote, "I reversed that ruling later after all the evidence was presented and permitted the jury to decide the main issue in the case . . .

"I felt if the jury adopted the concept of brain death in the case, it would have greater impact than if the trial judge had taken that issue away from the jury and had decided it was a matter of law."

When Anne wrote back, she thanked Compton for helping her conduct her research as a gift to Dick. She also sounded frustrated about the missing trial transcript.

"I was very disappointed to learn from [court reporter] Keith Crane in our final telephone conversation last month that he feels he disposed of all his court records on the Tucker case in November 1989."

As the years passed and the trial was largely forgotten, people on both sides of the case developed their own theories about the missing transcript. In early 2017, when Wilder was told there was no copy in the Richmond Circuit Court or Library of Virginia, he was adamant that it couldn't be lost to history. He insisted it must be *somewhere*.

"It's not in the file, you say?" When asked whether he thought it might have been destroyed, Wilder replied, "No, I didn't say that, but I think there was a transcript . . . Sure there was a transcript!" After all, he recalled that someone was "recording the whole damn thing!"[10]

The missing court record could serve as a metaphor for the mistreatment of Bruce Tucker. First, there was his brother's business card in his pants pocket that somehow escaped everyone's notice until it was too late. Then came the failed attempts by police to find his relatives. The final blow was delivered by MCV administrators with their callous treatment of William after his futile search for Bruce.

This lack of consideration of the family's feelings and the "social death" of Bruce Tucker continues today. A check of the online histories of heart research and transplantation on the website of the latter-day Medical College of Virginia—VCU Health—includes nothing about Bruce Tucker's contribution to the heart transplant program. Instead, it merely says, "In 1968, our transplant team performed its first heart transplant procedure, distinguishing our program as the longest running program on the East coast and the second oldest in the United States."[11] Other recent commemorations of MCV's first heart transplant also made no mention of the "donor."[12]

Still, despite the gaps in the institutional memory, today's medical students in Richmond are taught about the often-fraught history on campus—including the racial discrimination of the 1950s and 1960s, when the newly minted MD Charlie Christian, a Korean War veteran, wasn't allowed to join his classmates for a reception at a whites-only hotel.

They are shown photos of the rat-infested wards at the segregated St. Philip Hospital and other disturbing examples of racial discrimination. The information is shared during a class on the history of "cumulative wounding across generations" of Americans. VCU medical students learn that this shameful legacy was tolerated not only in Richmond, but also across the country—from the Tuskegee syphilis experiments in Alabama to Johns Hopkins Hospital in Baltimore, site of the cell-harvesting that was exposed in *The Immortal Life of Henrietta Lacks*.

Today's medical students also study Virginia's role in eugenics and its Racial Integrity Act of 1924. They learn about the forced sterilization of women at state-run hospitals from the 1920s into the late 1970s. It's a staggering amount of injustice and mistreatment to absorb at once. The class ends with slides about MCV's "Organ Transplant Legacy."

Old newspapers flash by with headlines from 1968 through 1972, along with photos of Wilder, Lower, and Hume. A headline declares "Questions Arise" about MCV's first heart transplant.

"Our goal has not been to indict MCV," the slide presentation concludes, "but to understand how our institution's history affects how people understand and experience their life and medical care."

★   ★   ★

Dr. Vigneshwar "Vig" Kasirajan, who followed Lower as chairman of the medical school's Division of Cardiothoracic Surgery, says he never knew his hospital had failed to contact the Tucker family after Bruce's death.[13]

"So they never told the family?" he asks incredulously. "They never met with the family?"

Told about the way William Tucker was treated by the hospital, and how he first learned about Bruce's missing organs from his funeral home director, Dr. Kasirajan looks dismayed and disappointed.

"So the family found out that the organs were taken only from the undertaker? I never heard that," he says somberly, removing his glasses.

The more he hears that strays from VCU's official narrative, the more interested he seems. "It will be important to write that story because that's never been written," he says.[14]

★   ★   ★

Across the United States, the medical college in Richmond is hardly alone in trying to come to terms with past injustices. Whether it involves medicine or other parts of a college's origin story, many institutions of higher learning have discovered their own skeletons in their historical closets. A partial list could include the slaves who built Thomas Jefferson's University of Virginia; segregationist figures such as Woodrow Wilson at Princeton; or the income from slave trading that helped finance construction of Georgetown University.

Yet many of these examples date back a century or more. More interesting, perhaps, are later cases of such injustices, such as the case of the unwilling heart donor, Bruce Tucker. Such queries remain as relevant in the twenty-first century as they were a half century ago. Consider, for instance, how altering the genetic makeup of babies to stave off disease can be used to create a "designer baby" to meet parental specifications—a consumer-age nightmare reminiscent of the eugenics movement and the medical horrors perpetrated by Nazi Germany. The list of current ethical challenges includes calls for physician-assisted suicide to the manipulation of human DNA to the ongoing debate over a woman's right to control her own body.

Such ethical quandaries test the limits of human understanding and wisdom in the face of life's pain and loss. No matter how sophisticated the latest scientific advances may appear, they inevitably pose fresh challenges for physicians and philosophers alike. Yet, as the story of Bruce Tucker shows, the Hippocratic oath's pledge to protect each patient from harm begins by treating everyone as worthy of respect and dignity.

Without this, medicine risks losing its very soul.

Unhealed History

December 14, 2018

ON A DREARY, DRIZZLY day in late fall, I drive along a two-lane blacktop past empty fields choked with weeds, scrub pines, and bare trees with skeletal branches raised to the gray sky. Traversing two rural Virginia counties—Sussex and Dinwiddie—I search for the farmhouse that once was home to Bruce and William Tucker.

My eyes strain to spot the address on a roadside mailbox for Bruce's son, Abraham. Some forty-six years ago, he'd been called on to testify in the civil suit against the MCV surgeons to show why the family deserved some compensation. Doug Wilder had submitted as evidence Bruce's pay stubs and tax returns to show the financial loss to his son in the wake of his father's death. After the family lost the suit, Abraham Tucker continued to live with his grandmother off Black Branch Road, near the town of Stony Creek. He'd graduated from high school and eventually joined the army. I was told he might be working at nearby Fort Lee.

Hoping to interview Bruce's son, I sent Abraham Tucker a registered letter to the property that had been recorded as delivered. Despite my efforts to convince him to help bring his father's story to life, he didn't respond. Other efforts to reach him through surviving relatives or other Tuckers in the area also failed.

Before driving down to try to visit, I'd noticed Abraham Tucker's photograph in a 2016 newsletter as he was honored for his service at the Fort Lee post exchange. Since he was in the public eye, I hoped to visit the base and perhaps explore the events of the 1972 trial. But after talking with army public affairs officials, I learned that he no longer worked there. If I wanted to meet Bruce Tucker's only son, it seemed, I'd have to go knock on his door.

In my letter, I tried—however feebly—to convey my condolences over the long-ago loss of his father, and to explain why I was contacting him.

> I am writing now to tell you about my work that I hope will help correct the historical record about how your father was mistreated at MCV in 1968. I realize this query is bound to stir up some sad memories, and for that I do apologize.
>
> I hope to provide a measure of justice where none was provided before.

I wanted to discuss his family's past in Dinwiddie County and in Richmond. Had Abraham visited his father much? Had he dropped by his uncle's shoe repair shop? Did he remember the 1972 trial when, in his midteens, he'd taken the stand? But my letters had gone unanswered. Like the missing trial transcript, this part of Bruce Tucker's story was proving elusive.

Slowly driving along rain-soaked Black Branch Road, I wonder if I'm meant to find Bruce Tucker's son.

"Arrived," my iPhone announces. Really? The mailbox on this small white-frame house doesn't match the address on file at the Dinwiddie County courthouse.

So I keep driving and looking for a hint of their name in this tidy rural community with white-frame and brick houses. "No Hunting" and "No Trespassing" signs are posted intermittently on fences, gates, and trees. With no one venturing outside in the rain, I have little choice but to circle back down the road to where the phone announced my arrival. I step out into a light rain and approach the white clapboard house. A window opens on the side of the house where someone's been watching.

"Are you lost?" a man calls.

Even at a distance I can see he's younger than the newsletter photo from Fort Lee.

Calling out the address, I ask if he knows a man named Tucker.

"Sorry," the man replies politely, "I have no idea who you're talking about." He suggests driving back up the road, in the direction of Little Bethel Church. Continuing along Black Branch Road, I see a bog choked with logs and branches. It serves as a reminder of how bogged down my search has become. So many unanswered letters to relatives and pastors and anyone named Tucker in the area; dozens of emails and calls that either bounced back or were never returned.

A few months earlier, I came to Stony Creek to visit the family's graves at Little Bethel Church. A sign on a nearby highway points the way with a dove carrying a twig, a hopeful message for those seeking refuge from the floods of life. The country road winds through thick forest before opening in a clearing. On the right is a large brick building with a white steeple topped by a small cross. The church has two white pillars and a stained-glass window. Peeking inside, I see thirty to forty rows of dark, wooden pews in the well-tended church.

I park across the road beside the cemetery, which is open to the public. Tiptoeing around the graves on this hot August day, I kneel down to scrape off traces of cut grass on the gravestones. I try to decipher names and dates that may be faded by rain, wind, and time. Despite my best efforts, I come up short on finding Bruce Tucker's grave. The midmorning sun and rising humidity start taking a toll on me.

Amid my doubts and sweat, a car pulls into the parking lot and a man—the pastor, maybe?—opens his door and seems to notice me.

Hoping he doesn't think I'm an intruder in the graveyard, I stand and wave. I'm relieved to see him wave back.

The slight, friendly man in the parking lot introduces himself as Wilbard Johnson, "the church sexton."

"Do you happen to know a man named Bruce Tucker?"

"Yes," he replies with a nod, "I know the whole family."

As I explain my research into the 1968 heart transplant, Johnson nods again and says, "First one down at MCV. I read it in the news."

He invites me to sit and chat in the shade of the church's front steps, below two colorful flower wreaths on the door. He tells me about the 1950s and 1960s and the Tucker boys, their parents, and some of their cousins. He grew up on a farm just a couple of miles away from them. His face lights up as he remembers some of the Tucker girls who danced to his rock-and-roll band as they performed in clubs "from Virginia up to the Apollo," the legendary music venue in Harlem.

In those days, the family patriarch, Spencer Tucker, grew what Johnson called "the average farmer's thing"—corn, peanuts, and possibly soybeans.

He attended the same elementary school as Bruce, William, and their siblings. Like other public schools in Virginia in those days, Little Bethel School was segregated. Strapped with limited resources, it stopped in the seventh grade and "then you graduated to high school."

William Tucker came down with polio—a scourge for thousands of Americans, from President Roosevelt to children growing up in the rural South. William managed to get around on crutches, Johnson recalls, and used them into adulthood in Richmond.

Over the years, the church sexton lost touch with most of the family except one, a niece in Florida, who had recently visited to make sure the Tuckers' graves were being maintained.

As he ponders the family's fate, he pauses. "Did you know Bruce had a son?"

I admit to knowing little about the son whose name was mentioned briefly in the court record and the judge's trial notes.

"He lives in his own place," Johnson says, pointing me in the right direction. Turn right at the crossroads, he says, and follow Black Branch Road.

"He's back in there somewhere," Johnson says.

He says he rarely sees him around Stony Creek, a mix of ranch-style homes and small farms.

★   ★   ★

Months later, as I drive along Black Branch Road, trying to find Abraham Tucker, two men appear in a driveway off to the right.

"I'm looking for Abraham Tucker," I shout out the passenger window. "Do you know where he lives?"

When the older of the pair nods, I turn off my engine and get out to introduce myself.

"We're kin," the man says, puffing thoughtfully on a small cigar. Pointing toward the first white house I'd visited, he tells me to drive past it, then turn right at the next mailbox. "Go up that road," he says. "He might be home."

Following his directions, I turn onto a seldom-used road into the woods, trying to avoid some deep, water-filled ruts. Besides finding Bruce's son, my biggest concern is getting stuck in a car without four-wheel drive. Would my iPhone even have service here if I had to call for a tow? The road is overgrown with weeds and it takes concentration to follow a nearly invisible path through what seems to be an old farm meadow. No houses are within view. A train whistle echoes mournfully in the distance, providing a soundtrack of isolation.

When the road levels out below two tall power lines, I spot a roof through a stand of trees off to the left. My heart races. The Tucker homestead? But it turns out to be another property, apparently deserted. I seem to have reached a dead end.

Or not.

Because on my way out, I notice another fork in the rutted road to another part of the farm. I know I have to see where this other path leads, though there's no mailbox or other sign of life.

Soon a stand of pines appears, and through the trees, a roof. Driving through the rain up the driveway, I spot a late-model vehicle parked in front of a white clapboard house. I pull in behind it and beep my anemic horn. Much to my amazement, a man opens the front door and steps out onto the porch. Even through the rain, I recognize the face from the base newsletter: Abraham Tucker. He looks younger than his work photo, wearing a stocking cap, green sweatshirt, and stylish glasses.

"Hello! Are you Abraham Tucker?" I apologize for arriving unannounced, and ask if I could get out of the rain and come up on his porch. I'm empty-handed, leaving my notebook and briefcase behind. I don't want to seem pushy.

"Tell me why you're here," he says.

The words pour out as I revisit some of the points I've already made in my previous letters: about the heart transplant history and his father's untold story; about my reporting background; and, recalling his army service, my own time growing up on military bases. Anything to make a connection.

He stops me, though, and asks me to get to the point. Flustered, I try to deliver a kind of elevator pitch and personal plea. It does no good, and he heads to the door.

Clearly my time is up. "You have my phone number if you change your mind," I say.

"I won't."

It's been more than forty-six years since he's been called as a witness in the Richmond trial. Now the tables are turned. He's the judge, I'm the witness. But my testimony has been weak.

ACKNOWLEDGMENTS

MY THANKS TO EVERYONE at Simon & Schuster and Gallery Books who made the writing of this book possible, including VP executive editor Jeremie Ruby-Strauss, whose guidance and insightful reading helped in so many ways. Also thanks to his able assistant, Andrew Nguyen, copy editor Erica Ferguson, and to Sydney Morris and Anne Jaconette of the marketing and publicity team, along with production editor Sherry Wasserman and designer Davina Mock.

My gratitude to Peter McGuigan and his staff at Foundry Literary + Media for nurturing the initial concept for this book and helping it reach fruition. Thanks for the invaluable assistance of Kelly Karczewski and Claire Harris.

As always, my wife, Deborah, provided invaluable support. Without her editorial insights, technical prowess, and boundless enthusiasm and energy, this book wouldn't have been written. Thanks as well to author Dean King, whose encouragement and advice kept me on track.

Special thanks to Jodi Koste, University Archivist and head of Special Collections at the Tompkins-McCaw Library at Virginia Commonwealth University. She guided me through the labyrinthine history of the Medical College of Virginia and American medicine. She also engaged in constructive debate to try to help me avoid the trap of judging the past by today's standards.

Dr. John Moeser, Professor Emeritus of Urban Studies and Planning at Virginia Commonwealth University, shared his research and insights about the institutional racism that has plagued the state of Virginia in general and the Richmond metropolitan area in particular.

I'm indebted to Deborah Elkins Froelich, former executive editor of Virginia Lawyers Weekly, for her skillful search of court and historical records. Attorney John Russell shared his stories of growing up with his father, Jack Russell, and the early days of medical malpractice law.

I'm in awe of the artistry and insights of Richmond graphic artist Christopher Hibben, who researched and designed the book's maps. Photographer Jay Paul captured some hidden figures still hovering in plain sight at the medical college.

Shirley Holmes Tucker, first cousin of Bruce and William Tucker, discussed life on the family farm in Dinwiddie County, Virginia, in the 1960s. Another family member, Wilma Malone of Petersburg, shared painful memories of the family's experience after the 1968 heart transplant.

Thanks to former Virginia Governor L. Douglas Wilder, who gave me what he called his first interview about the 1972 civil case over the transplant after more than four decades of not discussing it.

I was helped by the Hon. Theodore J. "Ted" Markow, a retired Richmond circuit court judge, who was on MCV's defense team as a young assistant Attorney General for the state of Virginia. Judge Markow's account of the 1972 trial, along with those of colleague William Crews, helped me better understand their legal defense of the Medical College of Virginia. I also was helped by a member of the jury in that case, Richmond stockbroker David Plageman.

A number of physicians provided helpful editorial suggestions on the history of medicine and clinical matters. They also discussed medical ethics with me. Dr. Mark H. Ryan, associate professor at the VCU School of Medicine, reviewed early drafts; he also allowed me to sit in on one of his classes on what's termed the "historical trauma" faced by patients and physicians alike from the sometimes unjust and insensitive practices of past health care in America.

Dr. Samuel T. Bartle, past president of the Virginia Chapter of the American Academy of Pediatrics, provided vital support and ideas.

Dr. Walter Lawrence Jr., director emeritus of the Massey Cancer Center at VCU, offered a front-row seat on the dramatic events that unfolded on May 25, 1968, during Virginia's first heart transplant. He also helped me better understand the complex personalities and surgical practices of Drs. David Hume and Richard Lower.

Thanks to Dr. Vigneshwar Kasirajan, chairman of the Division of Cardiothoracic Surgery at VCU, for discussing the legacy of the heart transplant and the importance of sharing the story of Bruce Tucker's treatment. Dr. I. N. Sporn helped me understand the culture at MCV in the 1960s and also shared his photos of Dick and Anne Lower enjoying themselves on their Montana ranch.

My brother-in-law, Dr. Donald W. Hatton Jr., of Lawrence, Kansas, a Master in the American College of Physicians, provided editorial assistance along with my sister, Carol Hatton.

Christopher Egghart, of the Virginia Department of Environmental Quality, gave a detailed account of the 1994 discovery of an abandoned well filled with human remains during the digging of a foundation to a new medical sciences building at VCU. Daniel Mouer, who was the university's lead archaeologist, also shared his recollections.

Paige Mudd, Executive Editor of the *Richmond Times-Dispatch*, generously gave me access to her newspaper's extensive collection of articles and photographs. Two talented former medical writers at the Richmond newspapers, Alberta Lindsey and Beverly "Bev" Orndorff, reflected on their coverage of the transplant saga.

Thanks to Dr. Shawn Utsey, chairman of VCU's Department of African-American Studies, for discussing the groundbreaking research that led to his documentary, *Meet Me in the Bottom: The Struggle to Reclaim Richmond's African Burial Ground*.

Dr. Michael L. Blakey, National Endowment of the Humanities Professor of Anthropology, Africana Studies, and American Studies at the College of William and Mary, discussed the complexities of his field of study. Dr. Douglas W. Owsley, Head of Physical Anthropology at the Smithsonian's National Museum of Natural History, shared his 2012 report on the findings at the VCU well site and other intriguing works about his field of forensic anthropology.

Thanks to the many librarians and archivists who assisted my research, including Gail Warren, Virginia State Law Librarian; John N. Jacob, Archivist and Special Collections Law Librarian at the Washington and Lee University School of Law; Selicia Gregory Allen, Archivist and Special Librarian at the L. Douglas Wilder Library at Virginia Union University; medical ethicist Chuck Hite; and the helpful staff of the Library of Virginia Archives.

The Hon. Ellen F. Robertson, a member of the Richmond City Council, discussed her experiences as a nurse and an African American dealing with the legacy of injustices in the health care system. Sandra Williamson, president of the Dinwiddie County Historical Society, helped me navigate the back roads of local and state history. Wilbard Johnson, sexton of Little Bethel Church in Stony Point, Virginia, welcomed a visitor to his church and shared his stories about the Tucker family. And thanks to Jim Beckner and Lisa Crutchfield at the Richmond Academy of Medicine. Adam Wilson, Director of Content at Inkubator Enterprises in New York City, provided a burst of early interest in telling the previously untold story of Bruce Tucker.

BIBLIOGRAPHY

Barnard, Christiaan, and Curtis Bill Pepper. *One Life.* Toronto: Macmillan, 1969.

Blake, William. *The Portable Blake.* New York: Viking, 1946, 1968.

Blanton, Wyndham B. *Medicine in Virginia in the Nineteenth Century.* Richmond, VA: Garrett & Massie, 1933.

Campbell, Benjamin. *Richmond's Unhealed History.* Richmond, VA: Brandylane, 2012.

Carmichael, Ann G., and Richard M. Ratzan, eds. *Medicine: A Treasury of Art and Literature.* New York: Hugh Lauter Levin/Macmillan, 1991.

Foner, Eric. *Reconstruction Updated Edition: America's Unfinished Revolution, 1863–1877.* New York: Harper Perennial Modern Classics, 1988, 2014.

Halberstam, David. *The Fifties.* New York: Random House, 1993.

Kimball, Gregg D. *American City, Southern Place: A Cultural History of Antebellum Richmond.* Athens: University of Georgia Press, 2000.

Larson, Erik. *The Devil in the White City: Murder, Magic, and Madness at the Fair That Changed America.* New York: Vintage Books, 2004.

Lederer, Susan E. *Flesh and Blood: Organ Transplantation and Blood Transfusion in Twentieth-Century America.* New York: Oxford University Press, 2008.

Lewis, C. S. *A Year with C. S. Lewis: Daily Reading from His Classic Works.* Edited by Patricia S. Klein. San Francisco: HarperSanFrancisco, 2003.

McRae, Donald. *Every Second Counts: The Race to Transplant the First Human Heart.* New York: G. P. Putnam's Sons, 2006.

Moeser, John V., and Rutledge M. Dennis. *The Politics of Annexation: Oligarchic Power in a Southern City.* Cambridge, MA: Schenkman, 1982.

Moore, Francis D., MD. *A Miracle and a Privilege: Recounting a Half Century of Surgical Advance.* Washington, DC: Joseph Henry, 1995.

337

Poe, Edgar Allan. *The Tell-Tale Heart and Other Writings*. New York: Bantam Books, 1982.

Robbins, Tom. *Even Cowgirls Get the Blues*. Boston: Houghton Mifflin, 1976.

Sappol, Michael. *A Traffic of Dead Bodies: Anatomy and Embodied Social Identity in Nineteenth-Century America*. Princeton, NJ: Princeton University Press, 2002.

Shultz, Suzanne M. *Body Snatching: The Robbing of Graves for the Education of Physicians in Early Nineteenth Century America*. Jefferson, NC: McFarland, 1992.

Skloot, Rebecca. *The Immortal Life of Henrietta Lacks*. New York: Crown, 2010.

Stark, Tony. *Knife to the Heart: The Story of Transplant Surgery*. London: Macmillan, 1996.

Veatch, Robert M., and Lainie F. Ross. *Transplantation Ethics*, 2nd ed. Washington, DC: Georgetown University Press, 2015.

Washington, Harriet A. *Medical Apartheid: The Dark History of Medical Experimentation on Black Americans from Colonial Times to the Present*. New York: Anchor Books, 2006.

Wilder, L. Douglas. *Son of Virginia: A Life in America's Political Arena*. Guilford, CT: Lyons Press, 2015.

Wolfe, Tom. *The Electric Kool-Aid Acid Test*. New York: Farrar, Straus & Giroux, 1968.

NOTES

CHAPTER ONE: Case of the Missing Heart

1 Governor L. Douglas Wilder, interview with the author, January 12, 2017, at the L. Douglas Wilder School of Government and Public Affairs, Virginia Commonwealth University.

2 The chronology of William Tucker's calls and subsequent visit to the Medical College of Virginia is drawn from my interview with Governor Wilder and from notes and court papers from the subsequent 1972 civil trial in Richmond.

3 Wilder interview.

4 In our interview, I asked Wilder if it was difficult arguing his case before an all-white jury. "I didn't have any problem with it. I did it all the time." Whether in civil or criminal cases, opposing attorneys could use preemptory challenges to prospective jurors without stating their reasons—even when race clearly played a role. "So even if you were lucky enough to have any" African American jurors on the panel, "the prosecutor would strike them," Wilder said.

5 "L. Douglas Wilder," Virginia Museum of History & Culture, accessed March 1, 2018. https://www.virginiahistory.org/collections-and-resources /virginia-history-explorer/l-douglas-wilder.

6 Wilder interview.

7 L. Douglas Wilder, *Son of Virginia: A Life in America's Political Arena* (Guilford, CT: Lyons Press, 2015), 47.

8 "Heart Transplant Operation Performed Here by MCV," *Richmond Times-Dispatch*, May 26, 1968, 1.

CHAPTER TWO: The Resurrectionists

1 C. S. Lewis, *A Year with C. S. Lewis: Daily Reading From His Classic Works*, edited by Patricia S. Klein (San Francisco: HarperSanFrancisco, 2003), 339. Lewis originally made this observation about magic and science in *The Abolition of Man*.

2 Edgar Allan Poe, *The Tell-Tale Heart and Other Writings* (New York: Bantam Books, 1982), 169.

3 Ibid., 170.

4 Michael Sappol, *A Traffic of Dead Bodies: Anatomy and Embodied Social Identity in Nineteenth-Century America* (Princeton, NJ: Princeton University Press, 2002), 2.

5 Jodi L. Koste, *Artifacts and Commingled Skeletal Remains from a Well on the Medical College of Virginia Campus: Anatomical and Surgical Training in Nineteenth-Century Richmond*, June 18, 2012, 5. In her in-depth paper about the founding of MCV, Koste cites the work of Wyndham B. Blanton, including "Augustus Lockman Warner, 1807–1847" from the *Annals of Medical History 4* (January 1942), 1–9, and Blanton's *Medicine in Virginia in the Nineteenth Century*, 38–39, 42–43.

6 Conversation with Koste, April 27, 2018, and her May 14, 2015, slideshow, *The East Marshall Street Well: What the Historical Record Tells Us*.

7 Koste, *Artifacts*, 5.

8 Benjamin Campbell, *Richmond's Unhealed History* (Richmond, VA: Brandylane, 2012), 17.

9 Ibid., 37.

10 Ibid., 33.

11 Ibid., 59.

12 Ibid., 109.

13 Koste, *Artifacts*, 6.

14 Wyndham B. Blanton, *Medicine in Virginia in the Nineteenth Century* (Richmond, VA: Garrett & Massie, 1933), 38.

15 Ibid., 38.

16 Ibid. Blanton notes this came from a report in one of the city's daily newspapers, the *Richmond Enquirer*, on June 6, 1837.

17 Ibid.

18 Ibid.

19 Ibid., 39.

20 Koste, *Artifacts*, 7. The Slavitt quote comes from "The Use of Blacks of Medical Experimentation and Demonstration in the Old South," *Journal of Southern History* 48 (August 1982), 331–35.

21 Campbell, 109.

22 Ibid.

23 Koste, *Artifacts*, 6.

24 Gregg D. Kimball, *American City, Southern Place: A Cultural History of Antebellum Richmond* (Athens: University of Georgia Press, 2000), 58.

25 Ibid. Kimball cites *Dickens' American Notes for General Circulation*, 1842, reprinted New York: D. Appleton & Co., 1868, 57–59.

26 Campbell, 109.

27 Koste, *Artifacts*, 7.

28 Ibid.

29 Ibid.

30 Koste, *Artifacts*, 6.

31 Suzanne M. Shultz, *Body Snatching: The Robbing of Graves for the Education of Physicians in Early Nineteenth Century America* (Jefferson, NC: McFarland, 1992), x.

32 Koste, *Artifacts*, 9.

33 Ibid.

34 Sappol, 117.

35 Koste, *Artifacts*, 14.

36 Ibid.

37 Blanton, 47.

38 "Wreck of the Steamship Arctic," *Mountain Democrat*, Placerville, California, November 18, 1854. Accessed online February 6, 2020, at Maritime heritage.org/ships/arctic.html.

CHAPTER THREE: The Anatomy Men

1 Edgar Allan Poe, "The Premature Burial" (New York: Bantam Classic Edition, 1982), 181.

2 Shultz, 26. She cites Ambrose Bierce's 1906 satirical work, *The Devil's Dictionary*.

3 Ibid., 45.

4 Sappol, 109.

5 Ibid., 106.

6 Ibid., 107.

7 Ibid.

8 Ibid. This account of what became known as "the Doctors' Mob of 13" is based on Sappol, 107–10.

9 Ibid., 107.

10 Ibid., 107.

11   Ibid., 108. Michael Sappol notes that "contemporary accounts differ in key details and almost certainly contain embellishments or misinformation on some points." His account is based on newspaper reports and certainly captures the spirit, if not exact details, of the public revulsion and subsequent riot.

12   Ibid., 108.

13   Ibid., 109.

14   Ibid.

15   Ibid., 99.

16   Ibid., 106.

17   Ibid.

18   Koste, *Artifacts*, 11.

19   Ibid.

20   A contemporary commentary on the often-misunderstood Hippocratic oath was written by Robert H. Schmerling, MD, "First, do no harm," *Harvard Health Publishing*, October 13, 2015, updated October 14, 2015, https://www.health.harvard.edu/blog/first-do-no-harm-201510138421.

21   Shultz, 1–2.

22   Ibid.

23   "Sweeney Todd," accessed February 8, 2020, https://yesterday.uktv.co.uk/history/historical figures/article/sweeney-todd/.

24   Sappol, 53.

25   Ibid., 98.

26   Ibid., 55.

CHAPTER FOUR: "The Limbo of the Unclaimed"

1   Koste, *Artifacts*. Virginia Commonwealth University medical archivist Jodi L. Koste detailed the history of what was then the first permanent home of the Medical Department of Hampden-Sydney College, which in 1854 became the Medical College of Virginia. The facility was first called College Building; it was formally the Egyptian Building in 1927 and later had extensive renovations in 1939 that added to its exotic look. Its exterior remains today largely unchanged from the original. Though the building was officially dedicated in 1845, it was used for anatomy classes the previous fall while still under construction.

2   "Egyptian Building," Wikipedia, accessed on July 1, 2018, https://en.wikipedia.org/wiki/Egyptian_Building.

3   Ibid. The "Herm figures" are actually of Greek origin, representing the fertility god, Hermes.

4   Blanton, Wyndham B., "The Egyptian Building and Its Place in Medicine," *Bulletin of the Medical College of Virginia* 37, no. 4 (February 15, 1940): 5.

5   Koste, *Artifacts*, 10.

6   Ibid.

7   Lois Leveen, "The North of the South," Opinionator, *New York Times*, January 24, 2011.

8   Kimball, 42.

9   Catalogue of the Officers, Students and Graduates of the Medical College of Virginia Session 1859–1860 and Announcement of Session 1860–61 (Richmond: Charles H. Wynne, Printer, 1860). Reviewed in the archives of Tompkins-McCaw Library, VCU.

10   Ibid.

11   Vince Brooks, "Chris Baker: Cheerful Among Corpses," Library of Virginia, October 27, 2010. Brooks, a senior local records archivist for the Library of Virginia, wrote this informative online article from the library's "Out of the Box" archives series.

12   Koste, *Artifacts*, 13.

13   Ibid.

14   Ibid.

15   Documents from Koste, VCU.

16   Ibid.

17   Dr. Shawn Utsey, interview with the author, October 26, 2018, at VCU.

18   Chris Baker's son, John, reportedly lived until 1972.

19   Eric Foner, *Reconstruction Updated Edition: America's Unfinished Revolution, 1863–1877* (New York: Harper Perennial Modern Classics, 2014), 111.

20   *The Virginia Star*, Vol. VI., Richmond, Va., Dec. 16, 1882. This article is in the Chris Baker file in the archives at VCU's Tompkins-McCaw Library. https://www.virginiahistory.org/what-you-can-see/story-virginia/explore-story-virginia/1861-1876/reconstruction.

21   Koste, *Artifacts*, *The Virginia Star*.

22   Blanton, 70.

23   *Virginia Star* article.

24   Blanton, 70.

25   Ibid., 71.

26   The wording of the law comes from "Acts and Joint Resolutions Passed by the General Assembly of the State of Virginia During the Session of 1883–84," on file at Tompkins-McCaw Library.

27   Brooks article on Chris Baker.

28   Sappol, 134.

29 Ibid., 135.

30 Koste, *Artifacts*; Sappol, 135.

CHAPTER FIVE: Breaking the Heart Barrier

1 Clyde F. Barker and James F. Markmann, "Historical Overview of Transplantation," *Cold Spring Harbor Perspectives in Medicine* 3, no. 4 (April 2013): a014977.

2 Ibid.

3 Ibid. Barker and Markmann explain: "In retrospect, the technical failure of autografts was not surprising because at first full-thickness skin grafts were used. These thick grafts never became established because their underlying layer of fat and other tissue prevented revascularization (that is, restoration of proper circulation)."

4 Ibid.

5 Ibid.

6 Ibid.

7 "Alexis Carrel," Wikipedia, accessed on August 1, 2018, https://en.wiki pedia.org/wiki/Alexis_Carrel.

8 Barker and Markmann.

9 Nicholas J. Fortuin, MD, "Difficult Cardiology III," *New England Journal of Medicine* 338 (June 4, 1998):1703–04. In the article, Fortuin reviews Clarence G. Lasby's *Eisenhower's Heart Attack: How Ike Beat Heart Disease and Held On to the Presidency.*

10 Ibid.

11 "Eisenhower Gives Tip on Quitting Cigarettes," *New York Times*, January 31, 1964, accessed at the *Times'* online archives, https://www .nytimes.com/1964/01/31/archives/eisenhower-gives-tip-on-quitting-cigarettes.html.

12 Ibid. The definition of acute coronary syndrome accessed at www .mayoclinic.org/diseases-conditions/acute-coronary-syndrome /symptoms-causes/syc-20352136.

13 The Centers for Disease Control and Prevention estimates that age-adjusted death rates for diseases of the heart (i.e., coronary heart disease, hypertensive heart disease, and rheumatic heart disease) reached a peak in 1950 with 307.4 per 100,000 persons to 134.6 in 1996, an overall decrease of 56 percent. Major risk factors cited were high blood cholesterol, high blood pressure, and smoking and dietary factors. "Achievements in Public Health, 1900–1999: Decline in Deaths from Heart Disease and

Stroke—United States, 1900–1999," *Morbidity and Mortality Weekly Report* 48, no. 30 (August 6, 1999): 649–56.

14   Accessed at the White House's official website, www.whitehouse.gov/about-the-white-house/first-ladies/edith-bolling-galt-wilson, which notes that nearly a century before voters ever considered a woman candidate for president, Edith Bolling Galt Wilson became what some called the "first woman to run the government."

15   Joel Achenbach and Lillian Cunningham, "The Hidden History of Presidential Disease, Sickness and Secrecy," *Washington Post*, September 12, 2016.

16   Ibid.

17   Sean Braswell, "President Eisenhower's $14 Billion Heart Attack," *Ozy*, April 13, 2016, https://www.ozy.com/flashback/president-eisenhowers-14-billion-heart-attack/65157/.

18   Barron H. Lerner, "An M.D.'s Guide to Ike's Heart and Hearth, *New York Times*, January 13, 2004.

19   Eisenhower's return to Washington, D.C., was viewed at www.historicfilms.com, "Eisenhower Suffers Heart Attack–1955."

20   Lerner. President Eisenhower suffered a total of seven heart attacks from 1955 until his death in 1969 at the age of seventy-eight from congestive heart failure.

21   Anne Lower, interviews with the author conducted in early 2018, at her home in Richmond, Virginia.

22   Dr. Richard Lower's quotes about his time at Stanford come from two oral histories conducted by the Virginia Commonwealth School of Medicine (earlier called the Medical College of Virginia). The first one was with medical school dean Stephen Ayres in late 1989; the second oral history was conducted on August 15, 2005, with Dr. Sheldon Retchin, vice president of health sciences and CEO of the VCU Health System.

CHAPTER SIX: Heart on Ice

1   David Halberstam, *The Fifties* (New York: Random House, 1993), 626.

2   Ibid., 617.

3   Ibid.

4   Maia Szalavitz, "The Legacy of the CIA's Secret LSD Experiments on America," *Time*, March 23, 2012, accessed online at healthland.time.com/2012/03/23/the-legacy-of-the-cias-secret-lsd-experiments-on-america/.

5   "Informed Consent," *Encyclopedia of Bioethics*, accessed on September 1, 2018, repository.library.georgetown.ed.

6   Richard Lower's memories about his time at Stanford are drawn from both oral histories at VCU.

7   Tracie White, "50 years ago, Stanford heart doctors made history," *Stanford Medicine*, January 4, 2018, accessed online September 1, 2019, med.stanford.edu.

8   Eugene Dong, MD, JD, "A Heart Transplantation Narrative: The Earliest Years," 1995, accessed on October 1, 2018, at web.stanford.edu/~genedong/httx/harttx.htm. This article was taken from *History of Transplantation: Thirty-Five Recollections*, Paul I. Terasaki, editor, (Oakland: Regents of the University of California, 1991).

9   Norman E. Shumway, MD; Richard R. Lower, MD; and Raymond C. Stofer, DVM, "Selective Hypothermia of the Heart in Anoxic Cardiac Arrest," *Surgery, Gynecology & Obstetrics* 109, no. 1 (December 1959): 750–54.

10   Dong.

11   Richard Lower oral history.

12   Ibid.

13   Dong.

14   Anne Lower, interviews with the author.

15   Donald McRae, *Every Second Counts: The Race to Transplant the First Human Heart* (New York: G. P. Putnam's Sons, 2006), 66.

16   Ibid.

17   Richard Lower oral history.

18   "Transplant Rejection," National Institutes of Health, U.S. National Library of Medicine, accessed January 28, 2019, medlineplus.gov/ency/article/000815.htm.

19   Ibid.

20   This hospital would merge in 1980 with two other Harvard teaching hospitals in Boston to become Brigham and Women's Hospital.

21   "Kidney Transplantation: Past, Present, and Future," Stanford University, accessed December 1, 2018, web.stanford.edu/dept/HPST/transplant/index.html.

22   Ibid.

23   Ibid., 82.

24   Ibid.

25   Richard Lower oral history.

CHAPTER SEVEN: Restless Genius

1   "New Chairman of Surgery Arrives for Duty at MCV," *Richmond News Leader*, August 21, 1956, 1.

2   It later became Brigham and Women's Hospital.

3   "Kidney Transplantation."

4   The recommendation letters from Hume's superiors and colleagues are on file at VCU's Tompkins-McCaw Library. These letters include those of Hume's mentor in Boston, Dr. Francis "Frannie" D. Moore, one of the early innovators in the field of kidney transplantation. They also contain Hume's early correspondence with MCV officials.

5   Ibid.

6   "Medicine in Richmond: The Hume Years, 1956–73," a 2003 slideshow presentation of the Richmond Academy of Medicine, is in Tompkins-McCaw Library archives at VCU.

7   Ibid.

8   Richard Lower shared Moore's account as part of a tribute to Dr. Hume to the Humera Surgery Society in 1991. (The Humera Surgical Society was founded after Dr. Hume's death to honor his memory.)

9   Barker and Markmann, 5.

10 Ibid.

11 Richard Lower's 1991 account of Moore and Hume in 1991 tribute.

12 Dr. Joseph E. Murray was a plastic surgeon who performed the first successful human kidney transplant on identical twins in 1954. In 1990, he shared the Nobel Prize in Physiology or Medicine with E. Donnall Thomas for their discoveries concerning "organ and cell transplantation in the treatment of human disease."

13 William L. Laurence, "Hormone is Indicated in Seat of Emotion," *New York Times*, October 21, 1949, 1.

14 Virginius Dabney's reflection comes from an early draft of *Virginia Commonwealth University: A Sesquicentennial History* (1987). This is in Tompkins-McCaw Library at VCU.

15 "Muskegon, Michigan," Wikipedia, accessed on December 15, 2018, https://en.wikipedia.org/wiki/Muskegon,_Michigan.

16 "Medicine in Richmond," slide 23.

17 Dr. Walter Lawrence, emeritus professor of surgery at the VCU School of Medicine, interview with the author, March 24, 2016, at VCU's Tompkins-McCall Library.

18 Martha Hume oral history, conducted by Richmond Academy of Medicine, September 25, 2002. On file in VCU's Tompkins-McCall archives.

19 "Medicine in Richmond," slide 3.

20 Dabney from Tompkins-McCaw archives.

21   VCU's archives contain Hume's early correspondence with MCV.

22   Ibid.

23   "Medicine in Richmond," slide 25.

24   Hume correspondence in VCU archives.

25   Ibid.

26   Kay Andrews Martine oral history, Tompkins-McCaw Library at VCU.

27   Ibid.

28   Ibid.

29   Ibid.

30   Dr. Hunter McGuire Jr. oral history, conducted by Richmond Academy of Medicine, September 24, 2002, at VCU's Tompkins-McCaw Library.

31   "H. H. Holmes," Wikipedia, accessed on October 1, 2018, en.wikipedia .org/wiki/h.h.holmes.

32   Hunter McGuire Jr. oral history.

33   Ibid.

34   Ibid.

35   Ibid.

36   Dr. I. N. Sporn, interview with the author, February 16, 2018, at Sporn's Richmond home.

37   Email from Dr. Sporn, August 8, 2019.

38   Ronald K. Davis, address to Humera Surgical Society, 1993. Text provided by Koste.

39   Ibid.

40   Rebecca Skloot, *The Immortal Life of Henrietta Lacks* (New York: Crown, 2010), 2.

41   Ibid., 150, 152.

42   "Medicine in Richmond," slide 54.

43   Correspondence between Dr. Bosher and Dr. Hume, along with related letters sent by MCV president Robert Blackwell Smith and dean William F. Maloney, from Tompkins-McCaw Library archives at VCU.

44   Ibid.

45   McGuire oral history.

46   Ibid.

47   "Medicine in Richmond," slide 35.

48   McRae, 95.

49   Ibid., 4.

50   Ibid., 135.

51   Ibid.

CHAPTER EIGHT: The Glass Jar

1 This account of Philip Morris USA's history in Richmond is based on the author's more than five years of reporting on the company and the entire tobacco industry for the *Richmond Times-Dispatch* between 1993 and 1998. The details about the Philip Morris USA research and development center in Richmond are drawn from the author's article, "Secrets within Secrets," *Richmond Times-Dispatch*, September 15, 1996, 1.

2 McGuire oral history.

3 "Negro Student Barred from Social Affairs. Leads M.C.V. Class," *Richmond News Leader*, May 28, 1962, 1.

4 "MCV Won't Bar Negroes from Functions," *Richmond Times-Dispatch*, May 30, 1962, 5.

5 Ibid.

6 Ibid.

7 The minutes of the MCV board of visitors from 1950 are in the archives of Tompkins-McCaw Library at VCU. Dr. Sanger's first remarks are part of a report of the board's executive committee on January 27, 1950; the follow-up on the first black applicant to the school of physical therapy comes from the March 10, 1950, board minutes.

8 Ibid., December 8, 1950, minutes of the executive committee.

9 Ibid., January 12, 1951, minutes of the board of visitors.

10 *Ebony*, July 1955, courtesy of Jodi Koste at VCU. Harris would later become Virginia's secretary of health and human resources from 1978 to 1982.

11 Dr. J. M. Tinsley letter, courtesy of Jodi L. Koste, VCU.

12 Larry Hall, "Ruth Nelson Tinsley," *Richmond Times-Dispatch*, February 1, 2006, https://www.richmond.com/ruth-nelson-tinsley/article_81d322ba-6af7-11e2-a9c1-001a4bcf6878.html.

13 Dr. I. N. Sporn, interview with the author, February 16, 2018.

14 Anne Lower interviews.

15 Richard Lower shared this story about the night at the Humes' house in a tribute to Dr. Hume given to the Humera Surgical Society in 1991 on file at VCU's Tompkins-McCaw Library.

16 Ibid.

17 "Medicine in Richmond," slide 64.

18 Richard Lower oral history.

19 Richard Lower oral history with Retchin.

20 Definition of heart-lung machine from "Cardiopulmonary bypass," Wikipedia, accessed on July 30, 2019, https://en.wikipedia.org/wiki/Cardiopulmonary_bypass.

21 "Controversies in the Determination of Death: A White Paper of the President's Council on Bioethics," Washington, DC, January 2009, https:// bioethicsarchive.georgetown.edu/pcbe/reports/death/pellegrino_ statement.html.

22 Ibid.

23 Ibid.

24 Richard Lower oral history with Ayres.

25 McRae, 123.

26 Ibid., 125.

27 Ibid., 126.

28 Ibid.

29 Richard Lower oral history with Retchin.

30 Ibid.

31 Richard Lower's talk to the Humera Surgical Society in 1991, on file at VCU's Tompkins-McCaw Library.

32 Ibid.

CHAPTER NINE: Foreign Exchange

1 The two letters quoted here are in the archives of VCU's Tompkins-McCaw Library.

2 Hume's reply was not part of the letters previously cited, and its existence is based on Barnard's swift reply.

3 Christiaan Barnard and Curtis Bill Pepper, *One Life* (Toronto: Macmillan, 1969), 291.

4 Ibid.

5 McRae, 158.

6 Ibid., 111. McRae cites *Time* magazine's thirteen-page spread about surgeons on May 3, 1963.

7 Ibid., 112.

8 Ibid.

9 Ibid., 158–59.

10 Barnard and Pepper, 12.

11 Ibid., 3.

12 McRae, 159

13 Richard Lower oral history with Ayres.

14 Lawrence interview.

15 Barnard and Pepper, 292.

16 Ibid., 293.

17 Ibid.

18 Ibid.

19 Ibid., 294.

20 Anne Lower interviews.

21 Ibid.

22 Richard Lower oral history with Retchin.

23 Ibid.

24 McRae, 166.

25 Richard Lower oral history with Ayres.

26 Ibid.

27 Ibid.

28 Richmond Academy of Medicine, oral history with Dr. Hunter McGuire.

29 Richard Lower oral history with Retchin.

CHAPTER TEN: Finish Line

1 Hanneke Weitering, "50th Anniversary of Apollo 1 Fire: What NASA Learned from the Tragic Accident," Space.com, January 27, 2017.

2 Ibid.

3 Ibid.

4 Ibid.

5 Ibid.

6 Anne Lower interviews.

7 Glenn Lower, phone interview with the author, February 16, 2018.

8 "Peace in Space Treaty Signed at White House," *Richmond Times-Dispatch*, January 28, 1967, 2.

9 Tom Robbins, *Even Cowgirls Get the Blues* (Boston: Houghton Mifflin, 1976), 4.

10 John V. Moeser and Rutledge M. Dennis, *The Politics of Annexation: Oligarchic Power in a Southern City* (Cambridge, MA: Schenkman, 1982), 8.

11 Ibid., 34.

12 Wilder, *Son of Virginia*, 45.

13 Ibid.

14 Moeser and Dennis, 6.

15 Ibid., 7.

16 Ibid., 77.

17 A 1904 law bars the removal or alteration of public war memorials in Virginia. This statute has allowed Confederate-heritage proponents to block cities such as Charlottesville and Richmond from taking down Confederate statues. It has been challenged by a recently elected Democratic majority in the Virginia general assembly. Gregory S. Schneider and Laura

Vozzella, "In Virginia, Democrats Set to Test the Blue Depths," *Washington Post*, November 7, 2019, A-1.

18 Richard Lower oral history.

19 McRae, 168.

20 Ibid.

21 Ibid., 169.

22 Ibid., 170.

23 Barnard and Pepper, 294.

24 Ibid., 295.

25 Ibid., 296.

26 Barnard and Pepper, 296.

27 Ibid., 297.

28 Ibid.

29 Ibid.

30 McCrae, 171. Edith Black felt "like a million dollars" and lived for twenty more years.

31 McRae, 172.

32 Ibid.

33 White, "50 years ago, Stanford heart doctors made history."

34 Associated Press, "Human Heart Transplant Held Success," *Richmond Times-Dispatch*, December 4, 1967, 1.

35 Ibid.

36 Beverly Orndorff, "Surgery Team Chief Worked at MCV in '66," *Richmond Times-Dispatch*, December 4, 1967, 1.

37 Richard Lower oral history.

38 Peter A. Alivizatos, MD, "Fiftieth Anniversary of the First Heart Transplant: The Progress of American Medical Research, the Ethical Dilemmas, and Christiaan Barnard," *Baylor University Medical Center Proceedings* 30, no. 4 (October 2017): 475–77.

39 John Illman, "Downfall of a Maverick Medical Genius: How the Man Who Carried Out the World's First Heart Transplant Was Gripped by a Lust for Fame, Money and Women That All but Destroyed His Reputation," *Daily Mail* (London), November 26, 2017, https://www.dailymail.co.uk/femail/article-5119557/Downfall-genius-performed-heart-transplant.html.

40 Alivizatos, "Fiftieth Anniversary of the First Heart Transplant."

41 Glenn Lower interview.

42 Beverly Orndorff, "Memories of Covering the Richmond Medical Scene: Early 1960s to late 1990s." This article was written in 2002 for the Rich-

mond Academy of Medicine and is in the archives at Tompkins-McCaw Library at VCU.

43 Ibid.

44 Ibid., 213.

45 "Gift of a Human Heart," *Life*, December 15, 1967.

46 *Life* gave short shrift to the heroic efforts of the surgeon in this second heart transplant, Dr. Adrian Kantrowitz. The Brooklyn surgeon's story is intimately recounted by Donald McRae in *Every Second Counts* (the baby transplant is described on pages 218–20). Among Dr. Kantrowitz's many trenchant comments—considering the carnival-like publicity around the South African operation—was this: "Dr. Kantrowitz said an attempt would be made to determine the cause of death and that this would be 'reported to medical colleagues through the medical literature.' The surgeon said he was disturbed and upset because news of the operation 'had been leaked to a newspaper' which he refused to identify. He added that newspaper headlines were not the place to disclose important operations, but they should first be reported to the medical authorities."

47 "Gift of a Human Heart," 27.

48 McRae, 226.

49 Ibid., 227.

50 Ibid., 227.

51 Ibid., 233.

52 Ibid.

53 Ibid., 192. One of the most difficult decisions Barnard never explained at the time was when he chose to inject his donor's heart with potassium to make it stop after they'd turned off the ventilator. This occurred after one of the staff surgeons refused to operate until there was no longer a heartbeat. The potassium injection, writes McRae, "was a decision that they swore would always remain secret from the world outside."

54 Ibid., 240.

55 Ibid., 248–49. The heart given to Philip Blaiberg, a fifty-eight-year-old retired dentist, came from a twenty-four-year-old South African, Clive Haupt, who died of a brain hemorrhage during a day at the beach. Though Haupt was classified by his government as "colored," Blaiberg, who was white, wasn't opposed to the multiracial operation. This would be Barnard's second, and the world's third, heart transplant operation. Blaiberg went on to live for more than nineteen months, until his death from heart complications the following August.

56 Ibid., 261.

57 Illman, who coauthored with Barnard the 1979 book *The Body Machine*, notes that Barnard divorced his first wife in 1969, only to marry a nineteen-year-old heiress one year later. After subsequent marriages and divorces, he confessed to Illman that he was "very much a sex-oriented man."

58 McRae, 265.

CHAPTER ELEVEN: The Fall

1 "Dr. Hinton Jailed in Police Spat," *Richmond Afro-American*, May 25, 1968, 1.

2 "18 of 'Poor' Arrested at Capitol," *Richmond Times-Dispatch*, May 24, 1968, 1.

3 According to the 1969 Richmond City Directory at the Library of Virginia, there were thirty-two listings for "shoe repairers" and "shoe shiners."

4 The details about Bruce Tucker's life, including his income and family commitments, are drawn from the 1972 case file in *Tucker's Administrator v. Dr. Richard R. Lower et al.* in the Law and Equity Court of the City of Richmond.

5 Biographical information about the Tuckers drawn from a November 1, 1971, court filing in the Law and Equity Court of the City of Richmond in *Tucker's Administrator v. Lower*.

6 Ibid. This information is from the May 25, 1968, autopsy report of assistant medical examiner Dr. Abdulleh Fatteh.

7 "Heart Transplant Performed Here by MCV," *Richmond Times-Dispatch*, May 26, 1968, 1.

8 White, "50 years ago, Stanford doctors made history."

9 Ibid.

10 A. Christian Compton, "Telling the Time of Human Death by Statute: An Essential and Progressive Trend," *Washington and Lee Law Review* 31, no. 3 (September 1, 1974): 525.

11 This account of the early-morning visit to Tucker's rooming house is based on multiple sources: the 1972 case file; Dr. Walter Lawrence, vice chairman of the surgery department; and two lawyers who worked for the Virginia attorney general's office—Theodore "Ted" Markow, who went on to become a judge in the Richmond Circuit Court, and William Crews.

CHAPTER TWELVE: His Brother's Heart

1 Lawrence interview.

2 Ibid.

3 Ibid.

4 Ibid.

5 The work of the Harvard Medical School's physician-led committee studying the issue resulted in an influential paper, "A Definition of Irreversible Coma." The group was grappling with how the "obsolete criteria for the definition of death can lead to controversy in obtaining organs for transplantation."

Ad Hoc Committee of the Harvard Medical School, "A Definition of Irreversible Coma," *Journal of the American Medical Association* 205, no. 6 (August 5, 1968): 337–40.

The paper's main conclusion was that patients who were comatose and had "no discernible central nervous system activity" may be pronounced dead before their heart stops beating.

6 Richard Lower oral history with Retchin, August 5, 2005.

7 This chronology is drawn from the case file in *Tucker's Administrator v. Lower*, May 23, 1972, in the Law and Equity Court of the City of Richmond, page 127.

8 Lisa J. Huriash, "Dr. Abdullah Fatteh, 82, Conducted Private Autopsies," *South Florida Sun Sentinel*, August 25, 2015, accessed at www.sun-sentinel .com/local/broward/fl-abdullah-fatteh-obituary-20150825-story.html.

9 *Virginia Circuit Court Opinions*, edited by William Hamilton Bryson (Richmond, VA: Dietz Press, 1985), 125.

10 Dr. David Sewell, phone interview on August 15, 2018, from his home in Kingsport, Tennessee. Though he said he was ailing at the time, Dr. Sewell was kind enough to spend about forty minutes discussing the Tucker case and his time at MCV with Lower and Hume.

11 Ibid.

12 Ibid.

13 Abdullah Fatteh, "A Lawsuit That Led to a Redefinition of Death," *Journal of Legal Medicine* 1, no. 3 (July/August 1973): 31.

14 The EEG used to be a front-line method for diagnosing brain tumors, strokes, and other disorders. This usage has decreased with the advent of high-resolution anatomical imaging techniques such as magnetic resonance imaging (MRI) and computed tomography (CT). The concept dates back to British physicians in the 1890s, but the first human EEG wouldn't be conducted until 1924 by the German psychiatrist and physiologist Hans Berger. "Electroencephalography," Wikipedia, accessed on October 1, 2019, en.wikipedia.org/wiki/Electroencephalography.

15 Fatteh, 31.

16 Tucker's vital signs were part of the testimony of Dr. J. G. Campbell, the MCV anesthesiologist, on May 25, 1968. The details were included in the handwritten notes of Judge Compton during the 1972 civil trial *Tucker's Administrator v. Lower* and are in his personal papers in the archives of the Washington and Lee University School of Law in Lexington, Virginia.

17 Fatteh, 31.

18 This eyewitness to the transplant was speaking broadly about the prevailing attitudes at MCV in 1968 but admitted he had "no firsthand knowledge" of the search for Bruce Tucker's family or friends.

19 Fatteh, 32.

20 Barry Barkan, "2nd St. Was on Powder Keg," *Richmond Afro-American*, May 25, 1968, 1.

21 Ibid.

22 Conversation is based on Compton's account of his ruling, 127–28.

23 The chronology of William Tucker's calls and subsequent visit to the Medical College of Virginia is drawn from my interview with Governor Wilder on January 12, 2017, and the notes of Richmond Circuit Court Judge A. Christian Compton in the aforementioned civil trial. Another helpful resource was Stuart Auerbach, "Dead Man's Kin Says Heart Was No Donation," *Las Vegas Sun*, June 26, 1968, 16.

24 Mrs. Gregory's search for Tucker is included in Compton's trial notes.

25 Ibid.

26 Compton, "Telling the Time of Death by Statute."

27 Sewell phone interview.

28 Beverly Orndorff, "First MCV Report Details Klett Heart Transplant," *Richmond Times-Dispatch*, May 31, 1968, 1.

29 Fatteh, 32. According to subsequent testimony by Dr. Lower, one of Tucker's kidneys was sent to Georgetown University, where it was intended for a female recipient, while the other kidney was used at MCV for scientific study.

30 Richard Lower oral history with Dr. Retchin.

31 Auerbach.

32 This chronology is drawn from the papers of A. Christian Compton in the archives of the Washington and Lee University School of Law. Compton kept copious handwritten notes from the landmark 1972 civil case *Tucker's Administrator v. Lower*. These notes on William Tucker's trial testimony provide an estimated time and place of when and how he received word of his brother's death at MCV.

33 Susan E. Lederer, *Flesh and Blood: Organ Transplantation and Blood Trans-*

fusion in Twentieth-Century America (New York: Oxford University Press, 2008), 176. Lederer is the Robert Turrell Professor of Medical History and Bioethics at the University of Wisconsin–Madison, where she chairs the Department of Medical History and Bioethics. In her discussion of the "social death" of patients, she cites David Sudnow's 1967 book, *Passing On: The Social Organization of Dying* (Englewood Cliffs, NJ: Prentice-Hall, 1967), 74.

34 Lederer, 176.

35 *Invisible Man* (New York: Vintage Books: 1995), 505.

CHAPTER THIRTEEN: The Scream

1 "Heart Transplant Operation Performed Here by MCV."

2 Ibid.

3 Ibid.

4 Jim Seymore went on to become a reporter and editor at *People* magazine and later became managing editor of *Entertainment Weekly*. Elizabeth Valk, "Publisher's Letter," *People*, June 25, 1990, accessed online at people .com/archive/publishers-letter-vol-33-no 25.

5 Orndorff, "Memories of Covering the Richmond Medical Scene."

6 Ibid.

7 "Heart Transplant Operation Performed Here by MCV."

8 Anne Lower interviews.

9 William Tucker's visit to his hometown of Stony Creek, Virginia, is chronicled in a November 1, 1971, memo filed by L. Douglas Wilder in the civil case *Tucker's Administrator v. Lower*, on file in the Richmond Circuit Court.

10 The story of James Jordan's lynching was accessed online at Frank Green, "Memories of 1925 Lynching Linger in Waverly," *Richmond Times-Dispatch*, March 2, 2014. This tragedy became a public relations nightmare for the state of Virginia, especially since it happened in broad daylight and in full view of a passenger train. Governor E. Lee Trinkle traveled to Waverly the next day, saying, "Virginia's record has been virtually washed clean of mob actions. I exhort you that the name of the Commonwealth not be brought again into the limelight of such publicity as she has received from this occurrence." The Waverly lynching—along with another mob murder in 1926—led to the passage of the Virginia Anti-Lynching Law of 1928.

11 Lawrence Mosher, "When Does Life End?" *National Observer*, June 3, 1972.

12 November 1, 1971, Wilder memo in *Tucker's Administrator v. Lower* case file.

13 William Tucker's visit to Jones Funeral Home in Stony Creek, Virginia, is described in the Nov. 1, 1971, Wilder memo.

14 Wilma Malone of Petersburg, Virginia, email to the author, September 18, 2018.

CHAPTER FOURTEEN: "Facts and Circumstances"

1 Beverly Orndorff, "MCV Patient Reported 'Satisfactory,'" *Richmond Times-Dispatch*, May 27, 1968.

2 "Heart Transplant Donor Indicated," *Richmond News Leader*, May 27, 1968.

3 Orndorff, "MCV Patient Reported 'Satisfactory.'"

4 Associated Press, "Heart Transplant Performed in Brazil," *Richmond Times-Dispatch*, May 27, 1968, A-2.

5 McRae, 274.

6 Ibid., 273.

7 Orndorff, "Memories of Covering the Richmond Medical Scene."

8 Beverly Orndorff, "Heart Donor Identified," *Richmond Times-Dispatch*, May 28, 1968, 1. This initial report had a couple of minor errors—Tucker was fifty-four, not fifty-three, when he died, and the location noted in the story—"between 11th and 12th St. on East Cary Street" appears to be the location of Bruce Tucker's workplace, the Esskay egg-packing plant. According to the May 25, 1968, *Report of Investigation by Medical Examiner*, signed by Dr. Abdullah Fatteh, Tucker suffered his injury at the 2200 block of Venable Street, the site of the Esso station where Tucker gathered with his friends.

9 It appears that "Grover" should have been spelled "Glover" Tucker, one of Bruce's three brothers. Glover Tucker resided in Dinwiddie County, according to court records.

10 This was another example of an error in the early reporting, with his age fluctuating between his forties and fifties.

11 A search of newspaper databases failed to find any evidence that either Richmond newspaper—the *Times-Dispatch* or the *News Leader*—ran Bruce Tucker's obituary. An obituary did run in the newspaper nearest his hometown of Stony Creek—*The Progress-Index* of Petersburg, May 27, 1968, 15.

12 The obituary misspelled the name of Bruce's youngest brother, Nathan, a Stony Creek resident who died at age forty-one in August 1971.

13   Orndorff, "Heart Donor Identified."

14   Ibid.

15   Orndorff, "Memories of Covering the Richmond Medical Scene." He also discussed the rising tensions with MCV's surgeons—"They thought I was glorifying Tucker"—in his oral history interview with the Richmond Academy of Medicine on June 27, 2002, on file at VCU's Tompkins-McCaw Library.

16   Victor Cohn, "Va. White Got Negro's Heart," *Washington Post*, May 28, 1968, B-1. Once again, this article shows how early news reports sometimes get basic facts wrong—in this case, though Tucker wasn't named, the age of the "donor" was incorrectly given as forty, when Bruce Tucker's age was fifty-four. The report also was off by a day on his death—which happened Saturday, not "Friday night."

17   Ibid.

18   Orndorff described this collective cold shoulder to the author on October 30, 2019. He said some of the early disappointment in his reporting was expressed by members of the surgery department staff loyal to Hume and Lower.

19   Beverly Orndorff, "Transplant Held Legal, Ethical," *Richmond Times-Dispatch*, May 29, 1968, 1.

20   Ibid.

21   Ibid.

22   On page 11 of his memoir, *Son of Virginia*, Wilder recalls, "My birth certificate has it spelled 'Laurence,' but because it was so often misspelled in school, I started spelling it in the more common way as Lawrence." The second "s" in "Douglass" apparently was initially left off his name.

23   Wilder would be elected to the Virginia senate the following year, 1969.

24   Asked about this unnamed source, Orndorff said in an email on November 8, 2019: "I honestly have no specific memory now of whether it was Mann, but I strongly think it was." Dr. Mann, who was respected by his professional peers across the United States, was a regular source for Orndorff and other reporters in Richmond at that time.

25   Ibid.

26   James E. Davis, "Heart Donor Law Asked by Carwile," *Richmond Times-Dispatch*, May 29, 1968, B-1.

27   Ibid.

28   Marsh would go on to become Richmond's first African American mayor and later serve for twenty-three years in the Virginia senate.

29   Davis, "Heart Donor Law Asked by Carwile."

30   Ibid.

31   Barry Barkan, "Hospital Refuses to Give Details," *Richmond Afro-American*, June 1, 1968, 1.

32   Ibid.

33   Orndorff, "Heart Donor Identified."

34   Cohn, "Va. White Got Negro's Heart."

35   Barkan, "Hospital Refuses to Give Details."

36   "Heart Case Was 146th Transplant," *Richmond Times-Dispatch*, June 1, 1968, B-1.

37   "New Laurels for MCV," *Richmond Times-Dispatch*, June 1, 1968, A-8.

38   Ibid.

39   Ibid.

40   Wilbard Johnson, sexton of Little Bethel Church for the past twenty-four years, interview with the author, August 16, 2018. Johnson, a retired civilian worker at nearby Fort Pickett army base, greeted me as I searched for Bruce Tucker's gravesite. He was kind enough to provide contact information for a family member taking care of the Tucker gravesites.

CHAPTER FIFTEEN: Rejection

1   Photo caption on *Richmond Times-Dispatch*, Saturday, June 1, 1968, 1.

2   Ian Shapira, "He was America's most famous pediatrician. Then Dr. Spock attacked the Vietnam Draft," Retropolis, *Washington Post*, January 5, 2018.

3   Ibid.

4   Ibid.

5   This editorial cartoon ran in the *Richmond Times-Dispatch*, Saturday, June 1, 1968.

6   Frank Walin, "Racial Housing Setup Ruled Factor in Assigning Pupils," *Richmond Times-Dispatch*, June 1, 1968, 1.

7   James E. Davis, "Richmond Forward's Record Vigorously Debated at Meeting," *Richmond Times-Dispatch*, June 1, 1968, B-1.

8   Ibid.

9   Ibid.

10 Richard R. Lower, MD, et al., "Rejection of the Cardiac Transplant," *American Journal of Cardiology* 24 (October 1968): 492–99.

11 Ibid.

12 Ibid.

13 Ibid.

14 Richard Lower oral history with Retchin.

15 Ibid.

16 "Heart Patient Joseph Klett Dies at MCV, Transplant Failure, Cause Unknown, Spokesman Says," *Richmond Times-Dispatch*, June 2, 1968, 1.

17 Lower et al., "Rejection of the Cardiac Transplant."

18 "Heart Patient Joseph Klett Dies at MCV, Transplant Failure, Cause Unknown, Spokesman Says," *Richmond Times-Dispatch*.

19 Ibid.

20 Ibid.

21 Joyce Kipps of Rochelle, Virginia, phone interview with the author, May 27, 2019.

22 Alivizatos, "Fiftieth anniversary of the first heart transplant."

23 Ibid.

24 Ibid.

25 B. D. Colen, "Heart Transplant on Wane Decade After 1st Operation," *Washington Post*, September 5, 1977.

CHAPTER SIXTEEN: The Making of a Medical Celebrity

1 Tom Whitford, "A Borrowed Heart Fails After Six Vigorous Years," *People*, December 16, 1974, accessed online at https://people.com/archive /a-borrowed-heart-fails-after-six-vigorous-years-vol-2-no-25/.

2 Beverly Orndorff, "Heart Transplant Performed at MCV," *Richmond Times-Dispatch*, August 25, 1968. Dr. Mann's role was explained in an article in the *Richmond News Leader*, the evening newspaper that, while owned by the same parent company, competed for daily news. The *News Leader* article by Alberta Lindsey ran on August 26, 1968, with the headline "Heart Patient is 'Satisfactory.'"

3 Beverly Orndorff, "I Knew That I Had to Have a New Heart or Die," *Richmond Times-Dispatch*, October 4, 1968.

4 Biographic information about Russell obtained at the web page of the Indianapolis public school named after him—Louis B. Russell Jr. School—https://myips.org/louisrussell/school-history/.

5 Ibid.

6 Orndorff, "Heart Transplant Performed at MCV."

7 Betty Parker Ashton, "Heart Patient's Wife Confident," *Richmond Times-Dispatch*, October 17, 1968, C-1.

8 Orndorff, "I Knew That I Had to Have a New Heart or Die."

9 Orndorff, "Heart Transplant Performed at MCV."

10 Ibid.

11   Ibid.

12   Ibid.

13   Ibid.

14   Orndorff, "I Knew That I Had to Have a New Heart or Die."

15   Ibid.

16   Ibid.

17   Sarah Jaffe, "From Women's Page to Style Section," *Columbia Journalism Review* (February 19, 2013), accessed online at archives.cjr.org/behind _the_news/womens_page_to_style_section.php.

18   Ashton, "Heart Patient's Wife Confident."

19   Ibid.

20   Alberta Lindsey shared her early experiences in journalism in an interview with the author on November 11, 2018. The *News Leader* and *Times-Dispatch* were owned by the same company, Media General. Like many evening dailies, its circulation declined in the face of increased competition from TV news, and the *News Leader* was closed in 1992.

21   Ibid.

22   Ibid.

23   Ibid.

24   Alberta Lindsey, "MCV Transplant Patient Keeps Busy," *Richmond News Leader*, October 23, 1968.

25   Beverly Orndorff, "Heart Recipient to Fly Home," *Richmond Times-Dispatch*, November 24, 1968.

26   Russell would return to MCV two times—once in December 1968 and again in March 1969—after two "relatively minor rejection episodes" that were easily reversed during brief hospitalizations, Orndorff wrote in a follow-up article on August 24, 1969. But Dr. Lower didn't sound quite as sanguine about Russell's rejection episodes. In a jointly written article, "Experiences in Heart Transplantation: Technic, Physiology and Rejection," in the *American Journal of Cardiology* 24 (October 1969), without naming Russell, he said his second heart transplant patient "experienced a significant episode of threatened rejection that was reversed with drugs," including steroids.

27   Valerie Jo Bradley, "First Black Man to Survive Heart Transplant: Indiana Teacher Thrills to New Life of Action," *Ebony*, May 1969, 82–89.

28   "Lawyer Probes Transplant Case," *Richmond Afro-American*, June 8, 1968, 1. This article, without a byline, has the look and feel of an editorial—a line that the historically black press felt freer to cross in its role as an ad-

vocate for African Americans as well as a counterpoint to the mainstream media.

29 Ibid.

30 Ibid.

31 Stuart Auerbach, "Dead Man's Kin Says Heart Was No Donation," *Las Vegas Sun*, June 26, 1968. This article first appeared in the *Washington Post*, which distributed the article across the country.

32 Ibid.

33 "Donor's Brother to Handle Estate," *Richmond Times-Dispatch*, June 28, 1968, B-1.

34 Bradley, "First Black Man to Survive Heart Transplant."

35 Ibid.

36 Lacy J. Banks, "World's Heart Transplant Sets Super Pace," *Ebony*, April 1971, 106-112.

37 Alivizatos, "Fiftieth anniversary of the first heart transplant."

38 That percentage would be cut by more than half by 2018, when about 25 percent of all deaths in the United States—or about 610,000—were attributed to heart disease. Despite the decline—a result of less smoking and generally improved diet and exercise—"heart disease is the leading cause of death for both men and women," according to the US Centers for Disease Control and Prevention (CDC), accessed online on September 10, 2019, at cdc.gov/nceh/tracking/Heart_Health.htm.

39 Banks, "World's Heart Transplant Sets Super Pace."

40 Ibid.

41 Whitford, "A Borrowed Heart Fails After Six Vigorous Years." In 1976, Indianapolis renamed a school Louis B. Russell Jr. School. His widow, Thelma, unveiled the school sign honoring her husband.

CHAPTER SEVENTEEN: The Defender

1 The recollections of Russell's life are courtesy of his son, John B. Russell Jr., during a lengthy interview on June 1, 2018, at his law offices in Chesterfield County, Virginia. He provided tapes of his father's speeches and described his father's burgeoning practice of defending physicians against malpractice litigation. John Russell also discussed the events surrounding the 1968 heart transplant at MCV and the civil trial in 1972.

2 Ibid.

3 John Russell proudly said of his grandfather John H. Russell: "He also

worked for the [Virginia] tax department. He actually devised a formula that the tax department still uses in computing some form of business tax."

4   Ibid.

5   Ibid.

6   Ibid.

7   Ibid.

8   Since 1976, Virginia has placed statutory limits on medical malpractice damage awards (Virginia Code 8.01-581.15).

9   John Russell interview.

10   Ibid.

11   Ibid.

12   Armstrong would later maintain that he said, "That's one small step for *a* man, one giant leap for mankind," but that it appears to have gotten lost in the radio transmission. Citation accessed online at Pallab Ghosh, "Armstrong's 'Poetic' Slip on Moon," BBC News, updated June 3, 2009, http://news.bbc.co.uk/2/hi/science/nature/8081817.stm.

13   The fan's death, other injuries, and the rock festival's general mayhem were captured in the 1970 documentary film *Gimme Shelter* about the Rolling Stones' tour of America.

14   Wilder, *Son of Virginia*, 3.

15   Ibid.

16   "Transplant Law Change Hit, Wilder Cites First Heart Case," *Richmond Times-Dispatch*, March 13, 1970, B-4.

17   Ibid.

18   McCandlish Phillips, "Dick Gregory in an Hour at Carnegie," *New York Times*, November 27, 1969, 51.

19   Lederer, 177.

20   Ibid.

21   Ibid., 177–78.

22   Ibid., 179. Lederer cites Sandra Haggerty, "Blacks Attitudes about Heart Transplants," *Los Angeles Times*, January 22, 1974, A-7.

23   Author's interview with Governor Wilder.

24   Karin Kapsidelis, "A Son of Virginia," *Richmond Times-Dispatch*, January 18, 2015.

25   In an interview with the author, Wilder underscored the importance of MCV prevailing in the case, especially at a time—1972—when race relations were still rocky in Virginia's capital. If he were to win the case, Wilder observed, "Do you understand what this does to the system?"

26 Ibid.

27 This account of Wilder's initial court filing, and the subsequent pretrial discovery process—including orders of the judge in the case, A. Christian Compton—is based on documents in the files of the clerk of Richmond Circuit Court.

28 This part of the suit would be dismissed because Wilder missed the one-year statute of limitations.

29 "Heart Donor's Brother Files $1 Million Suit," *Richmond Times-Dispatch*, May 23, 1970, 1.

30 Compton later wrote, "The case is believed to be the first damage suit involving a heart transplant which proceeded to final judgment wherein the central issue was a determination of the time of death. This action was brought under the Virginia Death by Wrongful Act statute." From Compton's article in the *Washington and Lee Law Review*, "Telling the Time of Human Death by Statute: An Essential and Progressive Trend," Sept. 1, 1974, Vol. 31, Issue 3.

31 "Heart Donor's Brother Files $1 Million Suit," *Richmond Times-Dispatch*.

CHAPTER EIGHTEEN: Relative Death

1 Interview with David Plageman on Nov. 7, 2018, at his office at Scott & Stringfellow, Richmond, Va.

2 The U.S. Supreme Court ruled against such race-based practices in 1986 based on the right to a fair trial under the Constitution's Sixth Amendment (guaranteeing the rights of defendants in criminal trials) and the Fourteenth Amendment promise of equal protection under the law. In 1991, such protections against race-based jury selection in civil cases were extended.

3 A. Christian Compton, "Telling the Time of Human Death by Statute: An Essential and Progressive Trend," *Washington and Lee Law Review* 31, no. 2 (June 1, 1974): 538. The jury's composition is described in footnote 29.

4 Wilder interview.

5 Ibid.

6 Judge Theodore "Ted" J. Markow and William Crews, interview with the author, October 29, 2018, at the Richmond Academy of Medicine.

7 Ibid.

8 The case that led to California's Uniform Simultaneous Death Act accessed online at law.justia.com/cases/california/court-of-appeal/2d/261/262.html.

9 Author's interview with John Russell.

10 Jack Russell discussed the significance of the case as part of a tribute to Dr. Hume to the Humera Surgical Society in 1991. It is on file at VCU's Tompkins-McCaw Library.

11 Richard Lower oral history with Ayres.

12 Richard Lower oral history with Retchin.

13 A copy of the insurance company's letter is on file at VCU's Tompkins-McCaw Library. It's based on Wilder suing for damages in the US District Court for the Eastern District of Virginia, a case dismissed in early 1973.

14 McRae, 279–80.

15 Lawrence interview.

16 Anne Lower interviews.

17 McRae, 278.

18 Markow and Crews interview.

CHAPTER NINETEEN: Time of Trial

1 Markow and Crews interview.

2 The state legislature passed a bill in 1973 that reorganized Virginia's court system, making Law and Equity Court part of the Richmond Circuit Court.

3 A. Christian Compton, "Telling the Time of Human Death by Statute," footnote 19.

4 Ibid.

5 James E. Woodson, "Heart Case Lawsuit Under Way," *Richmond Times-Dispatch*, May 17, 1972, B-1. Since no transcript of the trial was kept by the Richmond Circuit Court—a result of the lack of an appeal of the case—many quotes from the testimony are from the newspaper's extensive coverage and analysis. Quotes come from other sources noted separately.

6 Ibid.

7 Judge Compton mentions the missing trial transcript in footnote 18 of his law school article. "The synopsis of the case is prepared from the original court papers and from the notes of the writer taken during the course of the trial. A court reporter recorded the trial proceedings, but since no appeal was taken the transcript was not prepared."

The lack of a trial transcript or recording was confirmed by the author through multiple inquiries made to the Richmond Circuit Court. The court has an extensive case file made available by Edward F. Jewett, clerk of court. On October 2, 2017, Jewett wrote in an email about why the court reporter's record could not be found.

"We have reviewed the file itself to see if it mentions a transcript, which it does not," Jewett said. "Transcripts are normally prepared only when a case is on appeal. The recordings or any court reporter notes would have only been retained for approximately ten years. We do not have any recordings of this case now."

Other efforts to find even parts of the court record through Governor Wilder, John Russell, the Library of Virginia, and others proved to be futile.

8   Woodson, "Heart Case Lawsuit Under Way."
9   Judge Compton's trial notes and related journal articles, court papers, and correspondence are on file at the Washington and Lee University Law School Library archives.
10 These quotes come from Compton's ninety pages of handwritten notes on the yellow legal pads he filled throughout the trial. Along with providing a list of witnesses and key facts, Compton recorded his own thoughts and impressions during the weeklong proceeding.
11 Woodson, "Heart Case Lawsuit Under Way."
12 Jordan also was called as a witness on the third day of the trial. In his notes, Compton identified him as "Admin. Asst. for office of Chief Med. Exam" for "Com. Of Va."—that is, the Commonwealth of Virginia. Jordan was a legal counsel for the state medical examiner's office.
13 Compton notes.
14 Plageman interview.

CHAPTER TWENTY: Friends in High Places
1   Plageman interview. Based on press account and Judge Compton's notes, Wilder did most of the talking for the plaintiffs; he was aided by cocounsel Harrison Bruce, who appears to have only occasionally spoken during the trial.
2   Ibid.
3   "Proceedings of the First International Symposium on Clinical Organ Transplantation," *Transplantation Proceedings* 4, no. 4 (New York: Grune & Stratton, 1972): xix, 429–798.
4   Markow and Crews interview.
5   Russell's recollection of Hume's May 1972 transplantation symposium comes from an address he gave during a tribute to the surgeon for the Humera Surgical Society in 1991 in VCU's Tompkins-McCaw Library.
6   Ibid.

7   James N. Woodson, "Death of Donor Before Transplant Described," *Richmond Times-Dispatch*, May 18, 1972, B-1.

8   In *Every Second Counts*, page 280, Lower's biographer, Donald McRae, writes, "Lower won over some of the jury when he brushed aside Wilder's slur on his character and medical ethics." He describes an exchange in which Wilder "sputtered during his sneering cross-examination." Wilder, according to this version of events, purportedly asked the surgeon whether he would "actively go out to take hearts from dead folks and put them in your own patients." Lower responded "drily," according to McRae: "Now you got it." McRae cites Lower as his sole source for this scene in his book. "The death of Bruce Tucker and Lower's transplant of his heart on May 26, 1968 was recalled in close detail for me by the surgeon. Lower was also my main source for the subsequent court case . . ." However, the *Times-Dispatch* coverage of the third day of the trial, reported on May 19, 1972, does not mention a verbal confrontation between Wilder and Lower. And neither of the assistant attorneys general in the courtroom that day—Ted Markow or Bill Crews—remembered such a moment of high drama. For his part, juror David Plageman said Hume and Lower came across as "a little bit pompous on the stand" in their cross-examination by Doug Wilder, as if to say, *Who are you to question me?*

9   Ibid.; James N. Woodson, "Dominant Issue of Heart Case Emerges," *Richmond Times-Dispatch*, May 19, 1972, B-1.

10 Lederer, 176.

11 Sewell phone interview. At the time we spoke, Dr. Sewell had been retired for a decade as a professor of cardiac and thoracic surgery at East Tennessee State University in Johnson City, Tennessee.

12 Ibid.

13 Ibid.

14 James H. Hershman Jr., "Massive Resistance," Encyclopedia Virginia, accessed on August 15, 2019, encylopediavirginia.org/massive_resistance.

15 Sappol, 45.

16 Woodson, "Death of Donor Before Transplant Described."

17 Virginia has a long history of legal conservatism that follows the doctrine of stare decisis—that is, deciding cases based on legal precedent. Circuit court judges such as Christian Compton were reluctant to delve into matters of lawmaking they felt were the proper domain of the general assembly.

18 Woodson, "Dominant Issue of Heart Case Emerges."

CHAPTER TWENTY-ONE: Shaping a Verdict

1   James N. Woodson, "Definition of Death Ruled Legal Question," *Richmond Times-Dispatch*, May 24, 1972, B-1.

2   Italics the author's. The full text comes from Compton's "Motion to Strike" on May 23, 1972, 3. This comes from Compton's papers at the Washington and Lee School of Law archives. The headnote of the thirteen-page motion describes the judge's position at that point of the proceedings: "Death occurs at a precise time, and that is defined as the cessation of life, a total stoppage of the circulation of the blood, and a cessation of the vital functions consequent thereto such as respiration and pulsation."

3   The deep impression Fletcher made on the judge comes through in Compton's papers. The only surviving written transcript from the trial is the partial one the judge asked to be specially prepared for him, "Summary of Testimony of Dr. Joseph Fletcher."

4   James N. Woodson, "Medical Definition of Death Upheld in Transplant Case," *Richmond Times-Dispatch*, May 26, 1972, 1.

5   Italics the author's.

6   McRae, 281.

7   Woodson, "Dominant Issue of Heart Case Emerges."

8   Author's interview with Plageman, Nov. 7, 2018.

9   Ibid.

10   Woodson, "Dominant Issue of Heart Case Emerges."

11   Ibid.

12   Ibid.

13   "Virginia Jury Rules That Death Occurs When Brain Dies," Associated Press, May 27, 1972, accessed online from the *New York Times* archives, nytimes.com/1972/05/27/archives/virginia-jury-rules-that-death-occurs-when-brain-dies.html.

14   McRae, 281.

15   Anne Lower interviews.

16   Beverly Orndorff, "Doctor Finds Trial Reinforces His Faith," *Richmond Times-Dispatch*, May 27, 1972, 1.

17   Ibid.

18   Ibid.

19   Wilder, *Son of Virginia*, 48.

20   Ibid.

21   Ibid., 49.

22   The author's interview recorded at Wilder's office on January 12, 2017, at

the L. Douglas Wilder School of Government and Public Affairs proved to be the only one he gave for this book.

23   It's worth noting that the attorney general during the trial was a Democrat, Andrew P. Miller. In a split-party administration, the governor was a Republican, Linwood Holton, the last of Virginia's "Valley Republicans," known for being more progressive on racial issues than the old-line Democrats of the "Byrd Machine." Neither of the lawyers working for the attorney general—Ted Markow or Bill Crews—recalled any undue influence or outside interference on them during the case.

24   "Heart Suit Is Dismissed," *Richmond News Leader,* January 16, 1973. This brief article was provided by Jodi Koste, head of Tompkins-McCaw Library Special Collections and Archives. "Judge Merhige said William Tucker asserted the same factual allegations in his federal court complaint as were used in the Law and Equity Court action, and that he failed to prove sufficient factual allegations to bring the case under federal jurisdiction."

CHAPTER TWENTY-TWO: The Unresolved Case of Bruce Tucker

1   Compton, "Telling the Time of Human Death by Statute," 532.
2   Jeff E. Schapiro, "Both Parties Playing Race Card," *Richmond Times-Dispatch,* July 18, 2019, A-9.
3   Compton, "Telling the Time of Human Death by Statute," 535, footnote 60. Bill Crews helped shape the bill "with leaders of the medical profession in Virginia." This included David Hume, members of the Medical Society of Virginia, and the Virginia State Board of Medicine. Compton noted that his brief history of the legislation was aided by then Senator Wilder, who "gave active support to the bill in the legislature."
4   Ibid.
5   Ibid., 539–40.
6   Italics are the author's.
7   Compton, "Telling the Time of Human Death by Statute," 543.
8   Wilder interview.
9   Robert M. Veatch and Lainie F. Ross, *Transplantation Ethics,* 2nd ed. (Washington, DC: Georgetown University Press, 2015), 37.
10   Ibid., 38.
11   Ibid.
12   Ibid., 39.
13   Ibid.
14   Ibid., 45.

CHAPTER TWENTY-THREE: Down in the Well

1   Chris Egghart, interview with the author, June 17, 2018. Egghart had been interviewed by other journalists over the years and had vivid, often disturbing memories of the events of 1994. In early 2020, he was working for Virginia's Department of Environmental Quality as a cultural resources specialist.

2   Ibid.

3   Tina Griego, "Did VCU Break the Law?" sidebar to "Into the Light," *Richmond Magazine*, Sept. 8, 2015.

4   Forensic anthropology "is a special sub-field of physical anthropology (the study of human remains) that involves applying skeletal analysis in archaeology to solving criminal cases," according to the Smithsonian's definition at naturalhistory.si.edu/education/teaching-resources/social-studies/forensic-anthropology.

5   Mike Allen, "Well-Preserved Find at MCV Bones Give Clues to 1800s Practices," *Richmond Times-Dispatch*, May 11, 1994, B-1.

6   Ron Charles, "The Tenacity of Hope," *Washington Post*, August 7, 2019, C-1.

7   Author interview with Dan Mouer in June 2018.

8   Ibid.

9   Anna Barron Billingsley and Beverly Orndorff, "MCV, Corporation Discussing Deal," *Richmond Times-Dispatch*, April 28, 1994, 1.

10 The encounter between Eugene Trani and Dan Mouer has been described in various news reports. The author conducted lengthy interviews with Chris Egghart and his supervisor, Dan Mouer, in early June 2018. One of the most thorough accounts appears in the aforementioned article by Tina Griego in *Richmond Magazine*. "VCU's former president, Eugene Trani, declined to discuss his thinking at the time," she wrote. "In a statement sent by email, he said only that the Office of University Counsel in 1994 'provided legal advice based upon precedent for such an excavation. I followed that advice.'"

    For this book, Dr. Trani—now president emeritus of VCU—declined the author's invitations to discuss the events of April 1994. When contacted by phone at his VCU office on April 16, 2019, the response relayed by his personal assistant was "I don't want to be in your report."

11 Author interview with Mouer.

12 Griego.

13 Douglas W. Owsley, Karin S. Bruwelheide, Richard J. Jantz, Jodi L. Koste, and Merry Outlaw, "Skeletal Evidence of Anatomical and Surgical Train-

ing in Nineteenth-Century Richmond." A chapter on VCU's well discovery is included in Kenneth C. Nystrom, ed., *The Bioarchaeology of Dissection and Autopsy in the United States* (New York: Springer International Publishing, 2017).

14 Jodi L. Koste, "Artifacts and Commingles Skeletal Remains from a Well on the Medical College of Virginia Campus," June 18, 2012, scholarscompass .vcu.edu.

15 Ibid.

16 The Egyptian Building has been extensively renovated over the years, making it hard to say definitively whether its well was *in* or *under* the basement. Some descriptions of Chris Baker, the MCV caretaker of the late nineteenth and early twentieth centuries, mention him putting remains in his "vat." This may have been the well beneath the Egyptian Building.

17 Owsley et. al., 144.

18 Ibid., 159.

19 Ibid., 151.

20 Ibid., 162–163.

21 Karin Kapsidelis, "Draft Report Suggests Ways to Memorialize MCV Remains," *Richmond Times-Dispatch*, June 8, 2016, 1.

22 Michael Paul Williams, "On Well Project, VCU Has a Chance to Move Beyond Memorialization," *Richmond Times-Dispatch*, December 14, 2018, A-2.

23 The work of VCU and its Family Representative Council for the East Marshall Street Well Project continues. In November 2019, the human remains that had been studied and stored for more than two decades at the Smithsonian were returned to Richmond. They were placed at the Virginia Department of Historic Resources as planning for further commemoration continued. According to an article by Mel Leonor in the November 25, 2019, *Richmond Times-Dispatch*, options include "further research into the remains to understand their ancestry and their health before death; burial in the Richmond area that honors West African traditions; and physical memorials to mark the experiences of the people whose remains were disposed of in the well."

EPILOGUE: The Soul of Medicine

1 Jeremy Pearce, "Richard Lower Dies at 78; Transplanted Animal and Human Hearts," *New York Times*, May 31, 2008, A-15, https://www .nytimes.com/2008/05/31/health/31lower.html.

2 "Richard Lower," Wikipedia, accessed on November 2, 2018, https:// en.wikipedia.org/wiki/Richard_Lower_(surgeon).

3 Sandeep Jauhar, "Happy Anniversary, Heart Transplant," Opinion, *New York Times*, November 30, 2017, https://www.nytimes.com/2017/11 /30/opinion/sunday/anniversary-heart-transplant.html.

4 B. D. Colen, "Heart Transplant on Wane Decade After 1st Operation," *Washington Post*, September 5, 1977.

5 Ibid.

6 "David Milford Hume," *Richmond News Leader*, May 22, 1973, 18.

7 Martha Hume oral history.

8 This odd coupling was broken up in 2000, but in its own way, Wilder wrote, "perfectly symbolized the psychic divide that characterized the South." Wilder, *Son of Virginia*, 74.

9 This correspondence is included in the personal papers of A. Christian Compton in the archives of the Washington and Lee School of Law library.

10 See chapter 19, note 7.

11 "Cardiothoracic Surgery," Pauley Heart Center, VCU Health, accessed on November 1, 2019, vcuhealth.org/pauley-heart-center.

12 One such event was held March 14, 2018, in Richmond at the Virginia Museum of History & Culture. Some of the retired doctors and nurses who worked with Lower and Hume were in attendance. During a panel discussion, one of the current VCU faculty members mentioned concerns about manslaughter charges after the first heart transplant. "Hume just loved the publicity," the professor remarked. "Lower was very concerned [that] 'I'm going to jail.'" This drew laughter from the nearly all-white audience of about three hundred.

13 Dr. Vigneshwar "Vig" Kasirajan, interview with the author, October 25, 2018, at Kasirajan's office at West Hospital.

14 Ibid.

INDEX

Page numbers in *italics* refer to maps. Page numbers beginning with 339 refer to notes.